POSITIVE FRAGMENTATION

Polly Apfelbaum

Jennifer Bartlett

Christiane Baumgartner

Louise Bourgeois

Cecily Brown

Judy Chicago

Nicole Eisenman

Ellen Gallagher

Jenny Holzer

Nicola López

Julie Mehretu

Sarah Morris

Wangechi Mutu

Judy Pfaff

Wendy Red Star

Betye Saar

Lorna Simpson

Swoon

Barbara Takenaga

Mickalene Thomas

Kara Walker

POSITIVE FRAGMENTATION

From the Collections
of Jordan D. Schnitzer
and His Family
Foundation

Essays by Virginia Treanor
and William J. Simmons

Published by the Jordan Schnitzer Family Foundation in
association with the National Museum of Women in the Arts

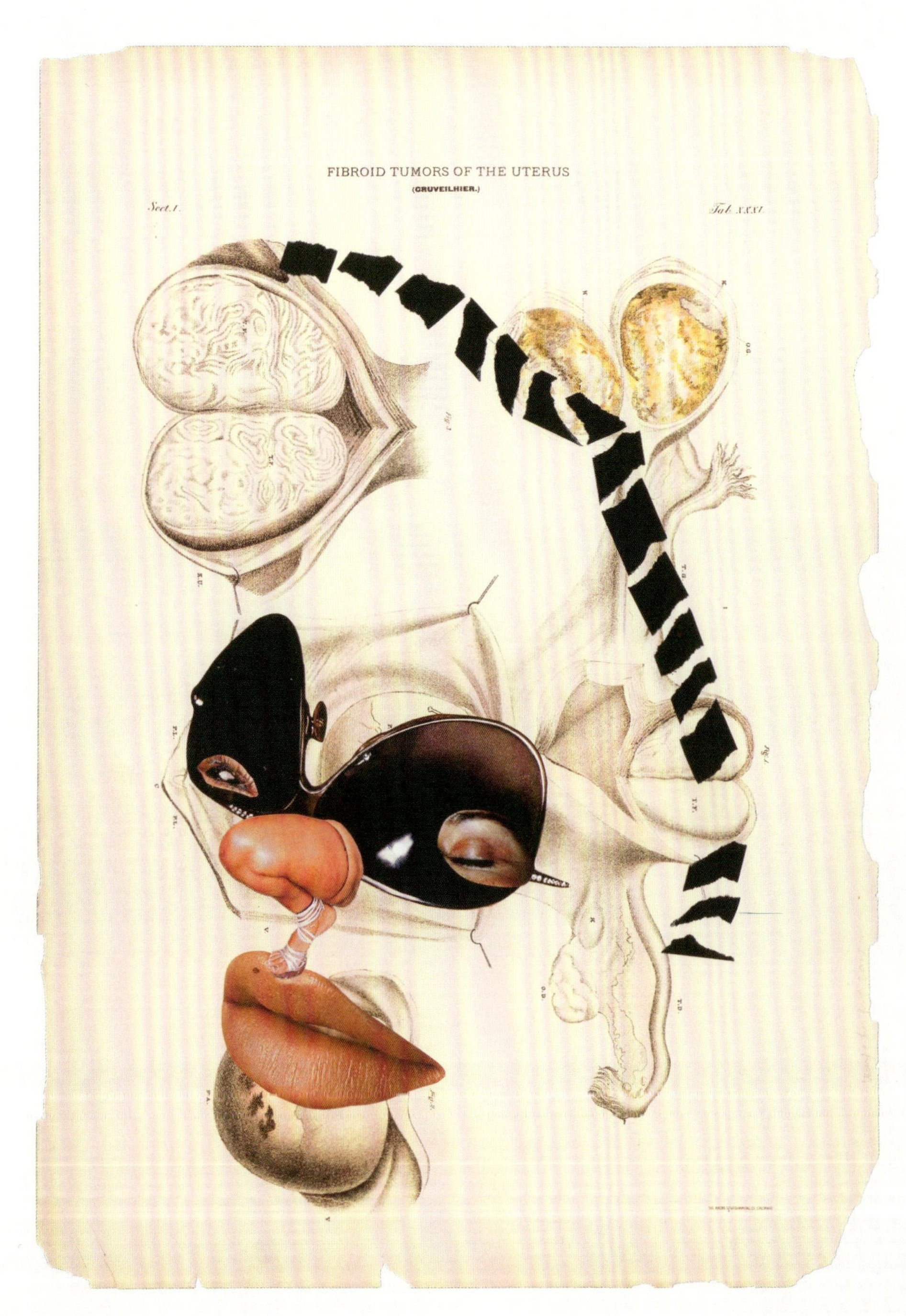
FIBROID TUMORS OF THE UTERUS
(CRUVEILHIER.)
Sect. I.
Tab. XXXI.

CONTENTS

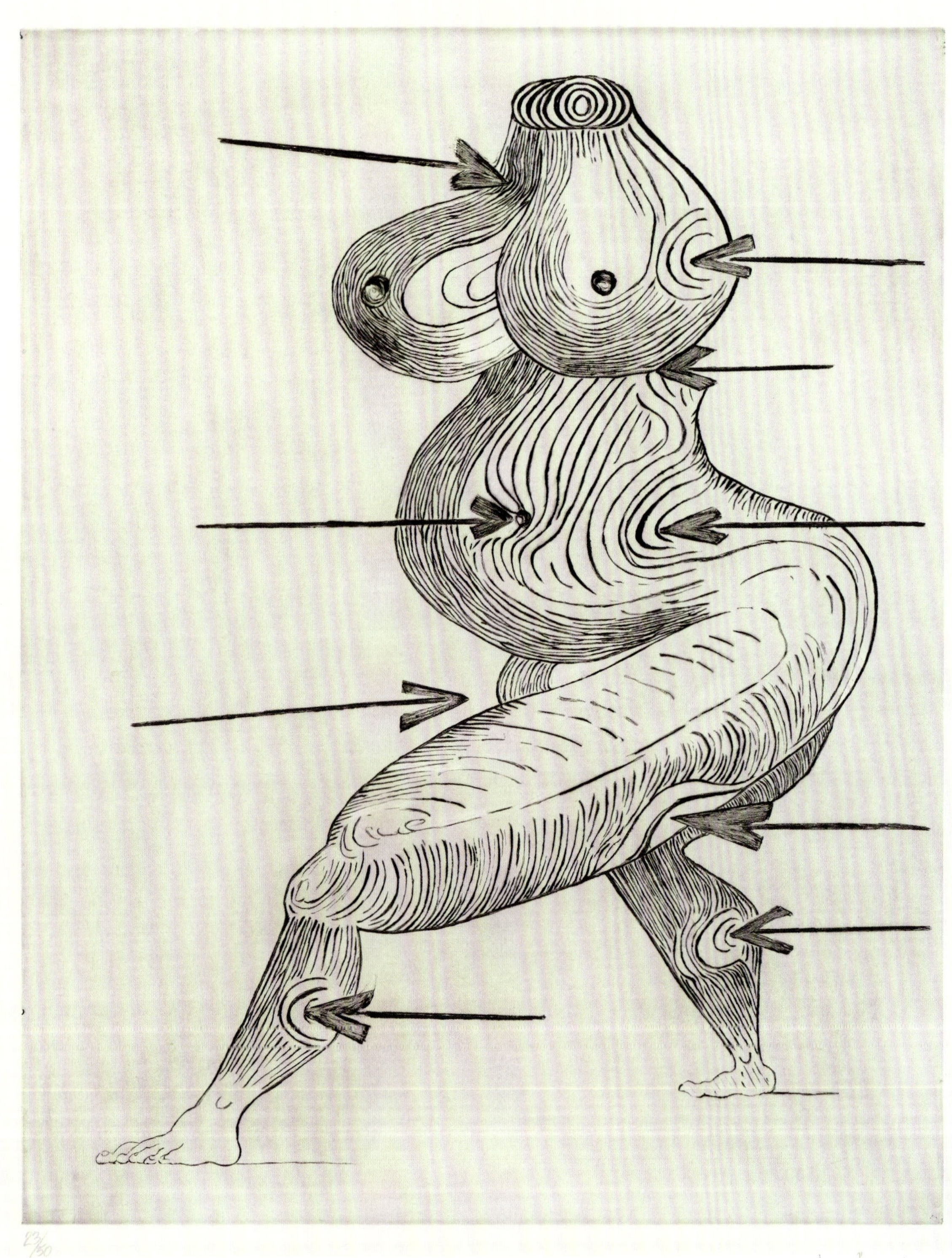

DIRECTOR'S STATEMENT

It is an honor to join Jordan Schnitzer in dedicating this catalogue to the memory of his mother, Arlene Schnitzer (1929–2020), a groundbreaking collector, tireless advocate for artists, and committed philanthropist.

Although I never met Arlene, I feel like I have come to know her through my friend and colleague Lucy Buchanan Garrett. Over the years, Lucy has shared the many lessons she learned from Arlene as well as the deep and abiding friendship she and her late husband, John Buchanan, had with Arlene and Harold Schnitzer and their son, Jordan. It is obvious from all these great stories that Arlene was true believer in the power of art to transform lives and communities. As the founder in 1961 of the celebrated Fountain Gallery of Art in Portland, she paved the way for Pacific Northwest artists to thrive in the region while also building national recognition for their work. After she closed the Fountain Gallery in 1987 to focus on philanthropy, Arlene was a major force behind the growth in prominence of the Portland Art Museum. She also supported Pacific Northwest College of Art, Oregon Health Sciences, University Women's Health, the Oregon Symphony, and countless other organizations throughout the rest of her long life.

It is clear that she passed on to Jordan her love of the arts and the responsibility she felt for supporting them directly. *Positive Fragmentation*, drawn from the collections of Jordan Schnitzer and his family foundation, is also dedicated to Arlene because she was the inspiration behind her son's own passion for collecting. Carrying on his mother's philanthropic work, Jordan generously makes his world-class collection of prints and multiples available for exhibition at institutions nationally and internationally. The passion they shared for contemporary art, and their personal relationships with so many great artists, is what makes their roles as collectors and advocates so special.

I know that Jordan has a close relationship with many, if not all, of the artists in his collection, and he has long been a champion of women and nonbinary artists. The works in this exhibition, *Positive Fragmentation*, represent a fraction of his holdings in this area but feature prominent artists such

Louise Bourgeois
(American, b. France, 1911–2011
Ste. Sebastienne, edition 23/50, 1992
drypoint, 47½ × 37 in. (120.6 × 94 cm)

as Louise Bourgeois, Judy Chicago, Nicola López, Sarah Morris, Wangechi Mutu, Lorna Simpson, Barbara Takenaga, and many others. As Jordan says often, artists are the chroniclers of our time, and we need them to help us untangle the complexities of our present and visualize where we might go next. This exhibition brings together works that engage in issues like gender, race, and sociopolitical polarization to aid us in thinking about and addressing these often-difficult subjects. In a world fragmented by a global pandemic that has laid bare existing inequalities, these artists and their works address hard truths. They also offer us entry points for discussing them. With their help, we can begin to have the conversations we need to have in order to move forward for the betterment of all.

Much of what I know about Arlene Schnitzer reminds me of NMWA's founder, Wilhelmina Cole Holladay (1922–2021). Of the same generation, "Billie" Holladay also was a champion of the arts. With her husband, Wallace, she began collecting art in the 1970s, just as scholars were beginning to focus on the underrepresentation of art by women. By 1980, she began devoting her energy and resources to creating the first museum solely dedicated to women artists' creative accomplishments, and, in 1987, the Holladay collection became the National Museum of Women in the Arts. Now, with her recent passing, we carry on her inestimable legacy.

So, it is as kindred spirits, building upon the genius and fortitude of our foremothers, Arlene and Billie, that we have entered into a unique partnership. At this moment when the loss of our founders is still deeply felt, we would like to thank Jordan Schnitzer for everything he has done to bring *Positive Fragmentation* to life. The wonderful staff at the Jordan Schnitzer Family Foundation has been a joy to work with, especially William Morrow, director of exhibitions; Catherine Malone, director of collections; Emily Kramer, exhibition registrar; and Caitlin Pihl, marketing director. We are grateful to our development consultant, Lucy Buchanan Garrett, for bringing us together to form this new artistic and personal relationship.

We further extend our gratitude to American University for their collaboration with NMWA in hosting *Positive Fragmentation* in the Katzen Arts Center while our building is undergoing renovation. Special thanks to Marc N. Duber, chair of the board of trustees at AU, and Nancy Duber, board member of NMWA, for facilitating this collaboration. We also appreciate the cooperation and teamwork with longtime friend Jack Rasmussen, director of the American University Art Museum, and his staff, including Sarah Leary, acting associate director; Jessica Pochesci, acting registrar; Sharon Christiansen, visitor services and operations manager; Kevin Runyon, preparator; and Elizabeth Cowgill, marketing and publications specialist.

Finally, it is my privilege to recognize NMWA's staff for their engagement with the Jordan Schnitzer Family Foundation and the AU Art Museum. Virginia (Ginny) Treanor, associate curator, selected the works in the exhibition and conceived of the theme. Catherine Bade, registrar; Neda Amouzadeh, assistant registrar; and Gregory Angelone, chief preparator, worked seamlessly with both the Schnitzer and AU teams to ensure the safe transit and installation of the exhibition at American University. I also thank Deborah Gaston, director of education and interpretation, and her team for working with the AU staff to develop complementary exhibition programming.

Thanks to the generosity and support of the Jordan Schnitzer Family Foundation and the American University Art Museum, the National Museum of Women in the Arts is able to continue championing the work of women and nonbinary artists through off-site exhibitions during the temporary closure of our own building. We look forward to the exhibition tour of *Positive Fragmentation* and we hope to continue important collaborations such as this one in the future.

Susan Fisher Sterling

Director, National Museum of Women in the Arts

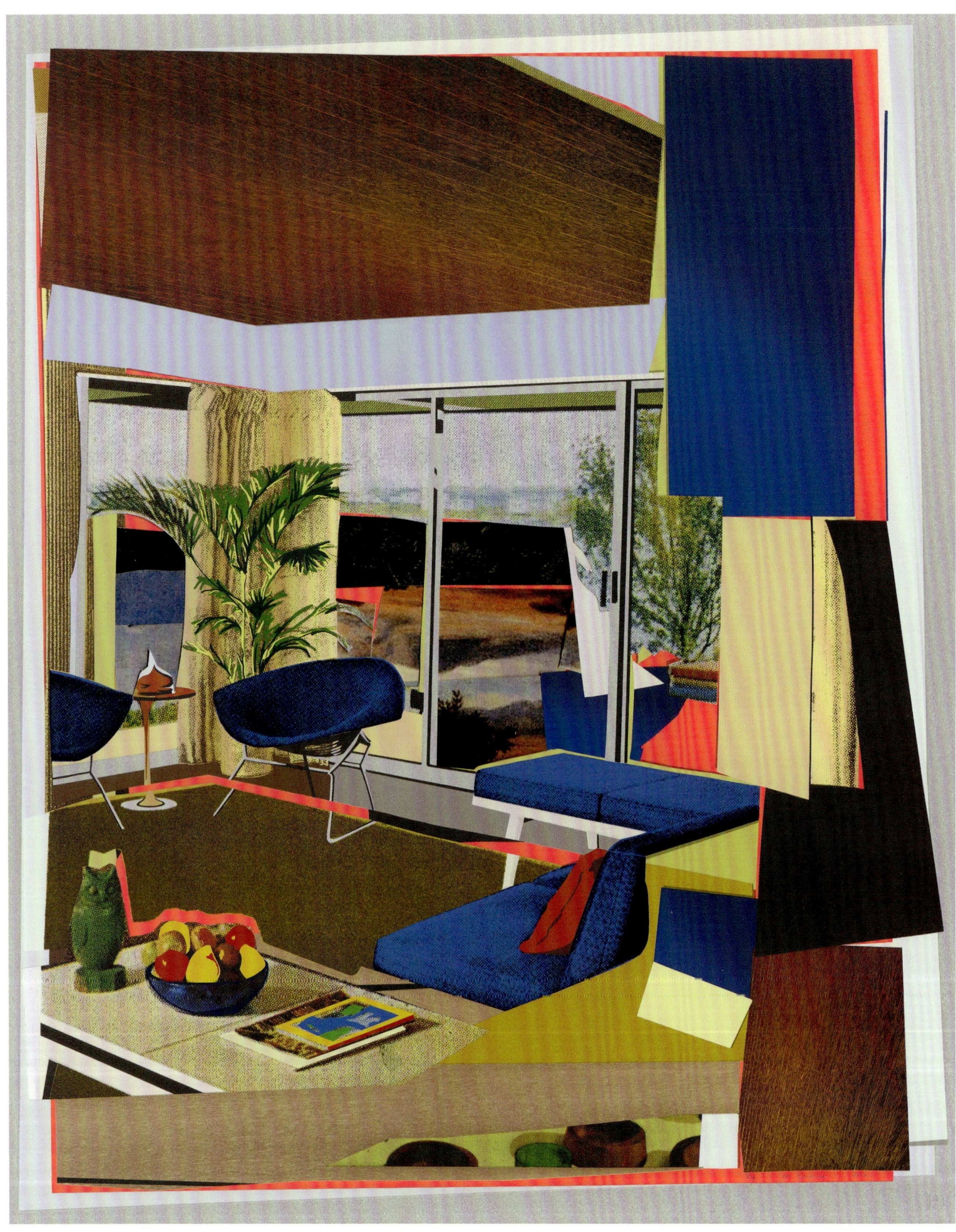

COLLECTOR'S STATEMENT

I grew up in Portland, Oregon, where I still reside. When I was in the third grade in 1961, my mother, Arlene Schnitzer, opened the first contemporary art gallery in Portland, the Fountain Gallery of Art, which featured artists from Portland, Seattle, and San Francisco. Over the twenty-five years that she operated the gallery, she helped many businesses and individuals appreciate the importance of having art in their offices and homes. She was totally committed to the art of our region, and although I now have a collection of prints, paintings, and sculpture in excess of 19,000 works by many of the most important artists of our time, I always preach the importance of supporting local artists!

It is because of my mother, who opened the door to the art world, that I developed a passion for collecting and sharing my collections with others. Since I bought my first piece of art when I was fourteen years old, my collection has grown dramatically. We are proud to have had over 160 exhibitions of art curated solely from our collections, which have traveled to over 110 museums across the country at no cost to those institutions.

In the fifty years that I have been collecting art, I have observed that it was always male artists who received the most attention, whether in gallery shows, auction sales, or museum exhibitions. Therefore, I have made an extra effort to collect art by women artists and artists of color. We have also had more exhibitions of women artists and artists of color at museums around the country than any other institution I am aware of.

We are also proud to have sponsored symposia and artist residencies, as well as funded the attendance of children and audiences from lesser-served neighborhoods at openings, panel discussions, and lectures. Through this program, I have tried to reach one individual at a time, whether they are two years old or 102, to help these amazing artists speak to them about issues facing our society.

Over a year ago, when Lucy Buchanan, a friend of many years, called and asked if I would be interested in an exhibition at the National Museum of

Mickalene Thomas
(American, b. 1971)
Interior: Blue Couch and Green Owl, edition 5/26, 2016
mixed-media collage, screenprint, woodblock, digital print, and flocking
42⅜ × 34¼ in. (107.6 × 87 cm)

Women in the Arts, I immediately said "Yes!" First of all, I would have said yes to anything Lucy asked, but especially for us to have the privilege of exhibiting many women artists in our collection at one of the important museums in the country—anyone would have said yes!

When Susan Fisher Sterling, the museum's director, and curator Virginia Treanor came up with the title *Positive Fragmentation*, I thought, "How brilliant." To me, it references how fragmented the role of women artists has been in society and therefore, makes a statement about how far we have come to advance the status of women, yet how much farther we need to go.

While I was not involved in selecting the artists in this exhibition, I applaud Susan and Virginia's choices. I can only imagine how hard it was for them to select twenty-one artists out of the more than four hundred female artists in our collection. So, for all those artists who were not chosen for this exhibition, I wish there were enough space so that every one of you could have had your art in these hallowed halls. The art that was selected showcases a remarkable representation of the best and brightest artists of our time who happen to be women.

While I could go on and on about each of the world-class artists in this exhibition, whose work I am honored have in our collection, I'll touch on the work of just a few, such as Lorna Simpson, Wangechi Mutu, and Kara Walker, whose art makes us feel the power and fury of their images and shows us new ways to understand race in today's world. Jenny Holzer's art for me is like poetry, making me think how carefully she chooses every word and how her words evoke thoughts we all share. Polly Apfelbaum, Jennifer Bartlett, and Judy Pfaff are masters of color. These artists, joined by Julie Mehretu, Mickalene Thomas, and Louise Bourgeois, haven't just broken through the glass ceiling but shattered it. Likewise, it gives me great satisfaction to have major works in our collection by Judy Chicago who, for over fifty years, has created images about many themes that force us to think about the inequities in society and the pursuit of social justice. To think, she just had her first retrospective in forty years, at the de Young Museum in San Francisco—it is heartening and yet shameful that she is only now receiving this well-deserved recognition.

I would like to thank Susan and Virginia, whose shared vision to support female artists and their work brought about this exhibition. A big thank you to the Jordan Schnitzer Family Foundation's fourteen hardworking art professionals, without whom the art would never make it from our warehouse to the walls of great institutions like the National Museum of Women in the

Arts. As always, I have the deepest respect and admiration for all the artists in the exhibition and for the work they do, which enlightens all of us. As I have said before, waking up without art around me would be like waking up without the sun! The artists in this exhibition, many of whose work I am fortunate to have hanging on my walls, illuminate my life every day.

Today, all of us are witnessing a change in the appreciation of all artists, regardless of race or gender. Let us celebrate these artists who have done so much to further this cause. While they stand on the shoulders of all women artists who have come before them, those in this exhibition, today, are leading the way for future generations to appreciate and revel in their amazing themes, messages, and designs.

Jordan D. Schnitzer

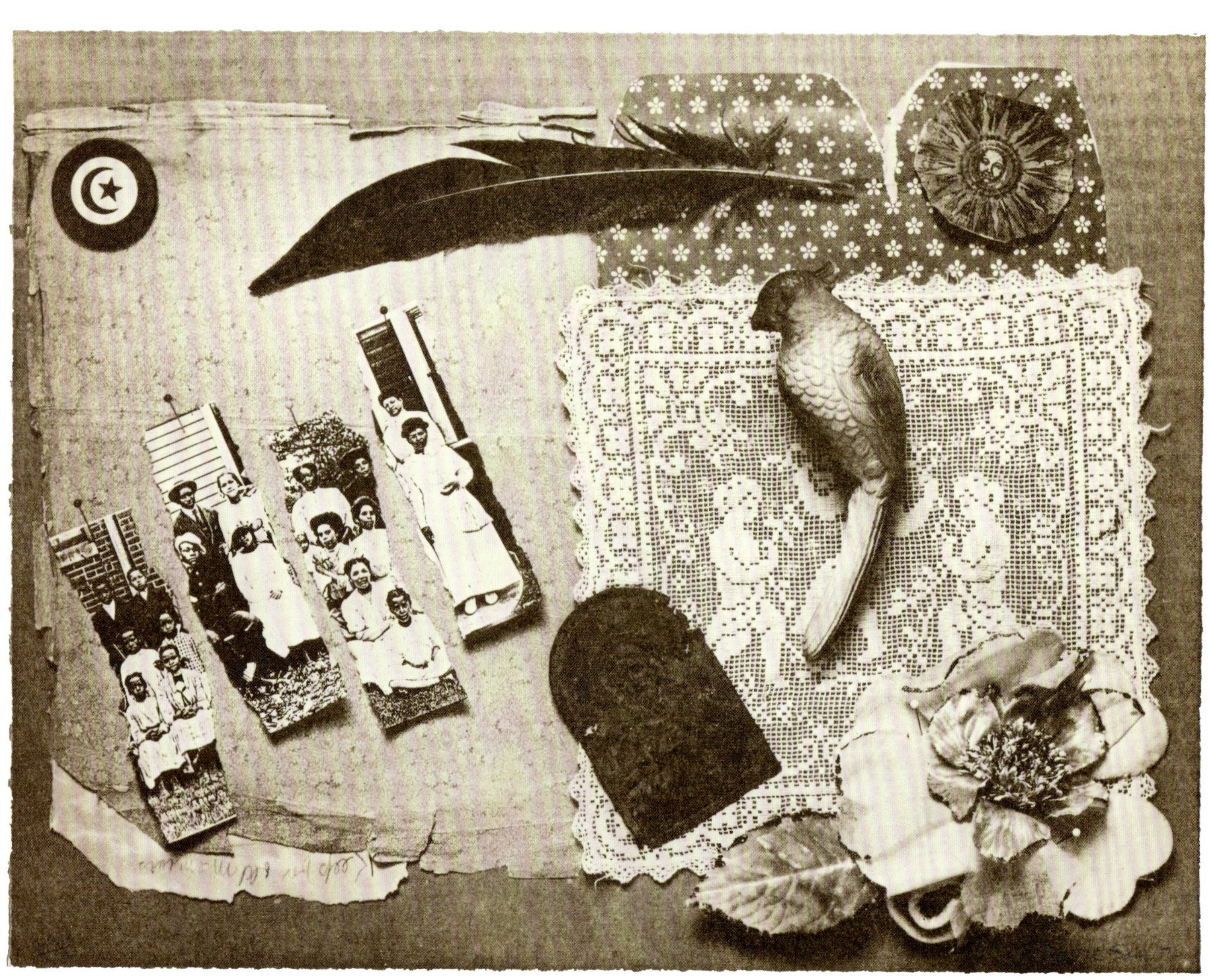

INTRODUCTION

Virginia Treanor

The title *Positive Fragmentation* comes from a term coined by the feminist scholar and critic Lucy Lippard in an essay published in 1978, in which she addresses the gender discrimination between the concepts of "high" art and "hobby" art.[1] She describes positive fragmentation, or the "collage aesthetic," as particularly suited to historically marginalized artists, as it "willfully takes apart what is or is supposed to be and rearranges it in ways that suggest what it could be." Taking that idea as a starting point, this exhibition and book showcase works by artists who have defined their careers by their exploration of fragmentation, whether literal or lyrical. The exhibition features more than one hundred works—all drawn from the collections of Jordan D. Schnitzer and his family foundation—by twenty-one artists who use fragmentation both stylistically and conceptually, to question and probe the status quo and to suggest and hypothesize different perspectives. In the same essay, Lippard also observed the tendency to see "high" or "fine" art as a rarity, while other modes of production are viewed as commodities and, therefore, as less valuable. In this regard, the works in this exhibition, which are all prints and multiples, collectively reject that notion by demonstrating that their power lies in the strength of their conception and the skill of their execution, and not the exclusiveness of their existence.

Betye Saar
(American, b. 1926)
Fragments, edition 226/250, 1976
lithograph
14½ × 18¾ in.
(36.8 × 47.6 cm)
© Betye Saar, Courtesy of the artist and Roberts Projects Los Angeles, California

Although chosen before the global pandemic of 2020, the theme of fragmentation is an apt one for the world as it has become. While on one level the interconnectedness and interdependency of the earth's population has been irrefutably highlighted by a virus that knows no borders, the pandemic has left societal infrastructures, institutions, and individual lives in pieces. In the United States and beyond, this havoc has laid bare the inequalities that have persisted in our societies and have led to impassioned calls for social justice. To build a more equitable way forward, systems must be taken apart and put back together again in a way that benefits everyone. The task at hand is enormous and overwhelming, but artists have been wrestling with these issues for years, and it is to them that we must look to guide us as we consider where the problems lie, how to untangle them, and how to move forward for the good of all.

Making New Meaning

Of all the artists in *Positive Fragmentation,* it is Betye Saar whose work, in her collective oeuvre and in the singular print included in this exhibition, exemplifies the taking apart and reconstituting of myriad objects and ideas. Saar is the undisputed champion of positive fragmentation, implementing it to cast a critical eye on constructs of race and gender. She uses it to pose probing questions and to generate new meaning. Saar's 1976 lithograph *Fragments* (p. 14), like her three-dimensional assemblages, relies on the collage aesthetic that Lippard would theorize just two years later in her article "Making Something from Nothing," where she first used the phrase "positive fragmentation."[2] In this lithograph, Saar makes something—art, memory, history—out of the assembled objects, creating new meanings and associations for them through their juxtapositions. Those meanings may be enigmatic for viewers, but they lead to questions, which in turn lead to the contemplation of the Black lives represented in the torn photograph on the left. Of Saar's use of found photographs, which the artist collects from flea markets and garage sales, Leslie King-Hammond says, "Countless individuals who were rendered invisible within their lifetimes and nearly lost to memory but for the remaining photographs of their presence find their images reborn in Saar's reconstructions."[3]

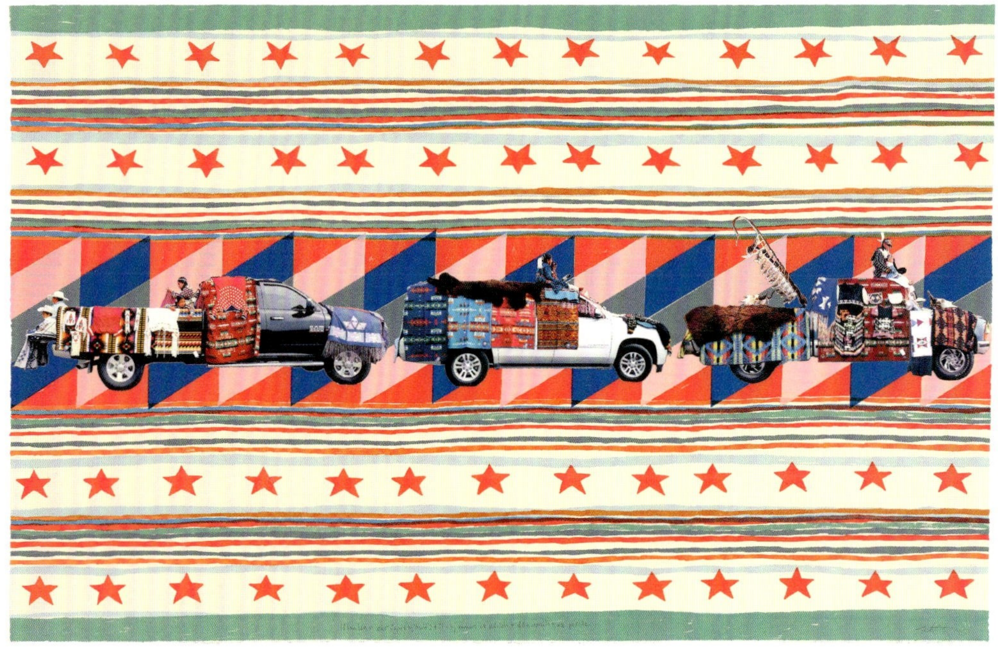

Wendy Red Star
(Apsáalooke [Crow], b. 1981)
iilaalée = car (goes by itself) + ii = by means of which + dáanniili = we parade, edition 1/20, 2015–16
lithograph with archival pigment ink photographs
24 × 38 in. (61 × 96.5 cm)

Similarly, Wendy Red Star's photo montages *iilaalée = car (goes by itself) + ii = by means of which + dáanniili = we parade* (2015–16, above and p. 107) and *Yakima or Yakama—Not For Me To Say* (2015, p. 109) use a combination of elements to create a new iconography for Indigenous American tribes that honors both the traditions of the past and the ingenuity of the present. Photographs of cars decorated for Crow Fair, an annual gathering of Great Plains tribes, are superimposed on geometric backgrounds whose designs are taken from Pendleton blankets. Although the company was founded by and is operated by Anglo-Americans, Pendleton blankets incorporate designs based on traditional motifs taken from many Indigenous cultures. The history of these blankets is inextricably linked to Native communities, and they have become objects of prestige and ceremonial importance within them. Together with the distinctly American-made cars and trucks that are often decorated for parade as horses would be, Red Star's images embody what Lippard observed about the collage aesthetic being a means for "putting things together without divesting them of their own identities."[4] In Red Star's works, the icons of modern American life, like pickup trucks, are as much a part of Native culture today as the parfleches that decorate their sides.

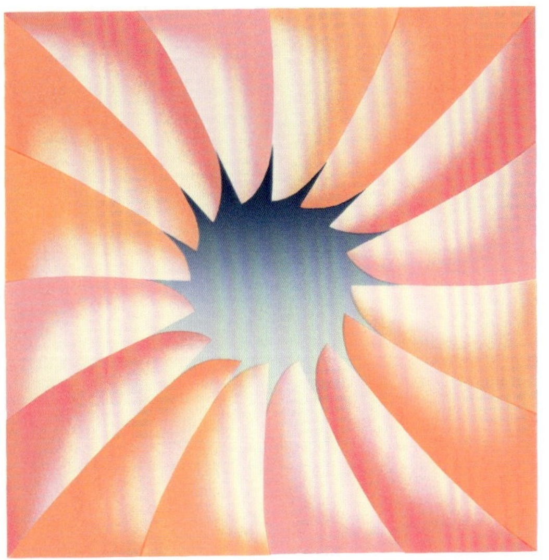

Judy Chicago
(American, b. 1939)
Through the Flower 3,
edition AP 1/1, 1972
lithograph
22 × 22 in. (55.9 × 55.9 cm)

Bodies

Representing the human body has historically been held as the highest achievement for artists. When rules for depicting the human form were challenged by artists like Pablo Picasso and Willem de Kooning in the first half of the twentieth century, the resulting fragmented forms often reduced women's bodies to sexualized elements: breasts, vaginas, and buttocks. However, when women and nonbinary artists fragment bodies in their work, it is toward a much different goal. In the 1970s, Judy Chicago, like Saar, was trying to deconstruct an existing visual vocabulary that was insufficient for communicating her lived realities. In both her *Through the Flower* (1972, above and pp. 29, 68–71) and *Great Ladies* (1973) series, Chicago uses geometric imagery and soft, pastel colors to create a woman-centric iconography, which she calls "central core imagery." Before the more explicit use of female genitalia in her work, Chicago formulated these abstracted references to the vaginal opening in direct opposition to what she saw as the phallocentric visual language of Western art.

The dissonance of not conforming to a white, cis-male norm, to be considered Other, is in itself a "collage experience."[5] This observation is visualized most precisely by Wangechi Mutu in her series *Histology of the Different Classes of Uterine Tumors* (2006, opposite and pp. 99–100). Women have long been, and troublingly still frequently are, defined by their reproductive organs. Using nineteenth-century medical illustrations of the uterus, ovaries,

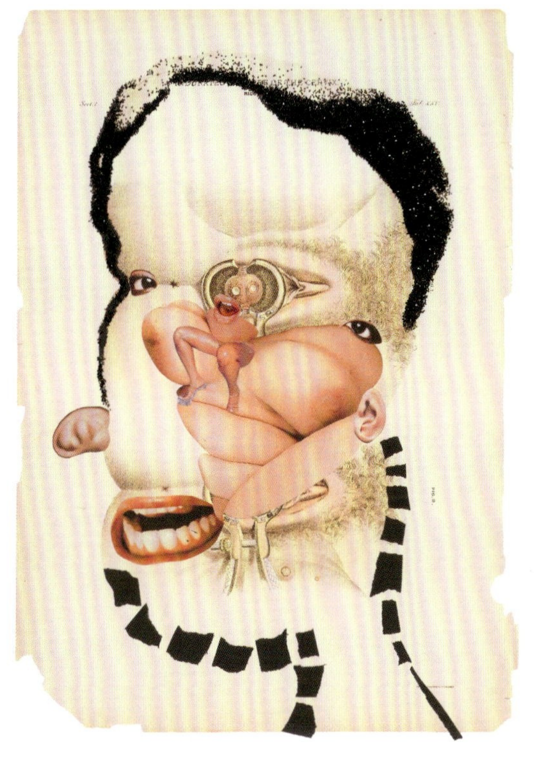

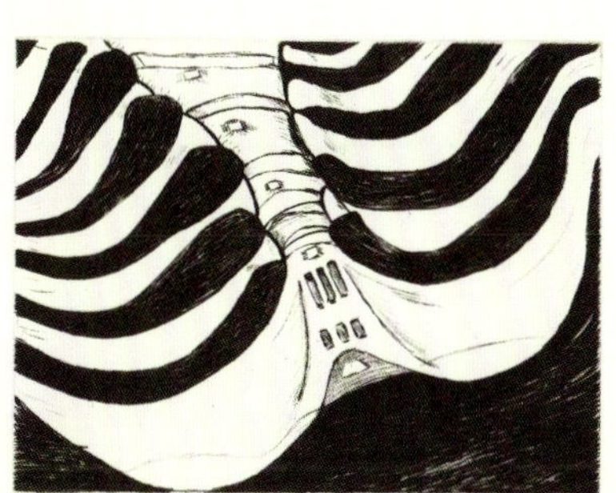

Wangechi Mutu
(Kenyan, b. 1972)
Histology of the Different Classes of Uterine Tumors: Indurated Ulcers of the Cervix,
edition 14/25, 2006
collage on found medical illustration paper
23 × 17 in. (58.4 × 43.2 cm)
Courtesy of the Artist.

Louise Bourgeois
(American, b. France, 1911–2010)
Anatomy, edition 37/44, 1990
etching
19½ × 14⅛ in. (49.5 × 35.9 cm)

and cervix as the foundation for her collages, Mutu creates faces from such disparate source material as fashion magazines and *National Geographic* photographs. Via this juxtaposition, Mutu demonstrates how the original illustrations, rife with the pseudoscience of colonialist thought, serve as the basis for contemporary constructions of gender and race. Importantly, however, Mutu gives each face a mouth, presumably so it can speak for itself.

Body parts are a familiar iconographic element throughout the oeuvre of Louise Bourgeois. Frequently depicting them in isolation from one another, as in her *Anatomy* series (1990, above and pp. 56–59), Bourgeois considers limbs, organs, and hair individually with an almost portrait-like approach, imbuing them with personalities all their own. While there is often a playfulness in her prints, there is also an element of the macabre, the nightmarish, the psychologically distraught. This is perhaps not surprising given the subject at hand. The gruesome connotation implicit in considering the fragmented body is utilized by other artists in the exhibition who, rather than shying away from the abject, embrace it to convey raw emotion. In one series

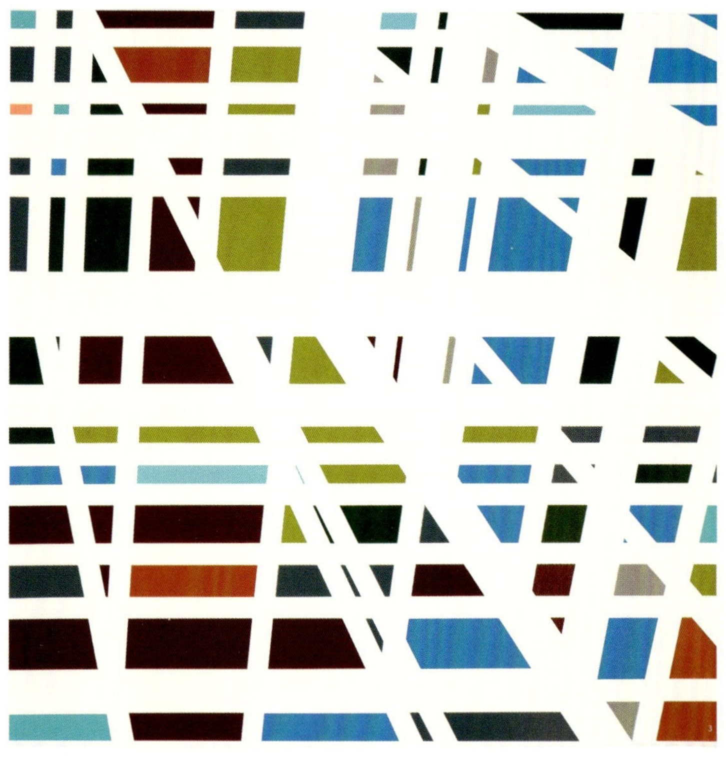

Sarah Morris
(American, b. Britain, 1967)
Dulles (Capital): Panel 3,
edition 32/45, 2001
screenprint
29 × 29 in. (73.7 × 73.7 cm)

of works from 2005, Kara Walker superimposes silhouetted dismembered hands, legs, and heads of Black bodies over nineteenth-century etchings reproduced from an 1866 publication, *Harper's Pictorial History of the Civil War* (pp. 131–33). By disrupting the view of the original, often saccharine vignette with silhouettes of maimed Black bodies that have at once nothing and everything to do with the scene onto which they are placed, Walker calls attention to the violence of slavery and war.

Environments

The spaces we inhabit—the architectural, the natural, and even the metaphysical—are also addressed by artists in *Positive Fragmentation*. Nicola López and Sarah Morris both use the urban environment and its architecture, whose elements—beams, girders, sheathing, wiring—they distill and rearrange to emphasize the visual interest of individual components as well as the unseen social forces that support, or destabilize, the city environment. Morris's work, both her films and two-dimensional pieces, are made up of fragments that, paradoxically, do not make up a "whole." Rather, the end result seems to be part of a never-ending expansiveness. It is easy to imagine *Dulles (Capital)* (2001, above and pp. 30, 97) continuing ad infinitum. For Morris, this obfuscation of the "whole," this intentional frustration of not being able to see the whole picture, relates to power, which, as she observes is "always in flux and up for grabs."[6] This is

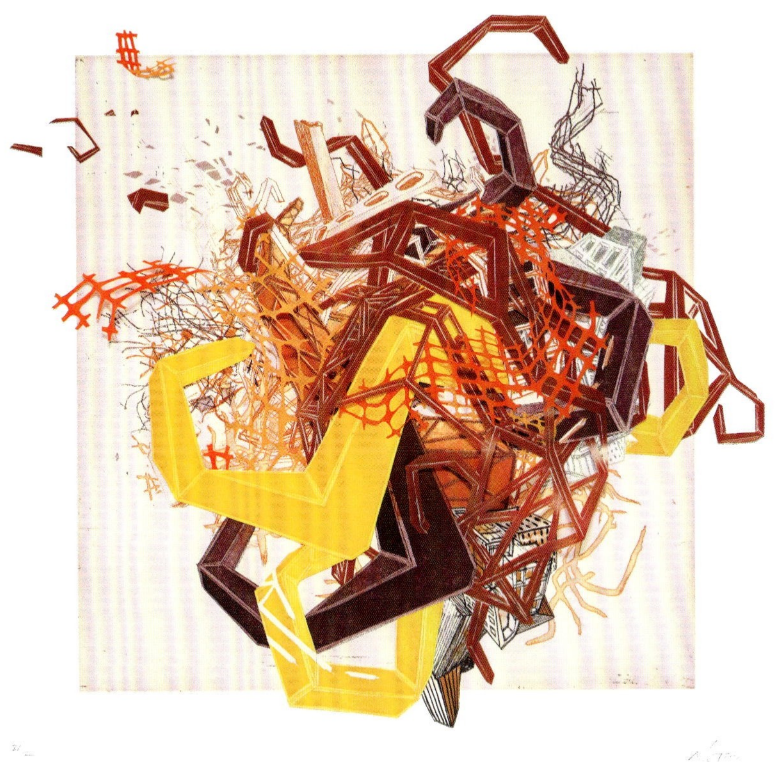

Nicola López
(American, b. 1975)
Urban Transformation #1,
edition 8/12, 2009
etching, lithography, and
woodcut with Mylar elements
30 × 30 in. (76.2 × 76.2 cm)

particularly true of the seat of the American government that is referenced in *Dulles (Capital)*—and was so violently demonstrated at the Capitol on January 6, 2021.

Seemingly the opposite of Morris's expansive grids are the works of López, who presents isolated, self-contained globes of compacted industrial building components. In her series *Urban Transformations* (2009, above and pp. 85–89), López, with the meticulous detail of architectural plans, presents kinetic masses of disordered elements whose frenetic energy suggests the hurried rhythms of life in cities. López also finds a synergy between her imagery and the process used to create it. She says of the intersection of her subject and printmaking: "It's a way of generating material and working with variations, and I think that it also resonates thematically with the work and with the environment that I'm talking about: this mass-produced, mechanized, technology-based, built landscape. There's a nice parallel with the process of printmaking in its capacity as a means of reproducing imagery."[7]

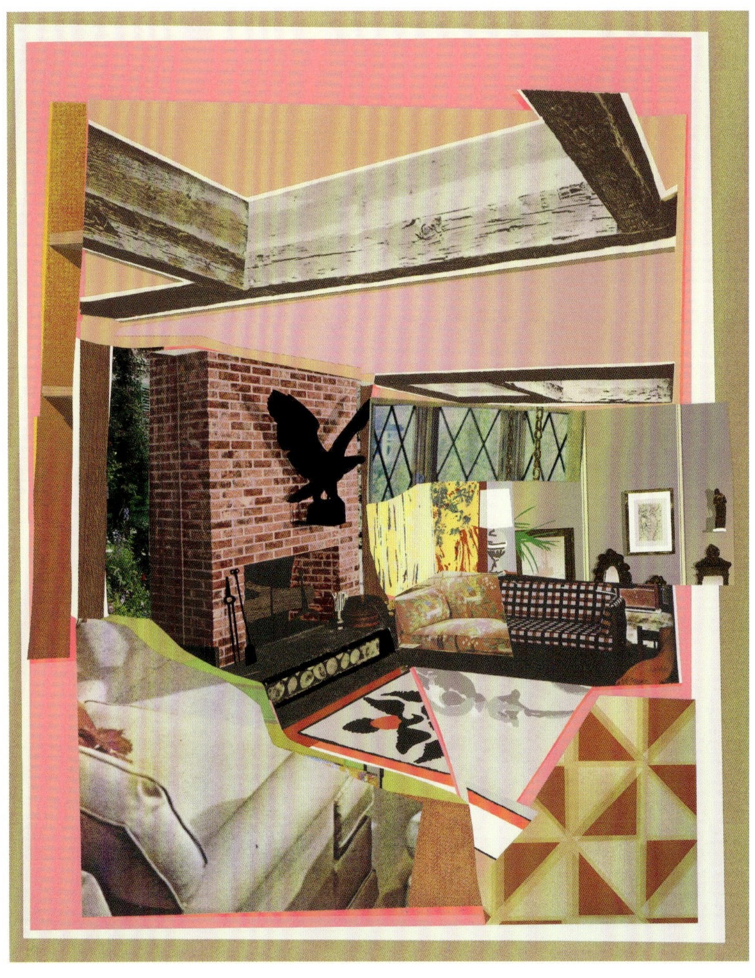

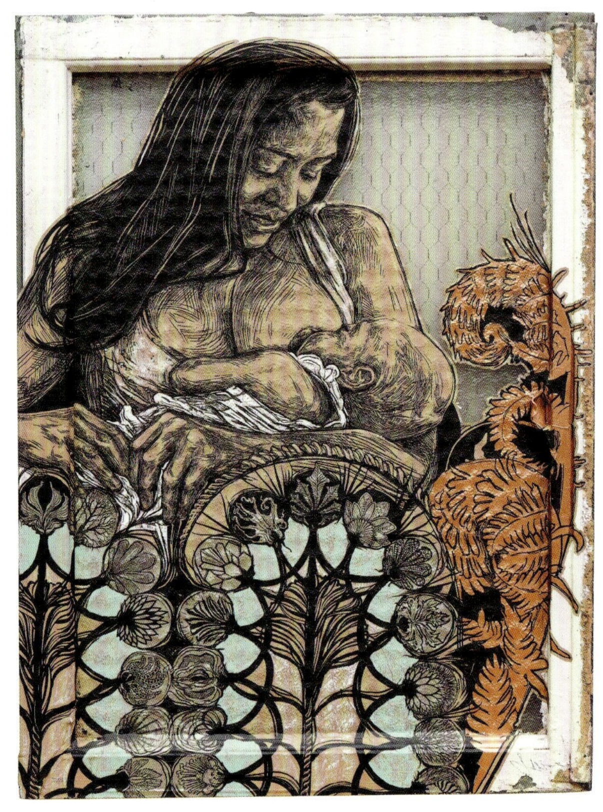

Mickalene Thomas
(American, b. 1971)
Interior: Fireplace with Blackbird, edition 5/26, 2016
mixed-media collage, screenprint, woodblock, digital print, etching, gold leaf, wood veneer, and flocking
42⅜ × 34¼ in. (107.6 × 87 cm)

Swoon
(Caledonia Dance Curry)
(American, b. 1977)
Dawn and Gemma, edition AP, 2017
silkscreen and acrylic gouache on paper and found object (glass and wood)
24 × 32 × 2 in.
(61 × 81.3 × 5.1 cm)

Disjointed architectural space is also present in the work of Mickalene Thomas. Often, in Thomas's work, bold interiors serve as the backdrop for figures; however, in her series of prints *Interiors* (2014 and 2016, above and pp. 125, 128–29), the space itself becomes the subject, full of as much personality as a portrait. Taking inspiration from a multivolume "manual" published in the 1970s on how to decorate the home, Thomas mixes and matches elements in puzzle-like configurations in a reflection of the very real way many of us approach home décor—as an expression of personality. Thomas also delights in mixing and matching styles from different art historical periods, like the bright bold colors of pop art and the shifting perspective of cubism. Her landscapes, in particular, are infused with these references, not only stylistically but thematically as well. In *Sleep: Deux Femmes Noires* (2013, p. 127), Thomas recalls the countless reclining nude women throughout art history from Titian to Manet in order to question and reevaluate those sources through the lens of queer, Black desire.

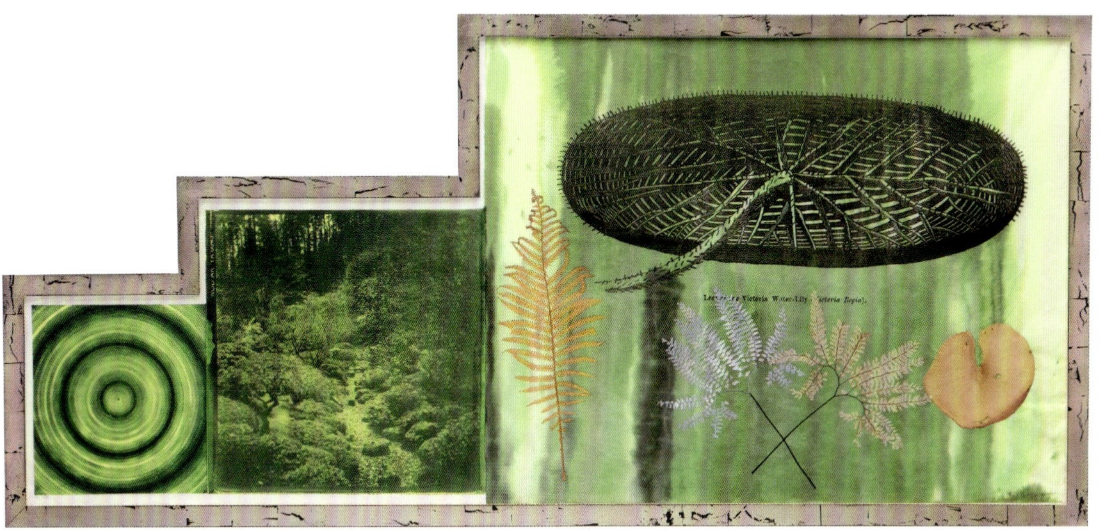

Judy Pfaff
(American, b. 1946)
Untitled (target, garden, lily pad), edition 16/30, 2000
photogravure, etching, lithograph, dye, applied leaves
37 × 84½ in. (94 × 214.6 cm)

The artistic roots of Swoon (Caledonia Curry) lie in street art. A believer in the power of art to uplift and inspire individuals and communities, Swoon transforms portraits of everyday people into archetypes of beauty and hope. Using supports like doors and windows for her imagery allows Swoon, in effect, to bring into the gallery space vestiges of the buildings onto which her artwork was first placed. There is, too, the symbolism inherent in such passageways, leading from one space—be it physical, emotional, or spiritual—to another (opposite and pp. 117–19).

The fragmentation we have wrought on the natural environment has irrefutably changed it and our relationship to it. Judy Pfaff's work is known for its response to particular environments. In her complex, large-scale installations, Pfaff utilizes a diverse array of materials to fuse the natural and the artificial, evoking the complex relationship between the two. The same aesthetic is prevalent in her two-dimensional works; in *Untitled (target, garden, lily pad)* (2000, above and p. 103), Pfaff uses multiple techniques including photogravure, etching, and lithography, as well as collaging actual plant specimens into the work. Far from presenting human intervention in the environment as a completely negative impact, Pfaff presents a more nuanced way of seeing the interaction of the two.

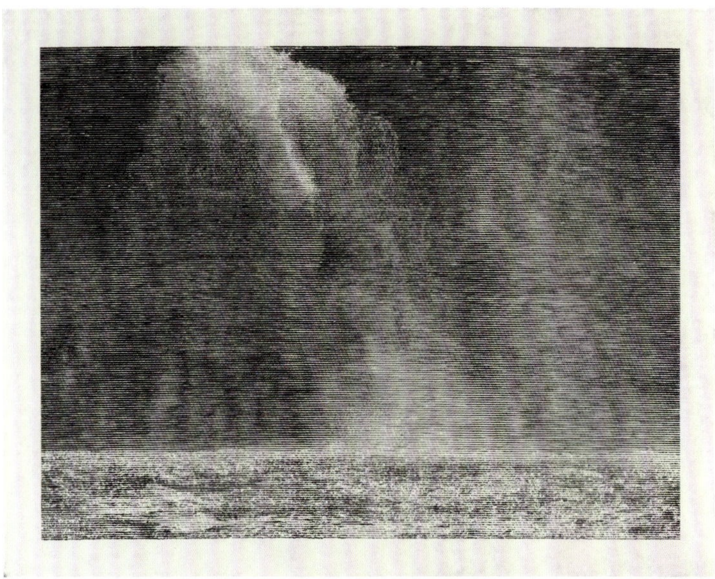

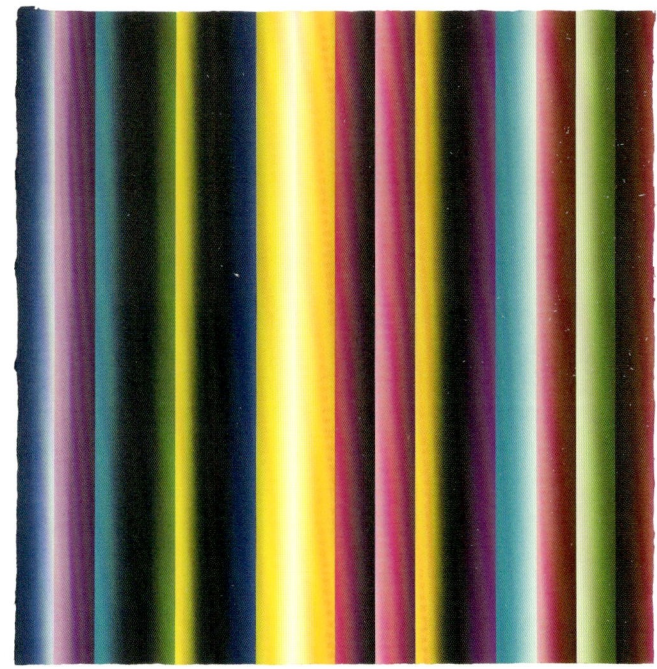

Christiane Baumgartner
(German, b. 1967)
Stairway to Heaven: Silver Rain I,
edition 1/3, 2019
woodcut
55⅛ × 70⅞ in. (140 × 180 cm)

Polly Apfelbaum
(American, b. 1955)
Baroque Time Machine 3, 2014
woodblock monoprint
79 × 79 in. (200.7 × 200.7 cm)

Time and (Sub)text

A seemingly straightforward, although bifurcated, view of the ocean horizon, Christiane Baumgartner's massive polyptych *Stairway to Heaven* (2019, above and pp. 47–49) is not so much a contemplation of the vastness of the ocean as a commentary on speed and the passage of time, subjects that are the focus of most of her work. Working from video stills, Baumgartner creates monumental woodblock prints, in effect taking the fleeting moments of time captured on film and re-creating them through labor-intensive hand carving. By translating a contemporary medium, film, into a print using centuries-old techniques, Baumgartner collapses the time between the two via the perennial view of sea and sky. Polly Apfelbaum likewise collapses time in *Baroque Time Machine* (2014, above and p. 41), which "simultaneously suggest[s] backward and forward temporal movement, signaling historical influences and new aesthetic directions."[8] Rather than taking inspiration from new media, as Baumgartner does, Apfelbaum draws on the saturated hues found in Baroque paintings and distills them into pure bands of color using a split fountain or "rainbow roll" printing technique, in which multiple colors are partially mixed to create a gradient effect.

Barbara Takenaga, too, finds inspiration in the art of the past. In *Angel (Little Egypt)* (2007, opposite), Takenaga takes her visual cue from an angel's wing painted by the Italian Renaissance artist Fra Angelico. Her repetitive motifs evoke the macrocosm of the infinite universe as well as the microcosm of molecular life. Of this plurality, Takenaga says: "I liked the way the feather

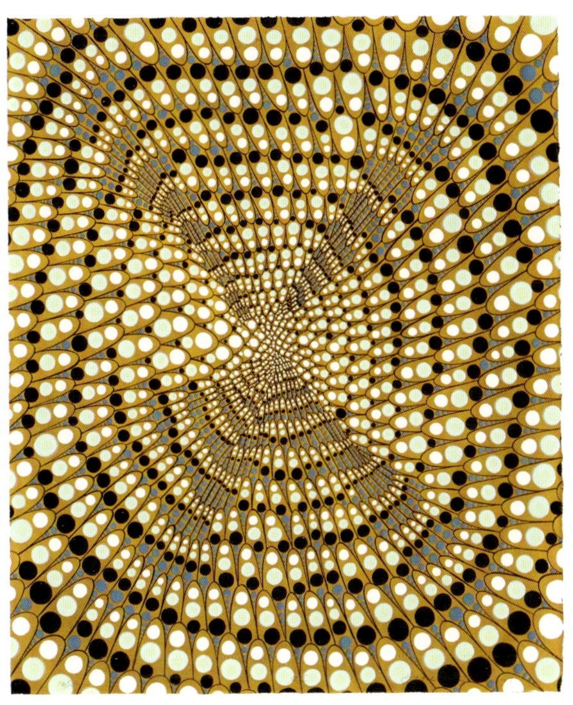

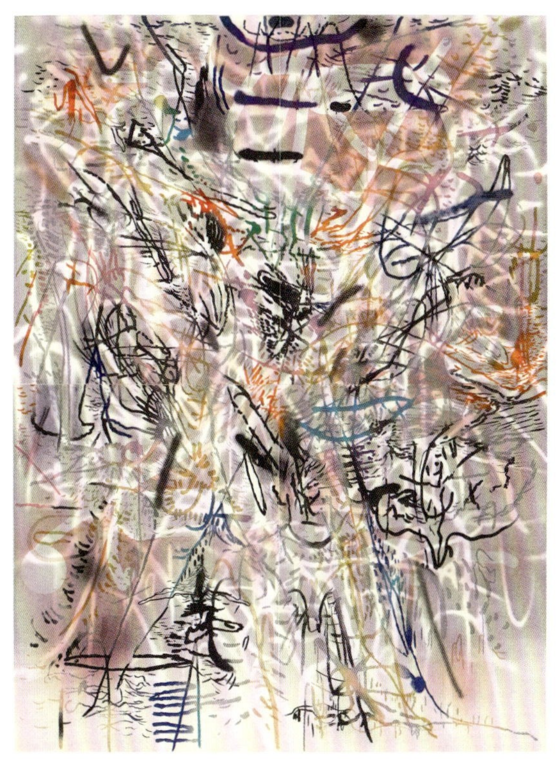

Barbara Takenaga
(American, b. 1949)
Angel (Little Egypt) State I,
edition 13/15, 2007
lithograph with metallic gold powder
24¼ × 20¼ in. (61.6 × 51.4 cm)
© Courtesy of the artist and Shark's Ink

Julie Mehretu
(American, b. Ethiopia, 1970)
Six Bardos: Transmigration,
edition 23/25, 2018
aquatint
98 × 74 in. (248.9 × 188 cm)
© 2018 Julie Mehretu and Gemini G.E.L. LLC

pattern [of the angel's wing] is similar to the Asian motif of fish scales or waves of water. There is a reference to the natural world, as well as the heavenly, but in an abstract, decorative approach."[9] The incommunicability of the universe, of time, and of the liminal space between life and death is a challenge that has tested religions, philosophers, and artists for centuries. Any attempt at the expression of these things is necessarily fragmented, seen through a glass darkly. Stylistically different from Takenaga's tightly controlled, geometrically ordered abstractions, Julie Mehretu's trademark wide gestural marks are equally suited to contemplating philosophical propositions. Titled after the six levels of transitional states between life and death in Tibetan Buddhism, Mehretu's *Six Bardos* (2018, above and pp. 37, 93–95), two of which are in this exhibition, use a combination of markings and lines that suggest at once ancient writing and contemporary graffiti. The familiarity of her forms gives viewers an entry point into Mehretu's works while their indecipherability prevents a singular interpretation.

Artists' use of legible text in their work can take many different forms. Chicago incorporates her textbook-perfect script in many of her prints,

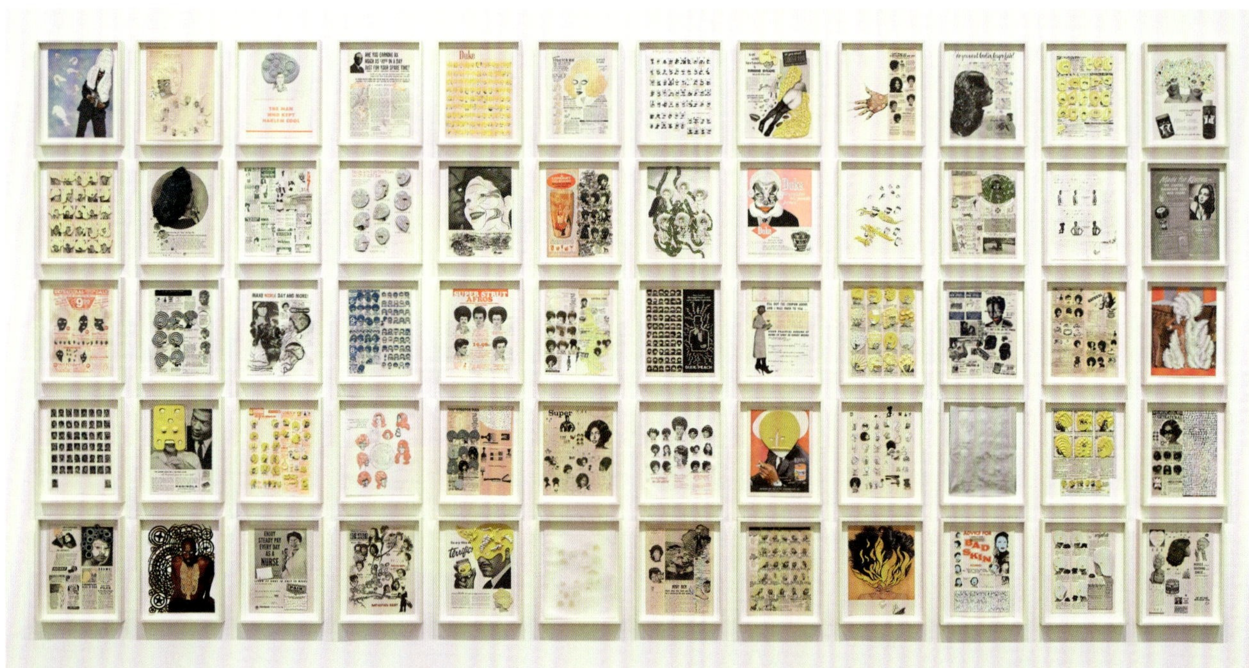

Ellen Gallagher
(American, b. 1965)
DeLuxe
2004–5
Edition 5/20
Grid of 60 photogravure, etching, aquatint, and drypoints with lithography, screenprint, embossing, tattoo-machine engraving, laser cutting, and chine collé; some with additions of Plasticine, paper collage, enamel, varnish, gouache, pencil, oil, polymer, watercolor, pomade, velvet, glitter, crystals, foil paper, gold leaf, toy eyeballs, and imitation ice cubes
13 × 10⅜ in.
(33 × 26.5 cm) each
84¾ × 176 in.
(215.3 cm × 447 cm) overall

as in *Mary Queen of Scots* (1973, p. 67), to elucidate the subject as well as her working process. Ellen Gallagher's text in *DeLuxe* (2004–5, above and pp. 75–79), taken from vintage African American periodicals and collaged together with imagery from the same publications, complicates rather than explicates. Mainly taken from advertisements, these words and images have been reassembled by Gallagher (who has also added her own handmade embellishments) into a barrage of hollow promises and dubious advice that in retrospect seems like an uncanny harbinger of social media newsfeeds of today. Equally prescient in that regard, Jenny Holzer's decontextualized fragments of text find a parallel in the bite-sized way we ingest information today. This analogy is all the more fitting considering that Holzer often placed her works in public spaces where people would encounter them in the course of their day-to-day activities. In her series *Inflammatory Essays* (1979–82, opposite and pp. 81–83), as in most of her work, Holzer uses only text, devoid of any visual clues. These blocks of text, written by the artist to emulate the urgent tone used by fanatics of all ideologies, reveal the absurdity and danger of such regimented thinking.

For the artists featured in *Positive Fragmentation*, creation begins with deconstruction as they dissect shape, color, perspective, text, idea, and stereotype. For some, meaning resides in the act of pulling apart and fragmenting images and ideas, exposing what lies beneath. Others assemble fragments to create a new whole defined by its different parts. Exploring the impulses that drive the creative approaches in the work of these artists through the lens of "positive fragmentation" can provide new ways of making sense of our own

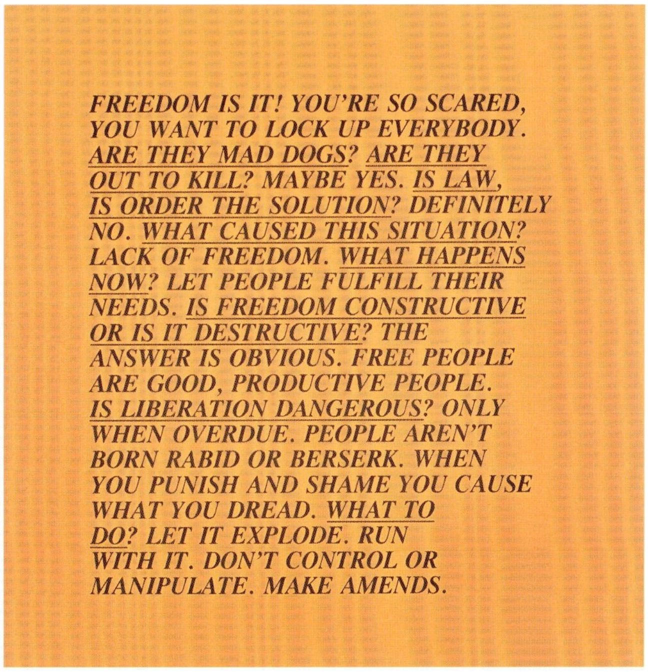

FREEDOM IS IT! YOU'RE SO SCARED, YOU WANT TO LOCK UP EVERYBODY. ARE THEY MAD DOGS? ARE THEY OUT TO KILL? MAYBE YES. IS LAW, IS ORDER THE SOLUTION? DEFINITELY NO. WHAT CAUSED THIS SITUATION? LACK OF FREEDOM. WHAT HAPPENS NOW? LET PEOPLE FULFILL THEIR NEEDS. IS FREEDOM CONSTRUCTIVE OR IS IT DESTRUCTIVE? THE ANSWER IS OBVIOUS. FREE PEOPLE ARE GOOD, PRODUCTIVE PEOPLE. IS LIBERATION DANGEROUS? ONLY WHEN OVERDUE. PEOPLE AREN'T BORN RABID OR BERSERK. WHEN YOU PUNISH AND SHAME YOU CAUSE WHAT YOU DREAD. WHAT TO DO? LET IT EXPLODE. RUN WITH IT. DON'T CONTROL OR MANIPULATE. MAKE AMENDS.

Jenny Holzer
(American, b. 1950)
Inflammatory Essays: Freedom Is It!..., 1979–82
offset print on colored paper
17 × 17 in. (43.2 × 43.2 cm)

fractured post-pandemic world and provide inspiration for how to navigate into the future.

Virginia Treanor is the associate curator at the National Museum of Women in the Arts.

NOTES

1 Lucy Lippard, "Making Something from Nothing," in *The Pink Glass Swan: Selected Feminist Essays on Art* (New York: New Press, 1995), 136. Originally published in *Heresies*, no. 4 (Winter 1978).

2 Lippard, "Making Something," 136.

3 Quoted in Deborah Willis, "Looks and Gazes: Photographic Fragmentation and the Found Object," in *Betye Saar: Extending the Frozen Moment* (Ann Arbor: University of Michigan Museum of Art, 2005), 22.

4 Lucy Lippard, "Feminist Space: Reclaiming Territory," in *Pink Glass Swan*, 209. Originally published in *The Event Horizon: Essays on Hope, Sexuality, Social Space, and Media(tion) in Art*, ed. Lorne Falke and Barbara Fischer (Toronto: Coach House Press, 1987).

5 Lucy Lippard, "Issue and Taboo," *Pink Glass Swan,* 168. Originally published in *Issue: Social Strategies by Women Artists* (London: Institute of Contemporary Art, 1980).

6 Quoted in Skye Sherwin, "My Work Is Related to Power," review of "Bye Bye Brazil," https://www.phaidon.com/agenda/art/articles/2013/july/18/sarah-morris-my-work-is-related-to-power/.

7 Clayton Porter, "Studio Visit, Nicola López," *Southwest Contemporary*, July 1, 2017, https://southwestcontemporary.com/studio-visit-nicola-lopez/.

8 "New Release: Polly Apfelbaum, *Emperor Twist & Empress Shout*," Durham Press, https://www.durhampress.com/2015/03/polly-apfelbaum-new-releases-and-in-the-studio/.

9 "*Angel (Little Egypt) State I*," Shark's Ink, https://sharksink.com/print/angel-little-egypt-state-i/.

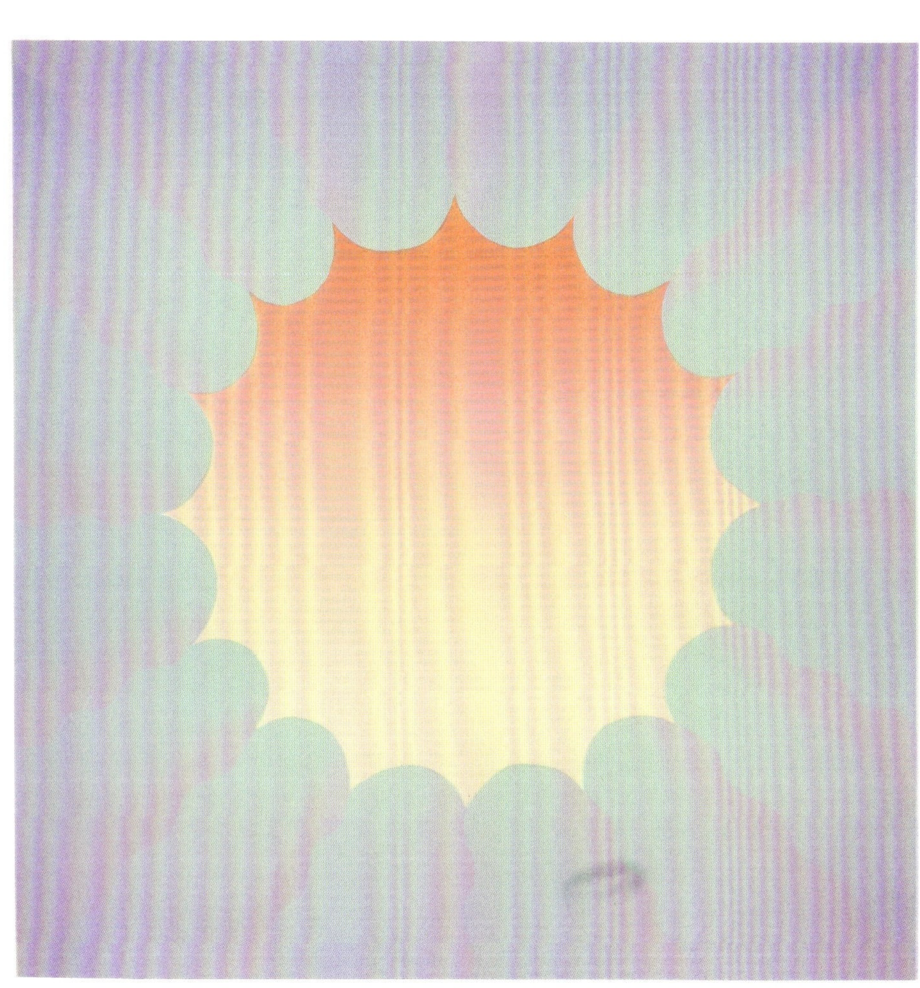

CRITIQUE AND THE ART HISTORICAL IMAGINATION

William J. Simmons

Any discussion of fragmentation necessarily engenders a variety of what appear to be its binary opposites: unity, universality, cohesion, love, sturdiness, and so on. Yet the queer/feminist/queer-of-color call for connectivity-within-difference, encapsulated by the title *Positive Fragmentation*, has taught us that within fragmentation is exactly the possibility of love, and within love is the possibility of inevitable fracture. Indeed, love is a form of fragmentation (an awareness of the singularity of the Other) that takes the form, knowingly or not, of unification. The urge to take apart is indistinguishable from the impulse for gentle rebuilding. A value judgment on love or its opposite, fragmentation or growth, is not made by the Print or by the Original or by the artist, but only by the critic or historian. The political implication often suggested by the critic or historian is that in order to thwart systems of power, we must deconstruct them and take them apart, but it is also true that, in some sense, we must love them, for who better to send us to the brink of positive disintegration than the lover who is indifferent to us, but whom we nevertheless feel we must understand? Indifference is at once more painful and more erotic. Despite its being an apathetic state, indifference feels more like violence than passivity, though of course those terms are likewise intertwined, and the implication that anything other than a critical relationship to art is tantamount to indifference. But what if the antidote to apathy is not deconstruction, which is another form of violence, but rather belief? Belief might sound saccharine or banal, or even fascist. It seems to me that all the artists in this exhibition, no matter how scathing their assessment of words and images and discourses might be, no matter how committed they may be to disintegration, all believe that there is the possibility of the shattered parts coming back together, that the art object, which is unconcerned with the viewer, critic, and historian, can at least feel, see some of the myriad emotions it produces.

Judy Chicago
(American, b. 1939)
Through the Flower 4,
edition 8/10, 1972
lithograph
22 × 22 in. (55.9 × 55.9 cm)

It is crucial therefore to recall that deconstruction/fragmentation is not an inherently avant-garde or politically progressive exercise, nor is love an inherently regressive and anti-critical relationship to objects of culture. This

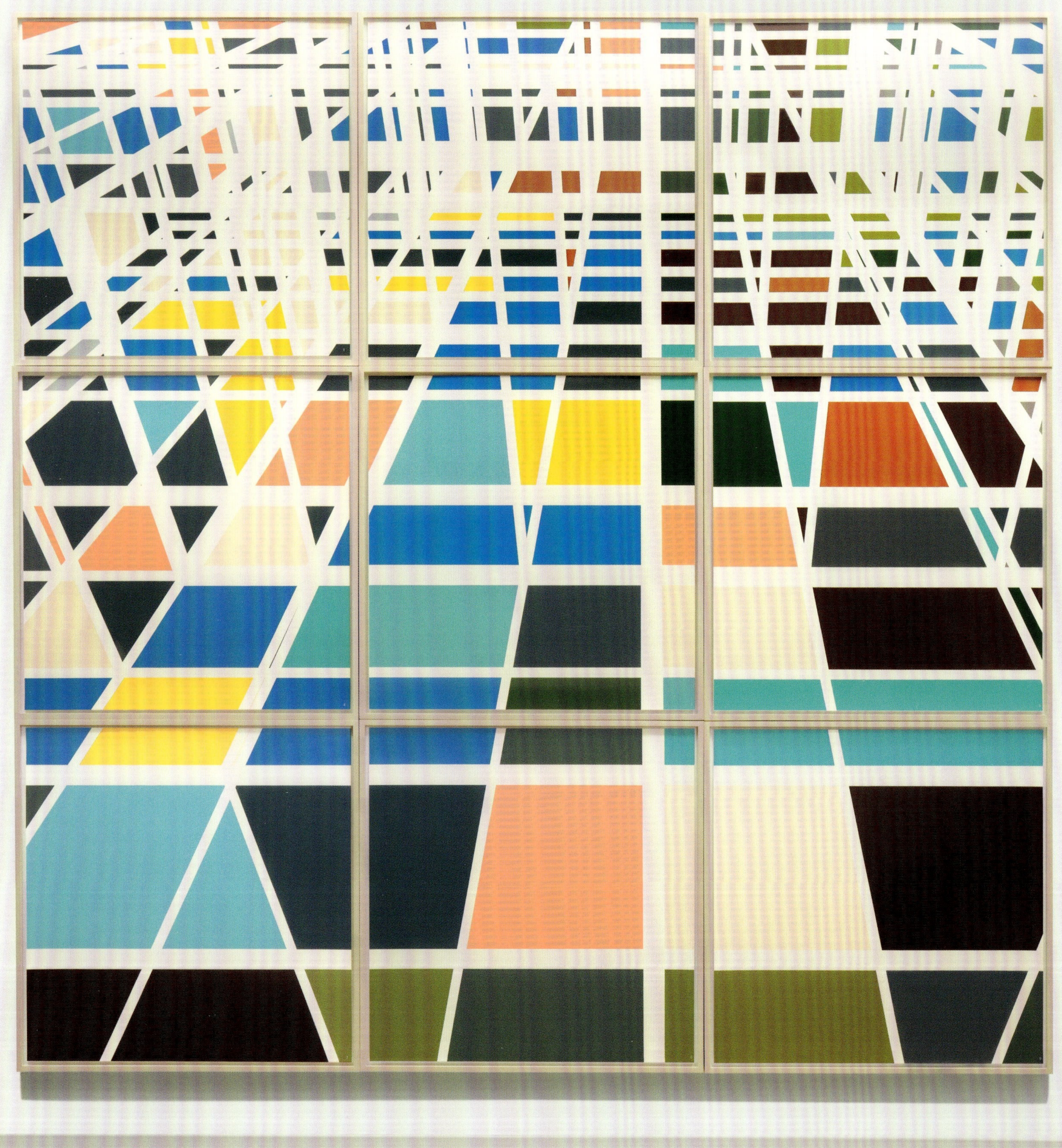

is especially true in the instance of prints, which are often treated as ersatz, selfsame reiterations of other media to which we might more quickly ascribe a degree of "genius," most notably painting and drawing. For Judy Chicago, however, lithography and other printing techniques were central to the development of feminist art, not only in terms of formal experimentation, but also in terms of an emotional experiment. She writes of her early lithograph *Red Flag* (1971), an image of a bloody tampon being removed from a vagina, that the act of making a print was a feminist gesture in itself: "I made the print for two reasons: first, I wanted to validate female subject matter by using a 'high art' process, which is what hand lithography is, and second, I think I was trying to test male reaction to overt female subject matter. . . . I can see now that I was slowly developing the confidence that I could, in fact, reveal my real feelings in my work and that nothing terrible would happen."[1] Luckily, it was a positive experience. The male printer she was working with was at best empathetic and at worst merely professional. This feminist testing Chicago mentions of the inherently collaborative printmaking process is a form of belief in the face of rejection: on the one hand, that there might be male solidarity for a feminist cause, and on the other, that the absence of that solidarity will not defeat her. The same is true of Chicago's *Great Ladies* and *Through the Flower* prints in this exhibition, which represent a deepening embrace of the "overt female subject matter" Chicago describes. Optimism therefore becomes Chicago's medium, ready to be replicated, like a print, in a multitude of situations that require cautious excitement, or at least some certainty that the Other will not disappoint you, in addition to paranoid dread—since, indeed, love and feminism require both of those emotional configurations.

Although she is rarely, if ever, categorized as a feminist artist, Sarah Morris works through a similar process of testing a potentially cruel hegemonic culture. It is true that Morris exposes the infrastructure of the nefarious systems of capitalism by abstracting and recontextualizing its conceptual and literal scaffolding. And yet Morris's work would be disserved by positioning it as a purely skeptical process of denuding faceless and selfish phenomena, thereby placing the viewer in the archetypal binary of good and evil. If it were so understood, she and the other artists of *Positive Fragmentation* would be biographers of morality (for which there is a place, no doubt). Morris's prints are revealing records of the built environment, culture, film, and so on, but they are also records of her own affective movements and attachments, not in the sense that the work is reductively "about" her in an autobiographical sense, but rather that it is "about" her and our conflicting, expanding choices and relationships with symbols of power, mobility, conflict, love, and loss.

Sarah Morris
(American, b. Britain, 1967)
Dulles (Capital), 2001,
edition 32/45
installation view
9 screenprints
29 × 29 in.
(73.7 × 73.7 cm) each
© Sarah Morris

It is no mistake that many of Morris's monographs contain production stills; indeed, her oeuvre is a sort of ongoing production still of a film comprising the artist's evolving interpolation and rejection of power as she disintegrates it and allows it to exist, precariously, in its alluring totality. Now, there is of course the issue of Woman-as-always-in-progress that must be addressed in any evocation of disintegration. That postmodernism as a state of liminality is really an adoption of a patriarchally defined "feminine" role is certainly of note here, since postmodernism thereby hopes to absorb difference and affect rather than engage them. Theory, at least as it is normatively practiced, authorizes certain kinds of accepted affects and not others, among them being those that are overly activist or essentialist. This is in part why postmodern art has largely rejected feminist art (and in some ways queer art) as reductive or otherwise precious in favor of the language of a universalized deconstruction that makes everything always-in-progress, a state usually connoted as non-male. Morris's work is therefore especially important because of its particularity, the particularity of her choices, her desires, and her relationships with place, even as they are all constantly shifting in time and space. This does not revive a modernist individualism centered on personal choice (made most explicit by the fragmentary and masculine picking-and-choosing of the Duchampian readymade). Instead, Morris presents the self as inherently activated through the desires set in motion by capital (which we may or may not choose to deconstruct), but always resistant to capital because of the necessarily unpredictable nature of desire, despite the ability to predict desire being the most feverish and hysterical goal of global capitalism, just as it is the goal of a desiring body.

Nicole Eisenman is likewise anything but indifferent, though at times they might choose to be indifferent (an affective requirement of total investment in the medium, in resistance, often plagues queer-feminist artists). In Eisenman's *Picabia Filter* prints, we are reminded that homage, which is a form of love that characterizes Morris's work as well, is often treated with fear by the language of appropriation, which we understand as an ironic, and therefore "good," act of distancing from a patriarchal tradition. Eisenman in particular has been precariously situated between a "queered" citational lineage of male traditions (i.e., Eisenman's "appropriation" of nineteenth-century beer-garden scenes so central to a Western and patriarchal history of painting) and a "queered" rejection thereof (i.e., their deflating use of humor or their centering of non-cis-male bodies). What has emerged is a positioning of artists who do not identify as straight cis men as purely a product of their antipathetic relationships to hegemonic discourses. So, it is equally important to suggest that Eisenman might and does have relationships with art history that are not purely ironic or irreverent or otherwise comical-as-critical, and that their world of non-cis-male bodies and queer activities is not just a response to their absence elsewhere. What if Eisenman really and truly *digs* Picabia, with no driving desire to "queer" him? If being queer actually centers on identifying at times with problematic or hegemonic elements of culture as a means of survival, such as a figurehead of a normative history of the avant-garde like Picabia, what would it mean to linger in that space of love for a historical figure without resorting

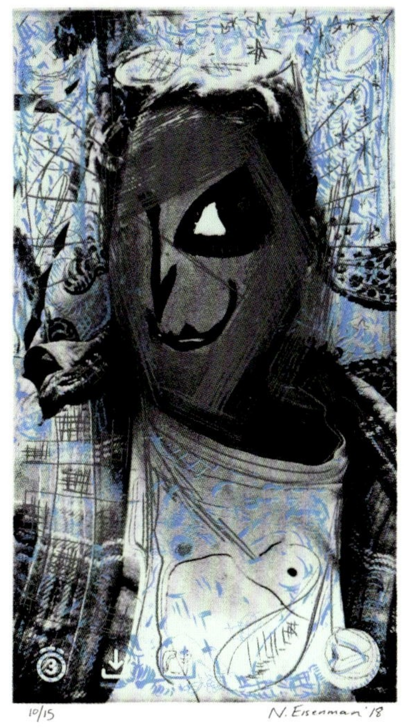

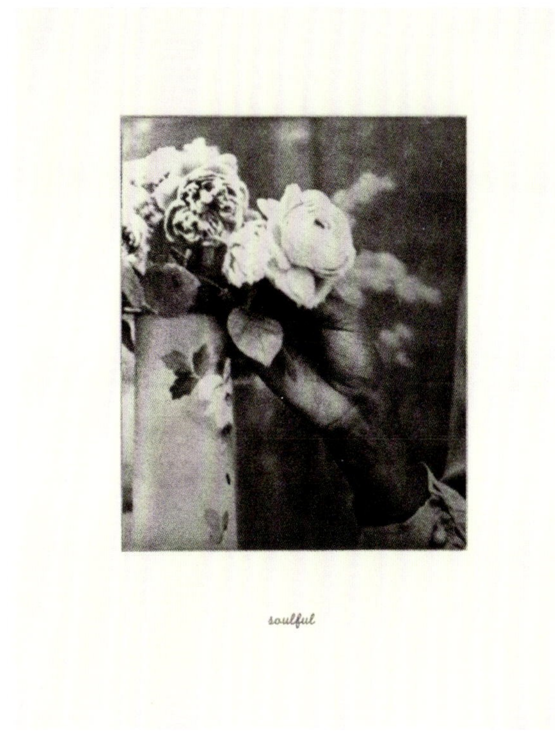

Nicole Eisenman
(American, b. 1965)
Picabia Filter I,
edition 10/15, 2018
intaglio with drypoint
22½ × 15 in. (57.2 × 38.1 cm)
© Nicole Eisenman. Courtesy
the artist and 10 Grand Press

Lorna Simpson
(American, b. 1960)
Details (soulful), edition 35/40,
1996
photogravure with text
10 × 8 in. (25.4 × 20.3 cm)
© Lorna Simpson
Courtesy the artist and
Hauser & Wirth

to immediate skepticism? How can we encounter a love for Picabia, or even a Picabia fandom, which may also include other artists that we might not immediately see as queer icons, without striving to disprove it as irony?

For Lorna Simpson, the moment of love and critique has been touch, not unlike the implied swipe of Eisenman's Instagram filter or the orchestral gesturality of Julie Mehretu's prints. Simpson's work is undeniably beautiful (as is Eisenman's, which we often neglect to acknowledge in favor of the grotesque-comical). Beauty has everything to do with its criticality. The point is not that beauty hides critique and therefore makes it more potent when the message finally creeps up on us. That tried-and-true Trojan horse argument purports that the viewer must be shocked into action, that they are not smart or empathetic enough to see the problematic within the seductive. By evoking beauty, I mean to suggest that there is something within the rigorous medium specificity of Simpson's work that is resistant to discourse, though it is certainly not pre- or post-discursive. For we cannot always use beauty as a metaphysical escape, though choosing to do so is not always cowardly or regressive. These prints by Simpson, in their intimacy and their distance, their discreteness and their interconnectivity, are indeed beautiful. They are beyond words despite the centrality of words. The hands of Black folk in countless iterations could indeed exit the beautiful and become metaphors for the history of photography itself, for which hand manipulation and, more obviously, photographs of hands have always been discursive loci that are inextricable from race. Yet non-cis-white-male touch (a possible effect of the hand but not the same as the hand) is simultaneously impossible to describe with the vocabulary given to us by history, which is a discipline of distance and of consolidation. A hand around a waist, modified and made sinister by cropping and text, is still an irreducible moment of skin-upon-skin remembered by someone somewhere, which discourse cannot flatten. Simpson's work, like others' in *Positive Fragmentation*, is not anti-interpretation because of the beautiful pause it gives, but there must be a moment between anti-interpretation and the directive (made most violently to artists of color, women artists, and/or queer artists) that their work be reduced to *only* interpretation.

At the same time, all this talk of the primacy of affect might be exactly beside the point because of the restrictive nature of autobiography when it comes to non-cis-male artists. As Rachel Cusk writes of Cecily Brown: "Since it is not yet possible to set aside femininity as affectless, the woman artist is often compelled to be at some level an autobiographer. The account of identity might present itself to some as a temptation and to others as a kind of sacred duty; at the very least it can seem somehow inextricable from the motivation to create art."[2] And indeed, for a good number of artists in this exhibition, principally among them Judy Chicago, identity is indeed a sacred duty, and that is a duty that must continue to be cherished and not sidelined as essentialist. Brown, like Eisenman, has the added duty of existing not only between autobiography and discourse but also in the over-theorized "interspace" between abstraction and figuration that non-cis-male artists have been forced to take up as the only way in which they can be legible, as if to touch upon abstraction at all as a woman must be a commentary on "liminality." More useful might be defining this archetypally "liminal" space in a way that is unequivocal, as Cusk does: "What will she make of it, what account will she give of it, this field of life that lies beyond the feminine known?"[3] It is true that Brown's canvases are vast and undecidable—chromatically, emotionally, historically, discursively—but Cusk notes a refreshing certainty here: that She, which we can read more widely as the non-cis-male Other, can create from the *informe*, or the disintegrated, a process of choice and self-theorization, which is not the same as autobiography. Brown's prints and paintings thereby become spaces of queer-feminist agency, one in which femininity is not affectless, to use Cusk's apt term, but rather some element of affect is retained as radically individual, and thereby opaque.

Opacity has likewise been of central interest to Julie Mehretu, whose technically rigorous *Six Bardos* prints refer to the spiritual steps taken as the soul transitions through reincarnation—a form of positive disintegration, to be sure. Mehretu's work has been understood as resolutely autobiographical, and from that autobiography emerges criticality, which is a formulation that

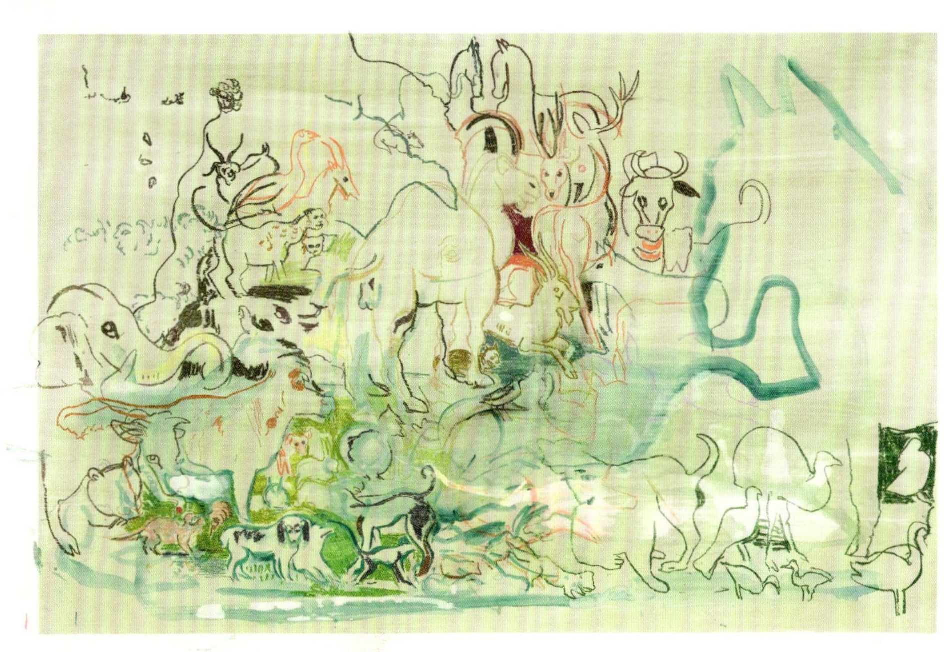

Cecily Brown
(British, b. 1969)
Untitled (Paradise), 2015
monotype in watercolor, pencil, and pastel
48 × 71 in. (121.9 × 180.3 cm)

often limits the avenues of signification available to non-white-male artists. Yet her autobiography and the way that it interacts with her criticality is, ultimately, her choice to make, despite an expectation of self- or sociocultural revelation. There is undoubtedly an almost intangible expansiveness to her prints and painting. However, additionally and simultaneously, part of Mehretu's ongoing optimism is that artworks can in some way offer an embodied, material glimpse into the unpredictable, individual, and collective phenomena to which she chooses to give curves and lines and chromatic density. Or if it is not optimism, it is at least at least a cautious hope that art can matter, in the most literal sense, to the incommunicable vastness of desire, identification, attachment, color, line, form, and disidentification. More than anything, it is a cautious hope that art can matter beyond being subsumed into buzzwords of "revolution" and "resistance" that do not always have to be manifest in the work itself, though the critical imagination might require them to be in order for the work to be considered of historical import. Mehretu needs to believe, in a spiritual sense, certainly, as evinced by the *Six Bardos* prints, but also in the ability of printmaking and painting to continue to signify across and along lines of difference. As Julia Kristeva writes of what she calls a "need to believe," belief is an inscrutable mixture of "joy and pain, expectation necessarily disappointed, and anguish nonetheless ever enlightening."[4] We might wonder about the possibility of empathy altogether, if the capaciously defined Other, be it a body or a piece of paper or a canvas, can receive our paradoxical emotions after all, and us theirs. There is some hope in this exhibition.

Finally, in her novel *History of the Universe,* Jennifer Bartlett writes of her painter-protagonist, “Some of the titles of her paintings are *Beerglass at Noon*, *Will*, *Mars Violet Cross*, *Red Arc Yellow Painting*, *Dark Heart*, *Pink Spiral*, *Leap*, *Middleground*, *Heartbeat*, *Flamingo*, *Benita*, *Harry*, *Southern California*, *Rise*, *Rolling Ball*, *Singing School*, *Back*, *Beginner*, and, most recently: *Desire, Searchin'*.”[5] By way of a normatively formal reading: not unlike Simpson's fractured narratives, here we have a variety of overlapping titles, almost grid-like, ranging from the hackneyed to the unexpectedly profound, that sound like false starts and invitations, a film noir. These titles are both critical-comical and earnest, and for all the insider laughs and groans they might produce from art world insiders, they nevertheless all end in desire, searching, searching for desire. And with that frankly stated goal, even the most saccharine titles—say, *Heartbeat* or *Southern California*—become sublime. The knee-jerk need to poke a hole in Barlett's protagonist's careless titling seems beside the point, for who can really deconstruct or fragment, as it were, metonyms of a life?

In the same way that it is easier to believe that Bartlett is being unserious for our amusement, it is easier to believe that Mehretu's prints that draw from Tibetan Buddhism have nothing to do with her work that is “about” globalism and/or race and/or self-referentiality or that can be easily understood by the historian or critic as critical, antagonistic, coded, referential, utopian, dystopian, revolutionary, or otherwise part of a rightful, unidirectional artistic “development.” It is likewise easier to believe in a host of negative affects, primary among them being evil, and with it violence, which could be seen as a form of fragmentation. As Toni Morrison writes: “I have never been interested in or impressed by evil itself, but I have been confounded by how attractive it is to others. . . . Is it its theatricality, its costume, its blood spray, the emotional satisfaction that comes with its investigation more than its collapse? (The ultimate detective story, the paradigm murder mystery.)”[6] The spray of blood, an atomization, a fragmentation. And what could be more of a paradigm murder mystery than the language of formal analysis of texts and images, the murder mystery of finding out what a work of art is “really” about? What emerges from the primacy of fragmentation, deconstruction, criticism, disintegration, skepticism, exposure, sleuthing, rejection, embarrassment, and unmasking? What is the emotional register or range of un-fragmentation, of positive fragmentation? The artists in *Positive Fragmentation*, whose work requires treatment as both murder mystery and bildungsroman, suggest that that there is not a hierarchy of emotions in terms of where and how we meet art objects that, like love, trust, murder mysteries, empathy, or prints, are both unique and replicable.

Above all, these artists remind us that love and choice and belief are, like a print, not a matter of singularity in a modernist sense of genius or neoliberal individualism. There is a fear that heartfelt feeling, like Art-with-a-capital-A, is always haunted by the inauthenticity of cliché, which is, in fact, a term that

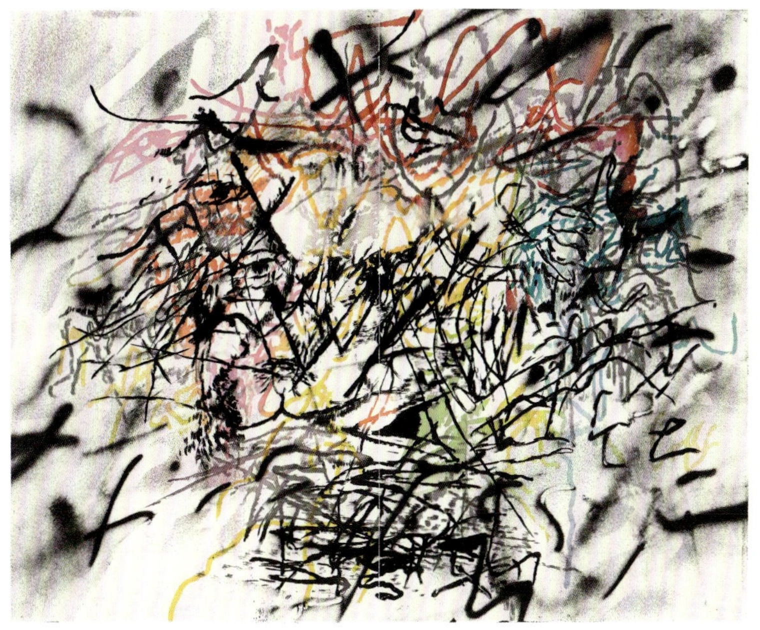

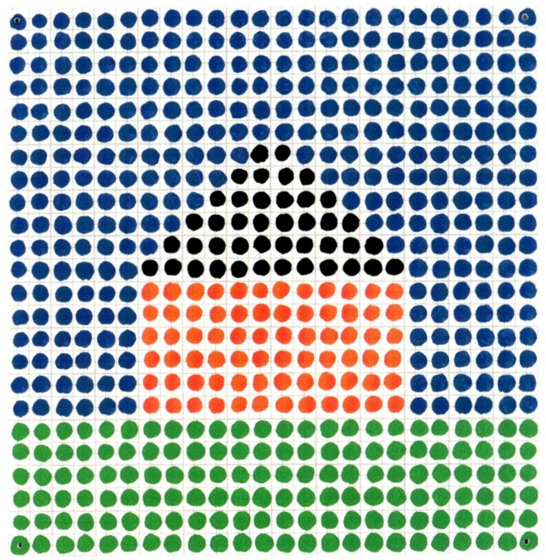

Julie Mehretu
(American, b. Ethiopia, 1970)
Six Bardos: Transmutation,
edition 23/45, 2018
aquatint
50½ × 61¼ in.
(128.3 × 155.6 cm)
© 2018 Julie Mehretu and
Gemini G.E.L. LLC

Jennifer Bartlett
(American, b. 1941)
House, edition PP 2/4, 2003
screenprint
14 × 14 in. (35.6 × 35.6 cm)
© Jennifer Bartlett. Courtesy
Marianne Boesky Gallery, New
York and Aspen, Paula Cooper
Gallery, New York, and The
Jennifer Bartlett 2013 Trust

comes from printmaking. "Cliché" was the sound that nineteenth-century French print workers used to mimic the sound of the press, so the word *cliché*, which denotes an allegedly ersatz emotion, is unexpectedly guttural and embodied and breathless, somewhere between an admonition and joy, banality and the extraordinary. Within the copy are endless versions of emotion, each of them recognizable and opaque. It is the viewer's radical opportunity to identify with or disidentify from those emotions as they are presented by the artist that allows for a conversation about a version of universality that is nevertheless driven by difference.

William J. Simmons is an art historian, curator, writer, and poet based in Los Angeles and New York.

NOTES

1 Judy Chicago, *Through the Flower: My Struggle as a Woman Artist* (New York: Anchor, 1977), 136.

2 Rachel Cusk, "We Didn't Mean to Go to Sea," in *We Didn't Mean to Go to Sea,* ed. Cecily Brown (London: Thomas Dane Gallery, 2019), iv.

3 Cusk, "We Didn't Mean," vi.

4 Julia Kristeva, *This Incredible Need to Believe* (New York: Columbia University Press, 2009), 9–10.

5 Klaus Ottman, *Jennifer Bartlett: History of the Universe* (New Haven and London: Yale University Press, 2013), 80.

6 David Carrasco, Stephanie Paulsell, and Maria Willard, eds., *Goodness and the Literary Imagination: Harvard Divinity School's 95th Ingersoll Lecture* (Charlottesville and London: University of Virginia Press, 2019), 15.

SELECTED WORKS FROM THE EXHIBITION

Polly Apfelbaum

Her signature use of bright colors, whether in ceramics, textiles, or installations, always distinguishes the aesthetic of the artist Polly Apfelbaum (American, b. 1955). For the work *Baroque Time Machine*, Apfelbaum collaborated with master printers at Durham Press in North Carolina to create a nearly seven-foot-wide monoprint, a unique image that, while created using printmaking techniques, is a singular irreproducible object. Ink was applied in a gradient fashion, known as a rainbow roll, to large wooden blocks of varying widths that were then pressed onto the large paper at the artist's discretion. The variance in tone within each colorful stripe creates a sense of dimensionality and heft similar to, as Apfelbaum has said, "the weight of drapery."[1]

Apfelbaum created this work shortly after spending a year in Italy as a recipient of of the American Academy of Rome Prize in 2012. She says, "Any work that operates beyond the scale of the body is also a physical experience; what someone has described as the fusion of feverish and dynamic baroque excesses with a rationalist geometry."[2] The expansive plane of vertical stripes engulfs the viewer's field of vision, recalling the frenzied and lush tapestries of the Italian Baroque period that the title references. —SD

---

1 "New Release: Polly Apfelbaum, *Emperor Twist* & *Empress Shout*," Durham Press, March 11, 2015, https://www.durhampress.com/2015/03/polly-apfelbaum-new-releases-and-in-the-studio/.

2 "Polly Apfelbaum," American Academy in Rome, Joseph H. Hazen Rome Prize, 2012, https://www.aarome.org/people/rome-prize-fellows/polly-apfelbaum.

Polly Apfelbaum
(American, b. 1955)
Baroque Time Machine 3, 2014
woodblock monoprint
79 × 79 in. (200.7 × 200.7 cm)

Jennifer Bartlett

Jennifer Bartlett (b. 1941) often creates her paintings, prints, and drawings according to a set of rules. In the early 1960s, minimalist artists like Donald Judd and Sol Lewitt championed the repetition of form and mechanical reproduction as a new way of making art—most famously, repeated stainless-steel blocks as sculpture or simply written instructions for serial pencil drawings on a wall. These artists used repetition as a way to question the individuality so lauded in the expressionist art of an earlier generation, expanding the notion of authorship and pushing the boundaries of abstraction. Responding to concurrent breakthroughs by minimalist artists in the late 1960s, Bartlett began fabricating identical twelve-inch-square steel plates that were coated with white enamel. Inspired by the signs she saw in New York City subway stations, Bartlett silkscreened images onto the modular panels and then layered hand-painted details onto those images. The resulting series was then hung in a grid similar to the muted sculpture hallmarked by her minimalist male counterparts; however, her interpretation of the grid emphasizes once again the handmade. As she has described: "I decided: 1) I didn't want to stretch a canvas again, 2) I wanted to be able to work on a lot of things at once. I didn't want to exercise my own taste, which seemed boring and hideous. I wanted something modular, a constant surface."[1] The twelve-inch panels generated creative limitations that allowed Bartlett to begin a lifetime of work, including her celebrated expandable paintings. Always working serially, Bartlett began each painting from a single-word prompt such as "tree" or "mountain," from which she created dozens of versions of that object, each unique in character. Where canonical minimalist works were purposely devoid of any sign of the artist's hand, Bartlett reinserted her colorful personal aesthetic into the grid, feminizing and reinvigorating the form.

For her editioned work *House* (2003), Bartlett created a paper-based version of her 1997–98 enameled panel piece of the same name. Each print in the portfolio attempts to find the most elementary way to visually describe a house through pixels, dots, squares, polygons, and lines. When seen together in a grid, the twenty-five screenprints speak to the ambivalent nature of what a house, or home, may be to each viewer, producing associations both cultural and personal. —SD

1 "Jennifer Bartlett: An Interview" (1976), Video Data Bank, 2010, http://www.vdb.org/titles/jennifer-bartlett-interview-0.

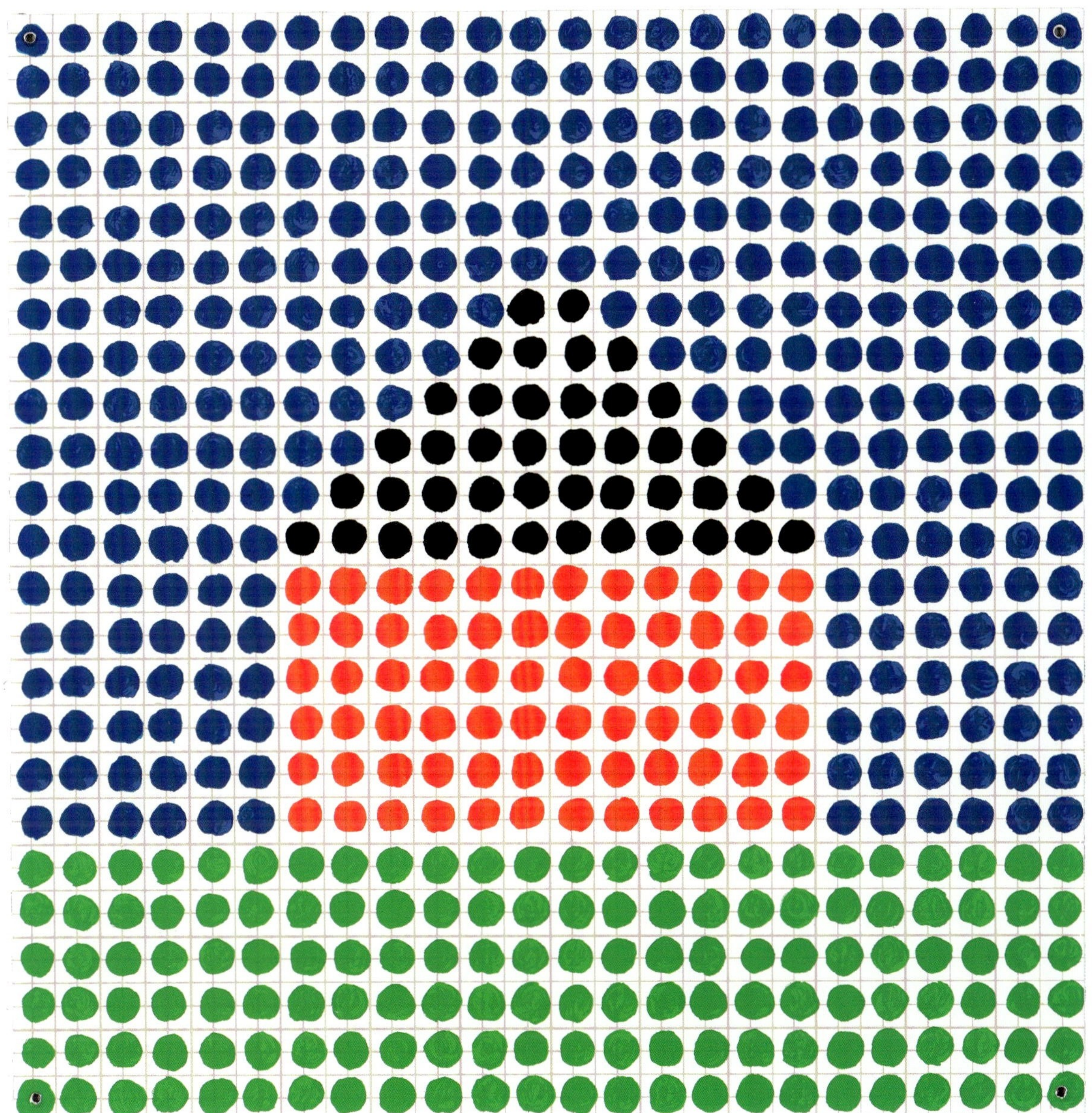

Jennifer Bartlett
(American, b. 1941)
House, edition PP 2/4, 2003
screenprint
14 × 14 in. (35.6 × 35.6 cm)

Jennifer Bartlett
(American, b. 1941)
House, edition PP 2/4, 2003
screenprints
14 × 14 in. (35.6 × 35.6 cm)
each

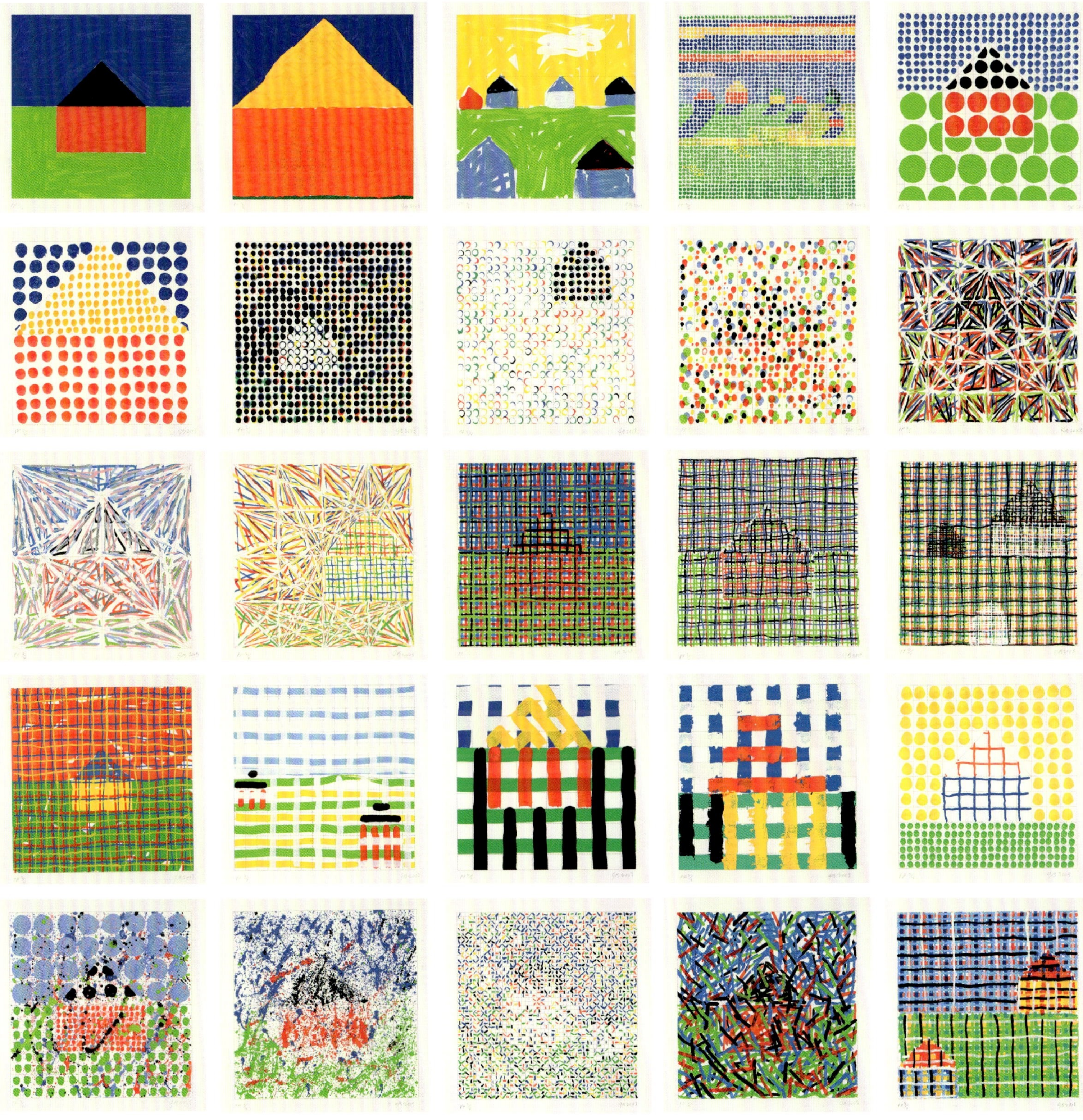

Christiane Baumgartner

The German artist Christiane Baumgartner (b. 1967) is known for her woodcuts of stills from video art and television. Having captured these stills by photographing the videos as they screened on an old television, Baumgartner translates their characteristic graininess by carving a series of horizontal lines across the entire surface of the woodblock. Her 2019 series of seascapes *Stairway to Heaven: Silver Rain I–V* evidences the way these lines—alternating positive and negative—come together to produce images with a haunting effect. Like much of Baumgartner's work, this series is printed on a large scale that requires the viewer to stand back in order to comprehend the subject matter; up close, the image disintegrates into its constituent array of abstracted horizontal lines.

Setting woodcuts into dynamic with digital media, Baumgartner is concerned with the crucial role each medium has played in replicating images; indeed, the woodcut is the earliest technique of image reproduction, while video and television are among the most recent.[1] The artist's hand-printing of her woodcuts further highlights the simplicity of the medium's reproductive function. While she identifies not as a printmaker but as "an artist working in print"[2]—shifting attention away from printmaking technique and, once again, toward larger questions of image, media, and replication—the process entailed in making woodcuts nonetheless remains crucial to her practice, sometimes even informing her choice of subject matter. Specifically, notions of pace have permeated much of Baumgartner's work, with the video stills she selects often containing speed-related imagery, which she understands as being in tension with the necessarily slow and laborious process of woodblock carving. —JO

Christiane Baumgartner
(German, b. 1967)
Stairway to Heaven: Silver Rain I (detail),
edition 1/3, 2019
woodcut
55⅛ × 70⅞ in. (140 × 180 cm)

1 Paul Coldwell, "Christiane Baumgartner Between States," *Art in Print* 1, no. 1 (May–June 2011): 4.

2 Thomas Marks, "'I Don't Call Myself a Printmaker'—An Interview with Christiane Baumgartner," *Apollo*, March 26, 2018, https://www.apollo-magazine.com/interview-with-christiane-baumgartner/.

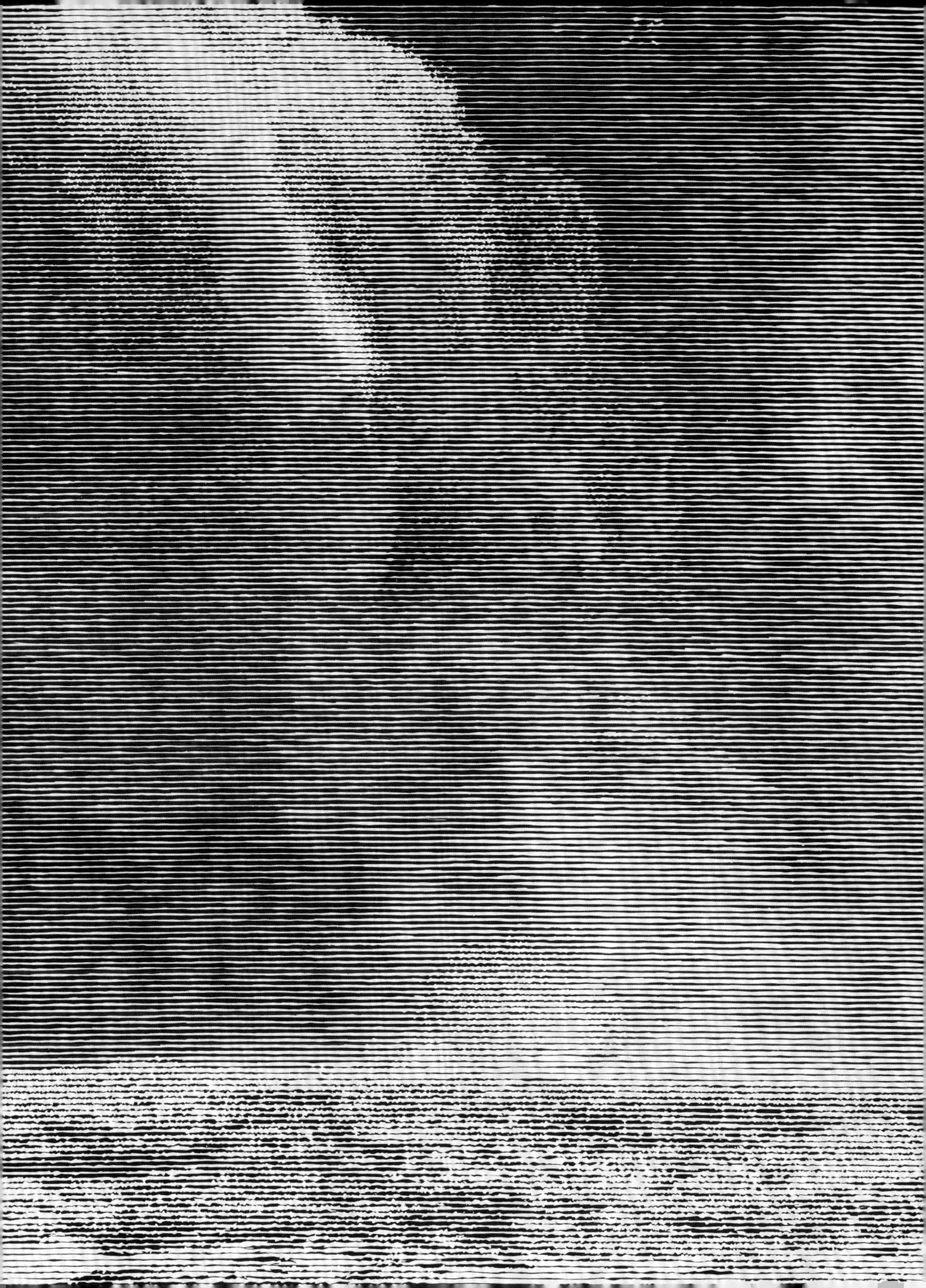

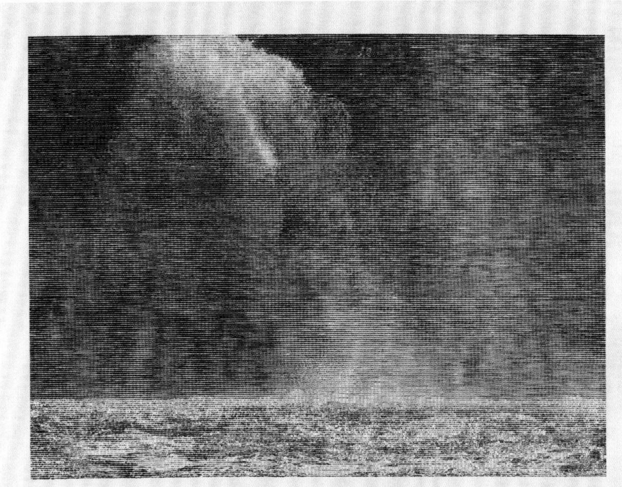
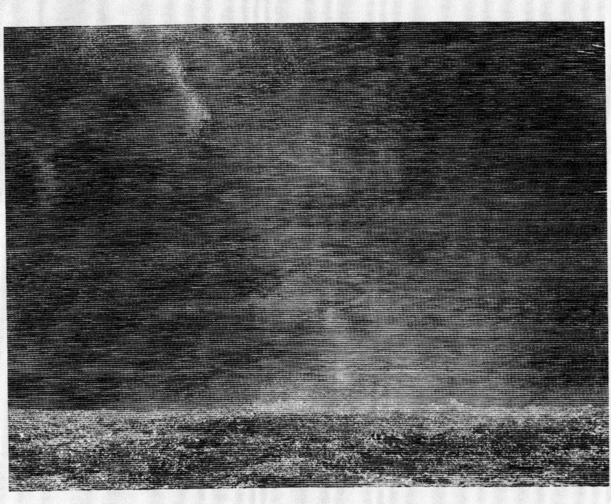
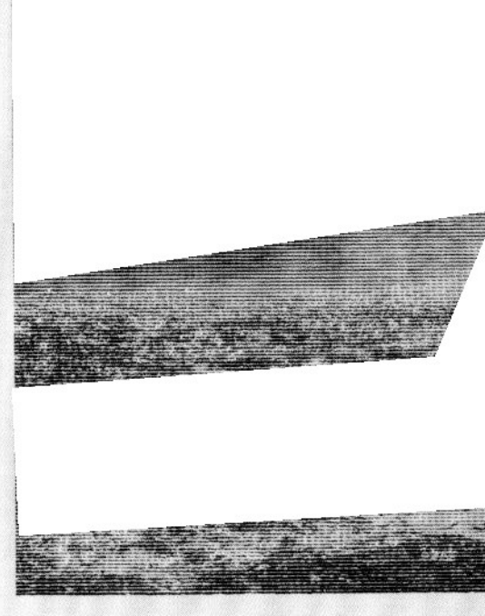

Christiane Baumgartner
(German, b. 1967)
Stairway to Heaven: Silver Rain I, edition 1/3, 2019
woodcuts
55⅛ × 70⅞ in. (140 × 180 cm) each

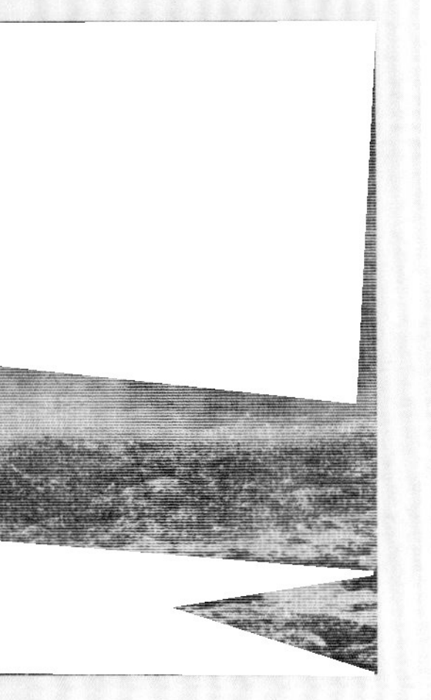

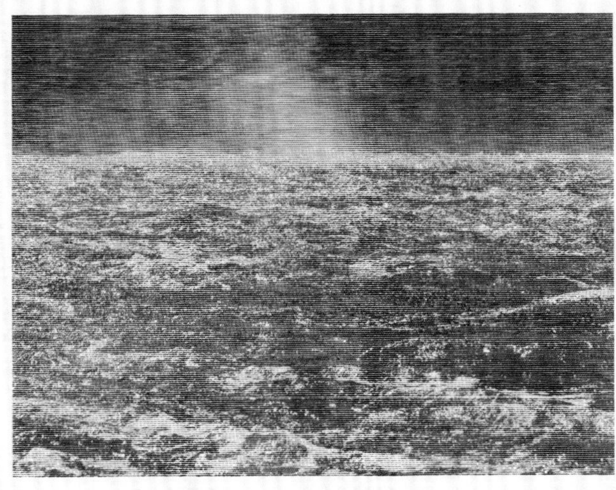

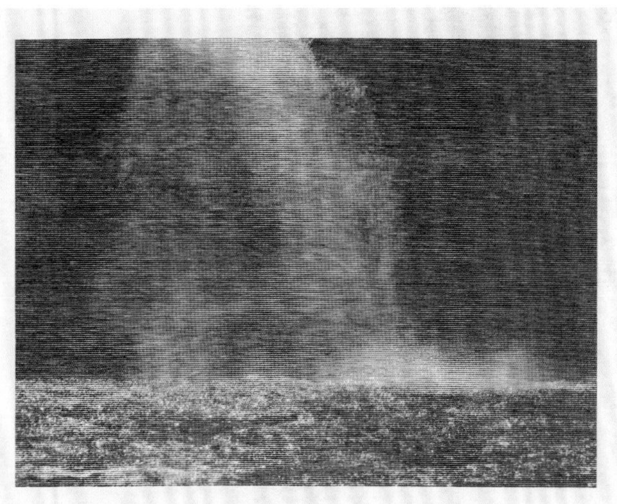

Louise Bourgeois

The influential avant-garde artist Louise Bourgeois (French-American, 1911–2010) began working on the *Anatomy* portfolio of prints with Judith Solodkin in 1989. Solodkin, the first woman to graduate from the acclaimed Tamarind Institute as a master printer, opened her own workshop, SOLO Impression, in 1975. The two women, both active in the feminist movement in New York City in the 1970s, worked closely to translate the artist's drawings into lithographs. As in her large-scale works in fabric, metal, wood, and other media, Bourgeois often drew upon her childhood memories of gender roles within her immediate family and her own sexuality to poetically capture her subjective experiences as a woman in modern society. Although a prolific sculptor, Bourgeois did not create large bodies of editioned works until later in life, and Solodkin became a key ally in that endeavor. For the *Anatomy* portfolio, though SOLO Impression specialized in lithography, Bourgeois had proofs from a nearby intaglio print workshop, Harlan & Weaver, brought to SOLO for her and Solodkin to inspect together as collaborators.

That portfolio is composed of twelve images that depict elements of the female body in motion: breasts multiplying and rotating around an axis, a pelvis depicted as if in an X-ray, hair braiding, and eyes crossing. Each image was made through an intaglio process, either etching or drypoint. The fine line of intaglio in this case allows for an intimate experience of the artist's hand as she imagines a reflection of herself and her body, from head to toe, moving through time and space, replicated and reproduced like the medium she has selected. As Bourgeois said at the time of creating this series: "These breasts go together with the heads. . . . This also could be hanging from a string and could turn. The person who does this is in a spirit of showing off . . . she is proud of her figure, so it is multiplied."[1]

Bourgeois began to fully incorporate printmaking into the breadth of her production, with the aid of established printmaking workshops that allowed for experimentation and complexity. *My Hand* (2002), completed with Solodkin at SOLO Impression, shows the artist's hand, scribbled on and transparent against a sheet of music, printed onto a vintage cloth that Bourgeois had embroidered with "LB" in the lower right corner. Already bearing the signs of memory and usage so important to the artist and her work, the cloth becomes a vehicle for other signifiers of meaning: the knobby knuckles of the artist's aging hand and the music sheet giving a

1 Deborah Wye, "Louise Bourgeois: The Complete Prints & Books," Museum of Modern Art, 2018, https://www.moma.org/s/lb/collection_lb/object/object_objid-63580.html.

natural rhythm to the page that referenced her early memories growing up near the piano. The artist frequently employed sheets of music in her prints, like *Untitled III* from the illustrated artist's book *Metamorfosis*, because, as she said: "It is very peaceful to look at the lines of the staff paper. It gives a rhythm . . . a passive direction to the horizontal . . . and an active direction to the vertical."[2]

Bourgeois preferred the delicate nature of drypoint, with its softer line, and she generated some fifteen hundred prints over the course of her career. Bourgeois continued to address the female body or her own body as her primary subject matter, sometimes adding textural elements that spoke to her sculptural practice. In *Ears* (2004), completed at Harlan & Weaver, a human ear repeats across the page, as if listening in the direction of the viewer. Bourgeois hole-punched the center of each ear, further blurring the distinction between body and art object. Similarly, for *Les Petites Sensations*, another drypoint etching printed at Harlan & Weaver, Bourgeois embellished the final image of a headless femme body with glass beads, a motif she frequently employed as a symbol of both pain and resilience, also seen in another Harlan & Weaver etching, *Sainte Sébastienne* (1992). Printmaking became an instrumental and cathartic part of her art practice at the end of her life, as she refined and repurposed content from her decades-long career of works on paper. —SD

---

2 Deborah Wye, "Louise Bourgeois: The Complete Prints & Books, Themes: Music," https://www.moma.org/s/lb/curated_lb/themes/music.html.

Louise Bourgeois
(American, b. France,
1911–2010)
Ears, edition 10/12, 2004
drypoint
17 × 15 in. (43.2 × 38.1 cm)

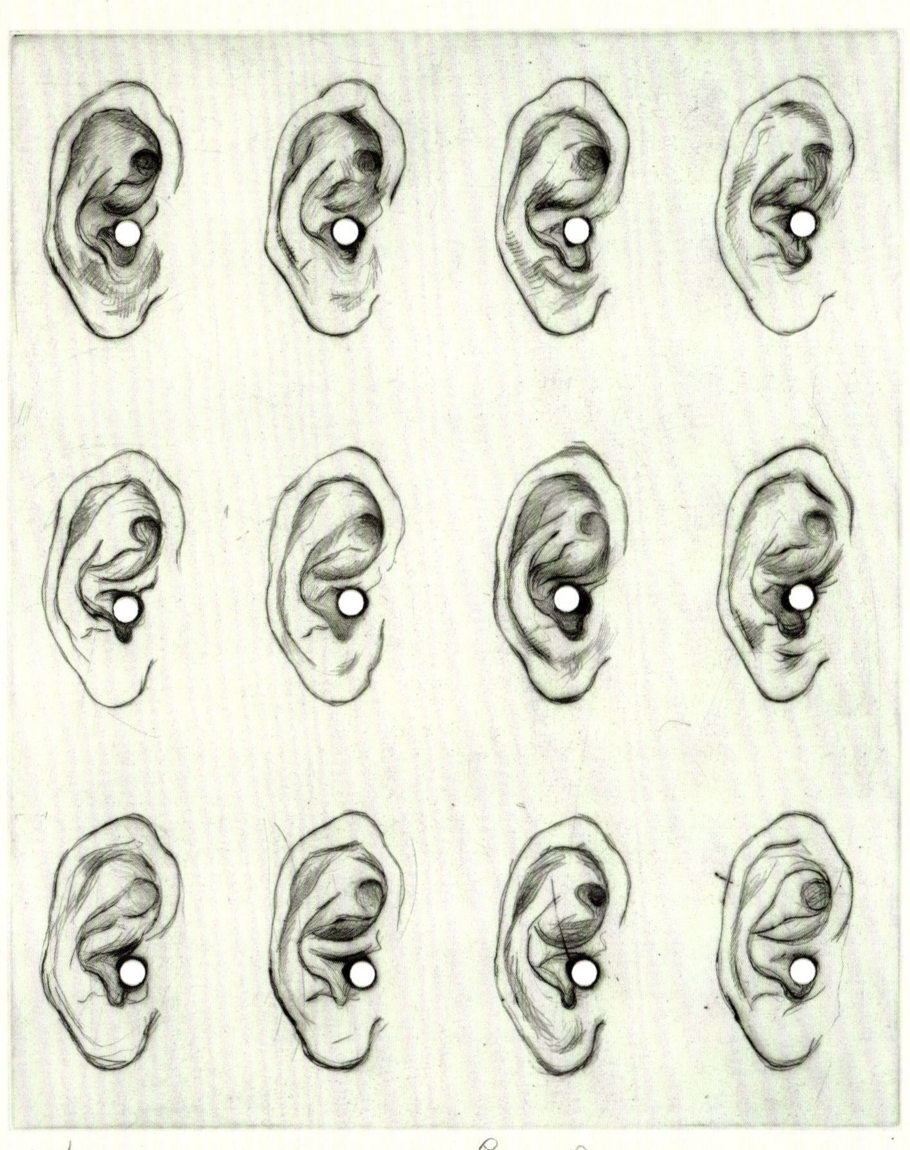

10/12

Louise Bourgeois 2004

Louise Bourgeois
(American, b. France,
1911–2010)
My Hand, edition of 10, 2002
lithograph on vintage cloth
11 × 8½ in. (27.9 × 21.6 cm)

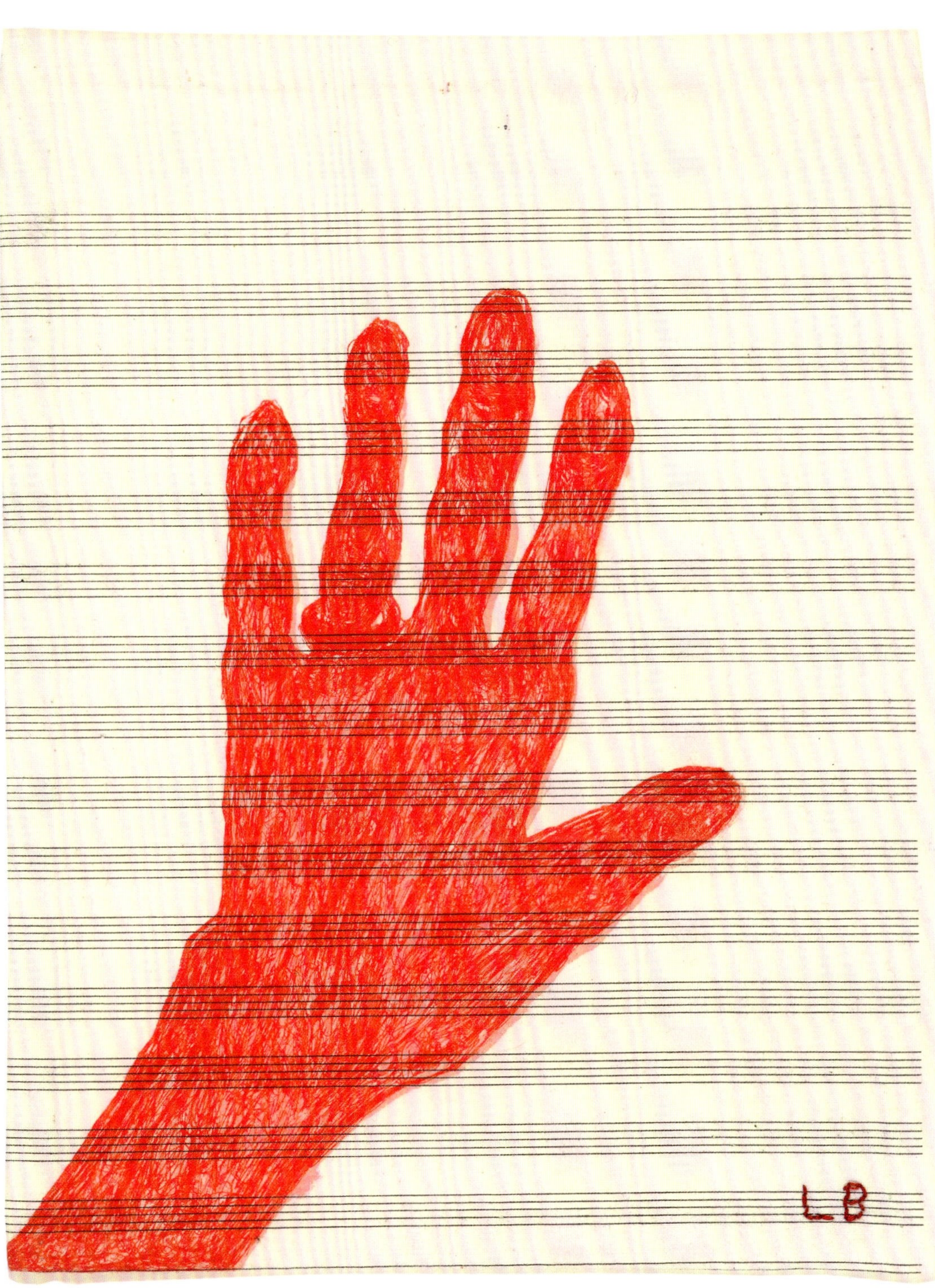
LB

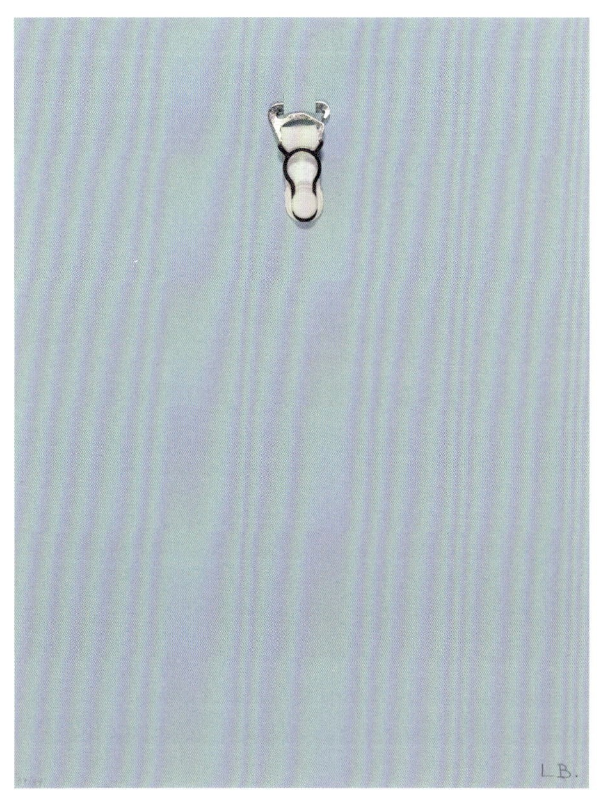

Louise Bourgeois
(American, b. France,
1911–2010)
Anatomy, edition 37/44, 1990
etching
19½ × 14⅛ in. (49.5 × 35.9 cm)

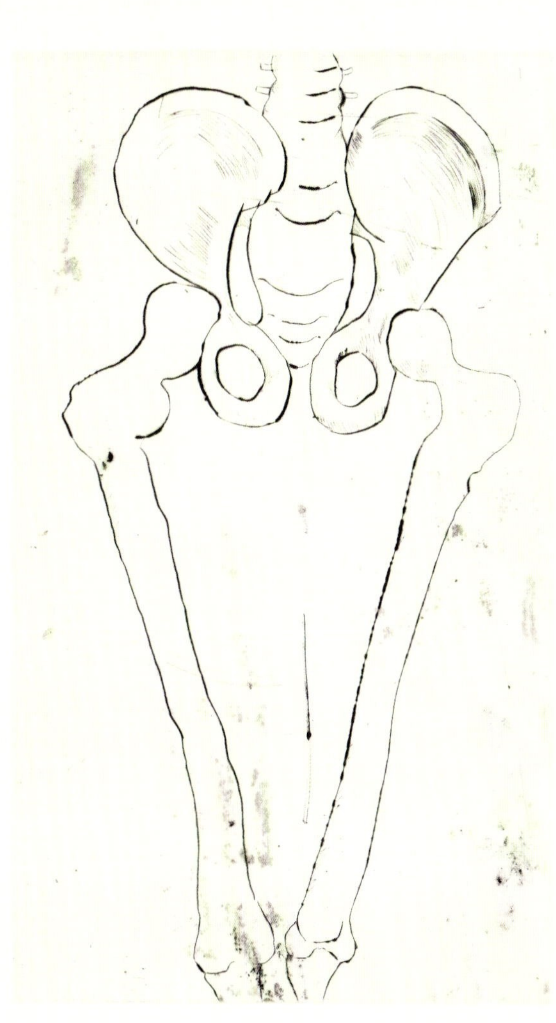

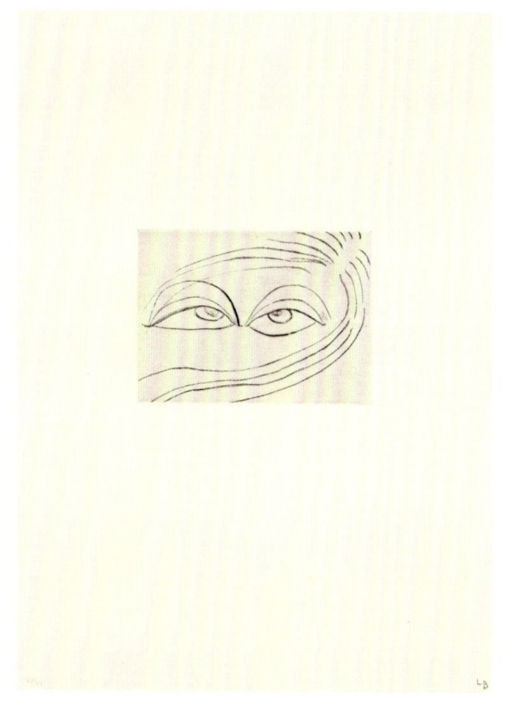
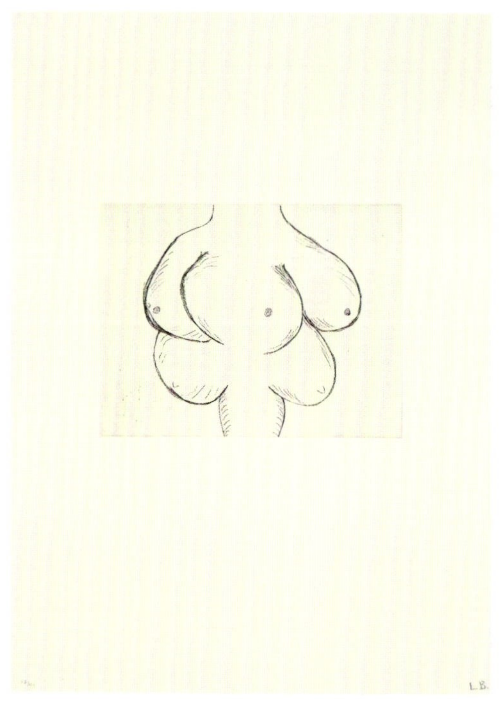
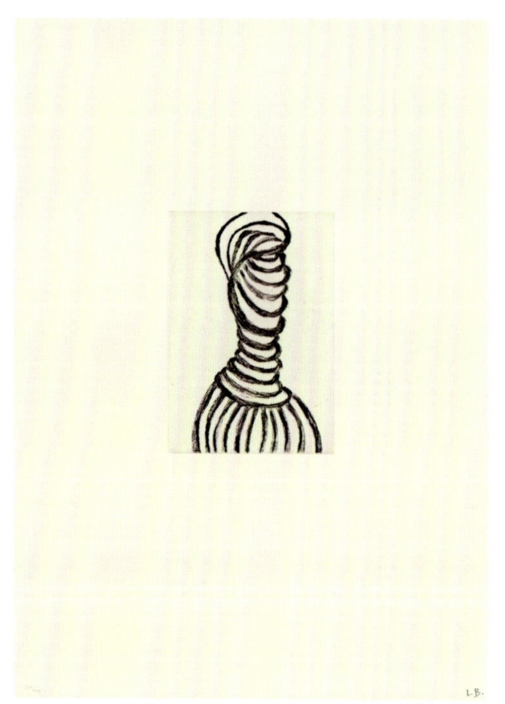
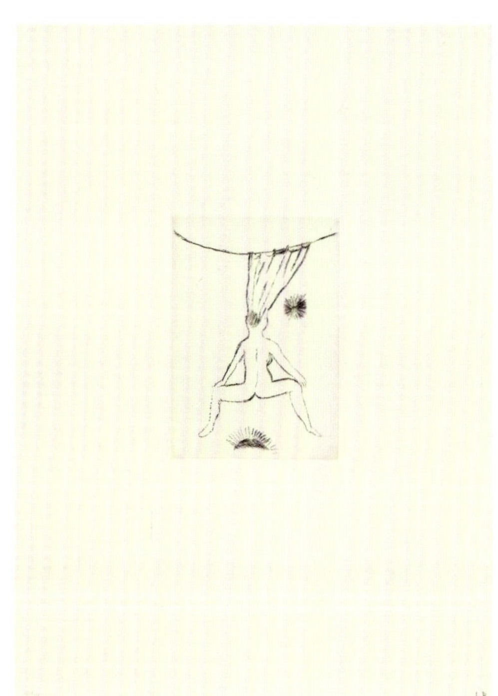

Louise Bourgeois
(American, b. France,
1911–2010)
Anatomy, edition 37/44, 1990
etchings
19½ × 14⅛ in. (49.5 × 35.9 cm)
each

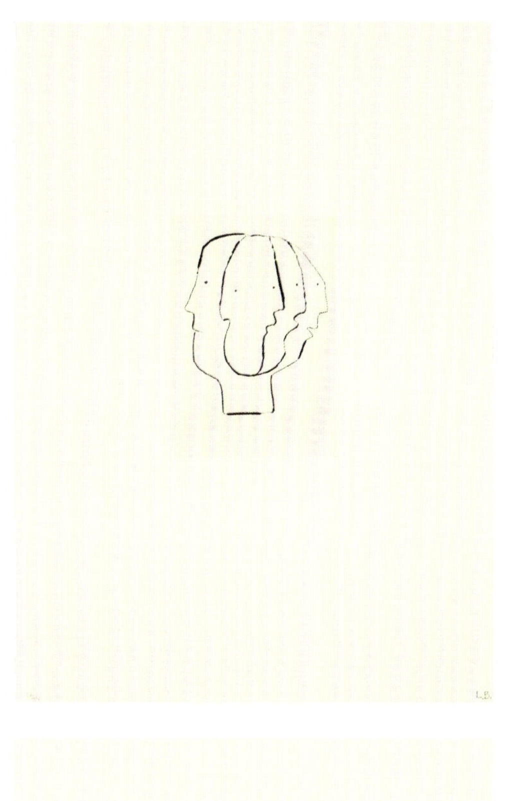
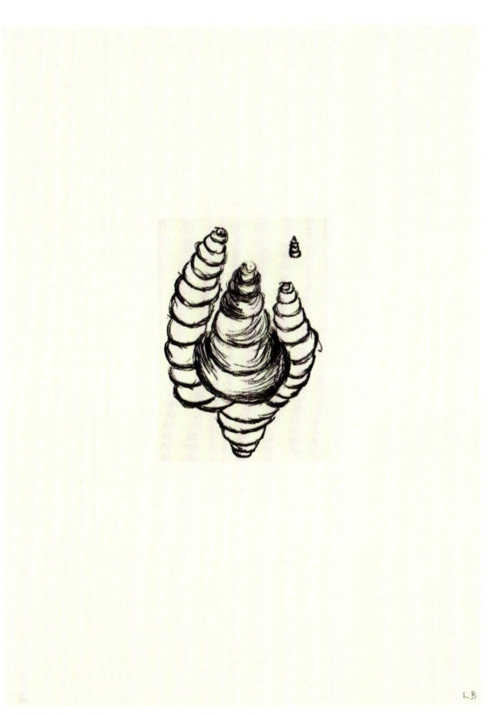
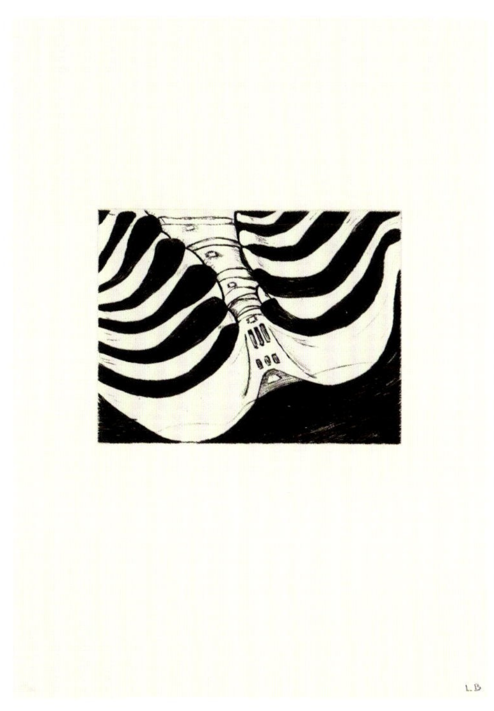
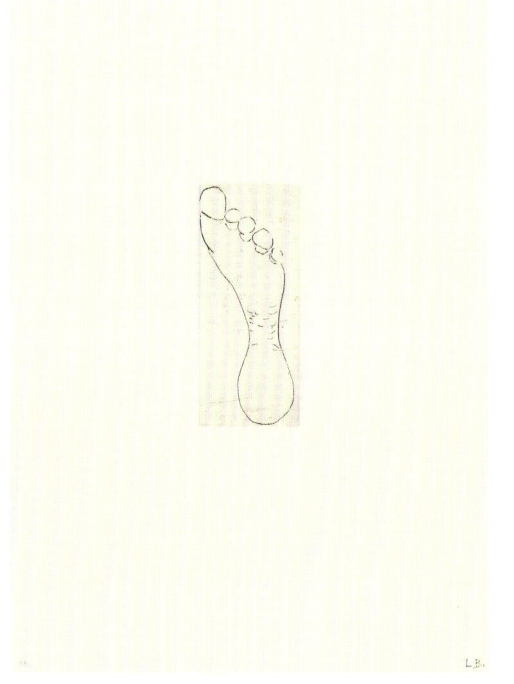
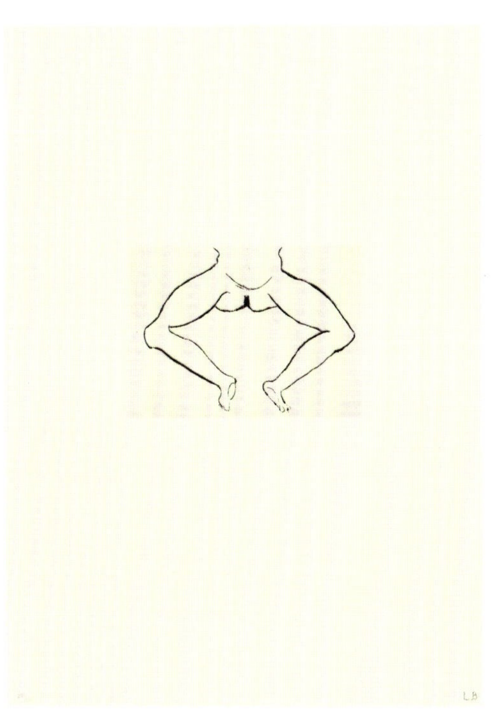
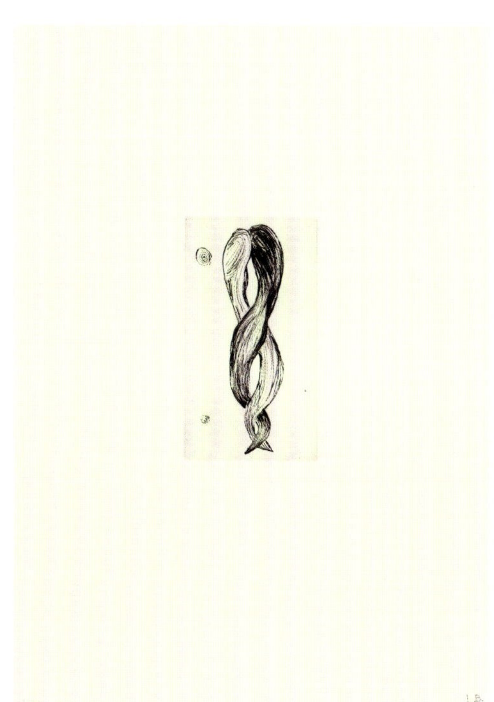

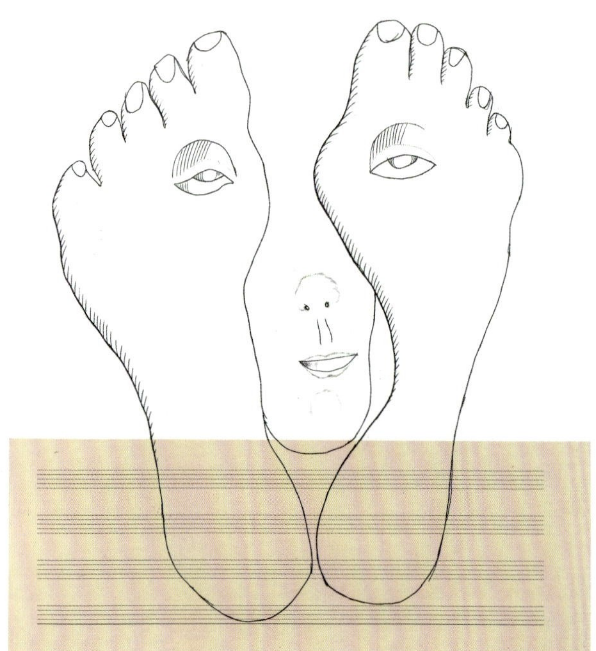

Louise Bourgeois
(American, b. France,
1911–2010)
Untitled, plate 3 of 5 from
Metamorfosis, edition of 85,
1999
etching, engraving, and
drypoint with chine collé
13 × 13 in. (33 × 33 cm)

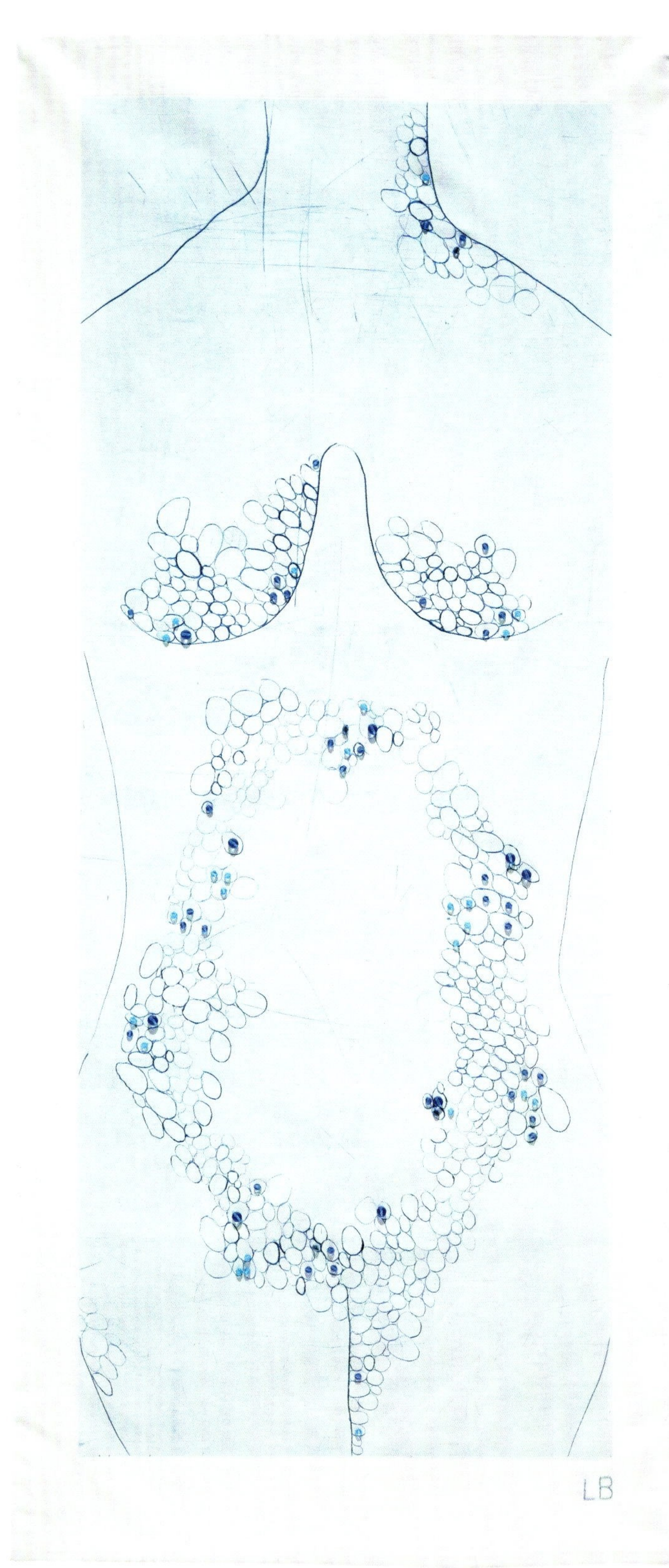

Louise Bourgeois
(American, b. France,
1911–2010)
Les Petites Sensations, edition
6/9 unique variants, 2008
drypoint on cloth with unique
glass beads appliqué
35⅝ × 16¼ in.
(90.5 × 41.3 cm)

Cecily Brown

The work of Cecily Brown (b. 1969) is always figurative yet, in its abstracted elements, turns definitively away from description. The British artist has been active in New York since the early 1990s, when she completed her art education in London amid the ascendance of the Young British Artists. Naming Titian, Rubens, and Caravaggio as among the first artists that she gravitated toward, and taking a particular interest in their treatment of human flesh,[1] Brown self-consciously engages the legacy of Western European and American figurative painting. The art world has often sought her commentary on exhibitions in this arena, whether Baroque or modern in scope.[2] Yet, Brown's own work stands at the meeting point of figuration and abstraction, as evident in the 2005 lithograph *Aujourd'hui Rose*, which presents a double image that can be read either as a skull or as a portrait of two young girls.

Brown tends to draw recurrently from the same art-historical source imagery. One such source is representations of the earthly paradise, whether the Garden of Eden or Orpheus playing to the animals, as taken up in her watercolor-monotype *Untitled (Paradise)*. Its clustering of outlined forms evokes recombination and, arguably, encapsulates the artist's process of reworking source imagery. A 2016 exhibition of Brown's works on paper, at the Drawing Center, New York, emphasized precisely this dimension of her practice by thematizing the etymology of the term "rehearsal," meaning to go over something repeatedly in order to come to a fuller understanding of it.[3] —JO

---

1 "An Evening with Cecily Brown," conversation with Jasper Sharp, Contemporary Talks, Kunsthistorisches Museum Vienna, February 2, 2018, https://www.youtube.com/watch?v=zuiaXaJ0TLI.

2 For Brown on Rubens, see Vienna, "An Evening." For Brown on Soutine and De Kooning, see "A Conversation Between Cecily Brown and Simonetta Fraquelli," Barnes Foundation, July 22, 2021, https://www.youtube.com/watch?v=umKREuerWqI

3 *Cecily Brown: Rehearsal*, Drawing Center, October 7–December 18, 2016; Museum of Contemporary Art Santa Barbara, January 28–June 3, 2018.

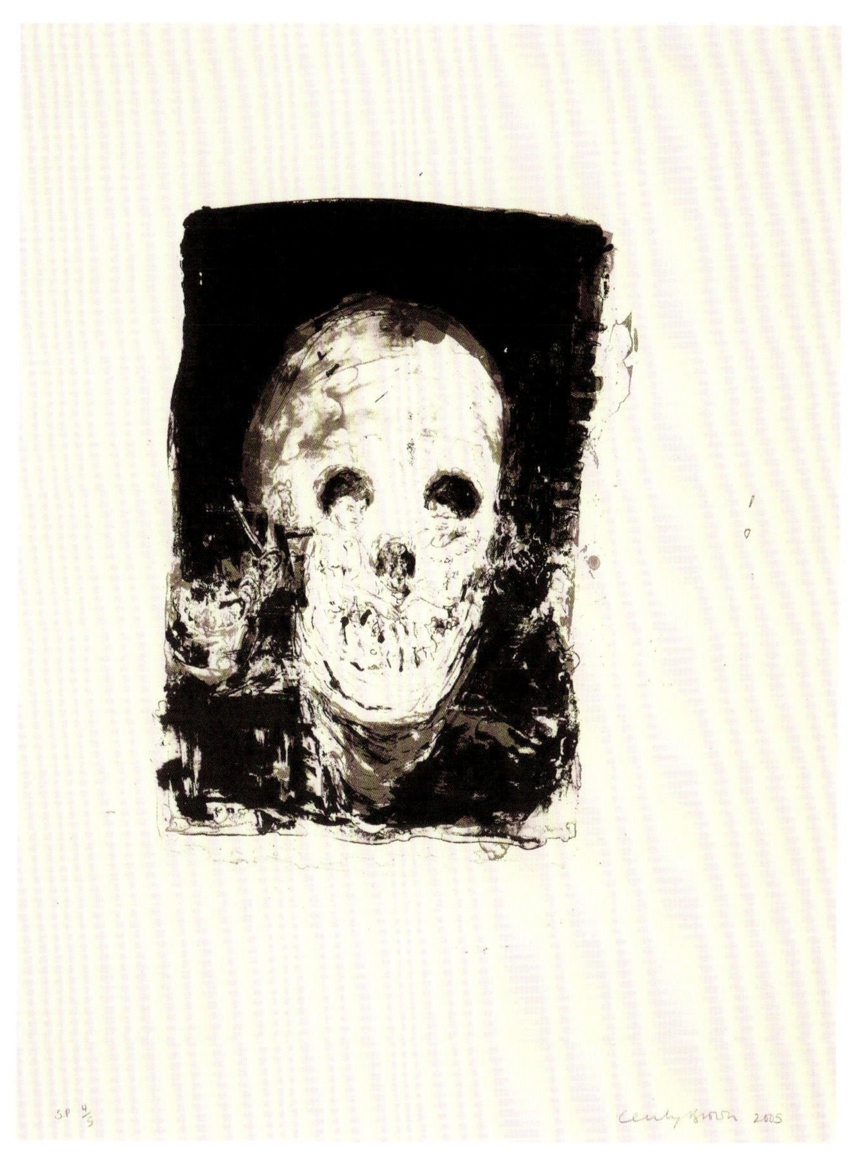

Cecily Brown
(British, b. 1969)
Aujourd'hui Rose, edition SP 4,
2005
lithograph
39 × 29½ in. (99.1 × 74.9 cm)

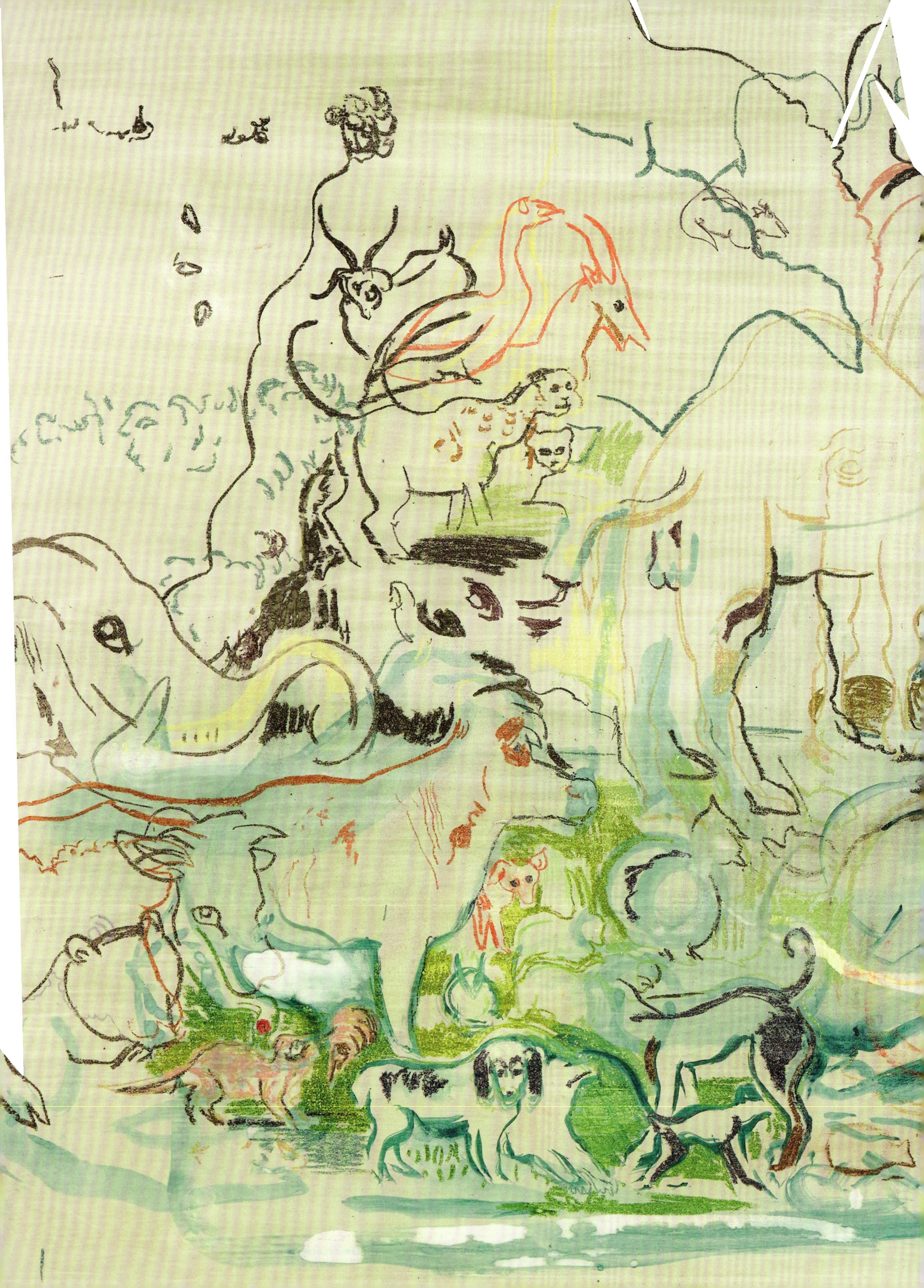

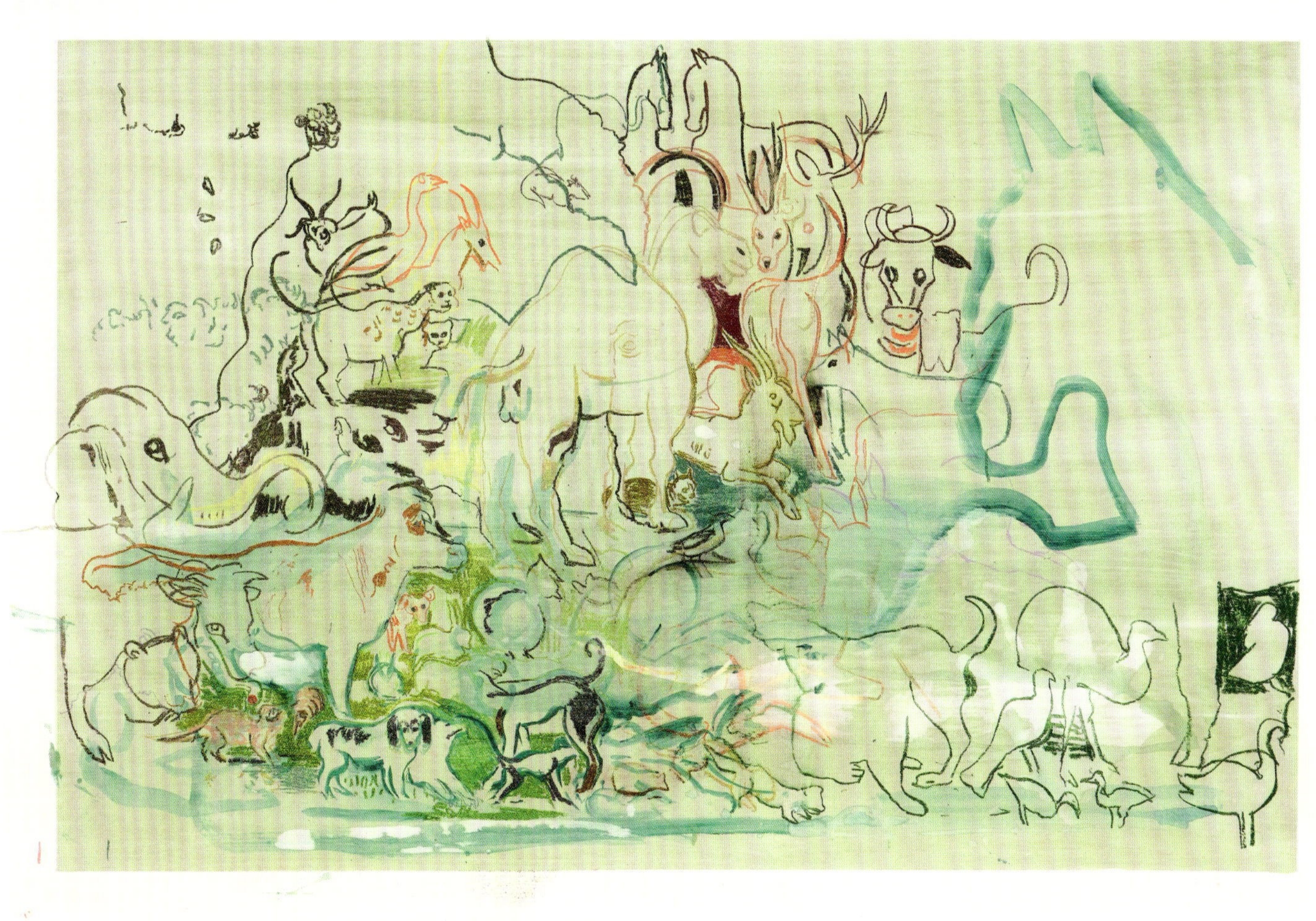

Cecily Brown
(British, b. 1969)
Untitled (Paradise), 2015
monotype in watercolor,
pencil, and pastel
48 × 71 in. (121.9 × 180.3 cm)

Judy Chicago

Though perhaps best known for *The Dinner Party* (1979), the pioneering feminist artist Judy Chicago (b. 1939) began making prints at age twenty-six while an art student in Los Angeles. As a reaction to the sexism and hypermasculine culture she encountered surrounding the all-male group of LA-based minimalists, in the late 1960s Chicago began to explore emphatically female-centered iconography, which she called "central core imagery." Chicago and other artists working at the time, like Hannah Wilke, Carolee Schneemann, and Miriam Schapiro, strove to proclaim the vagina, a woman's "core" literally and metaphorically, as a source of power and identity by asserting its form in artworks. Concurrently, Chicago and Schapiro began collaborating with other female artists to create a sense of community and to push the boundaries of artmaking, as in the 1972 multiroom installation project *Womanhouse*, which occupied a six-room repurposed home.

Chicago's leadership in the early days of the feminist art movement informed her early printmaking as well. In her *Through the Flower* series, within which she made multiple variations, Chicago offers a central colorful expanse encircled by pastel-colored petals of soft pinks, yellows, and blues. Now the recognized name for Chicago's nonprofit and subsequent titles of her autobiographies, in these early iterations *Through the Flower* was a visual assertion equating the vagina's form with that of an unfolding flower, a political declaration of a woman's right to represent and celebrate her own body. In the 1960s and '70s, printmaking studios, like most art spaces, were male-dominated arenas. Chicago's early prints thus not only assert the quintessential feature of the female body as a symbol of beauty and strength but also challenge the gendered hierarchical spaces inherent to the act of printing as the artist interfaced with male master printers and commercial printers. Through the collaborative nature of the lithography studio, as well the accessible nature of prints as art objects, printmaking served as an important modality of Chicago's early feminist practice. As she later reflected, printmaking "also allowed me the opportunity to share my ideas in entirely new technical modes and to introduce people to my work in a more accessible way, something that has always been important to me."[1] —SD

1 William J. Simmons, "Judy Chicago on Printmaking," *Chicago in Ink: An Autobiography*, 2020, https://chicagoinink.com/ABOUT.

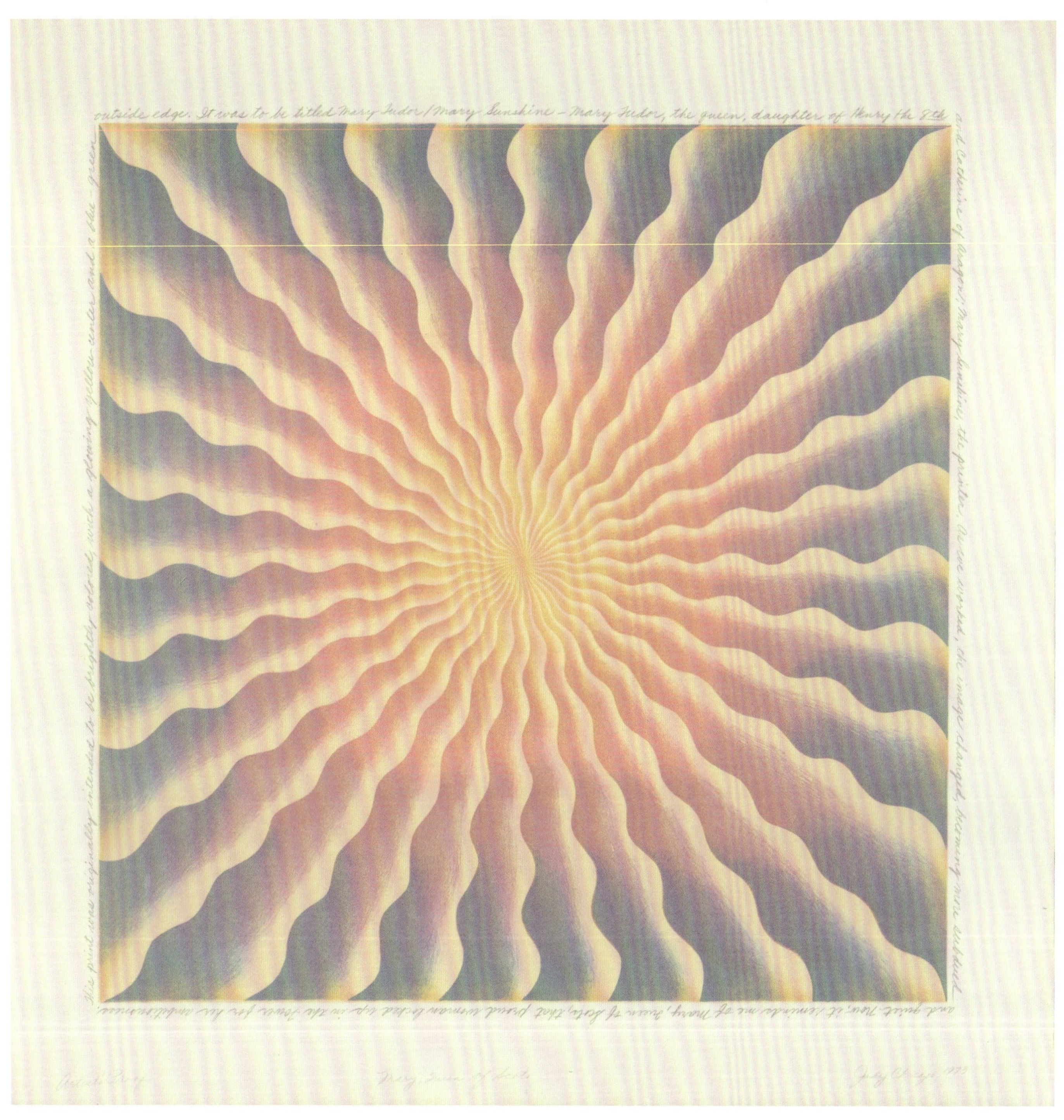

Judy Chicago
(American, b. 1939)
Mary Queen of Scots, edition
AP 1/7, 1973
lithograph and serigraph
25 × 25 in. (63.5 × 63.5 cm)

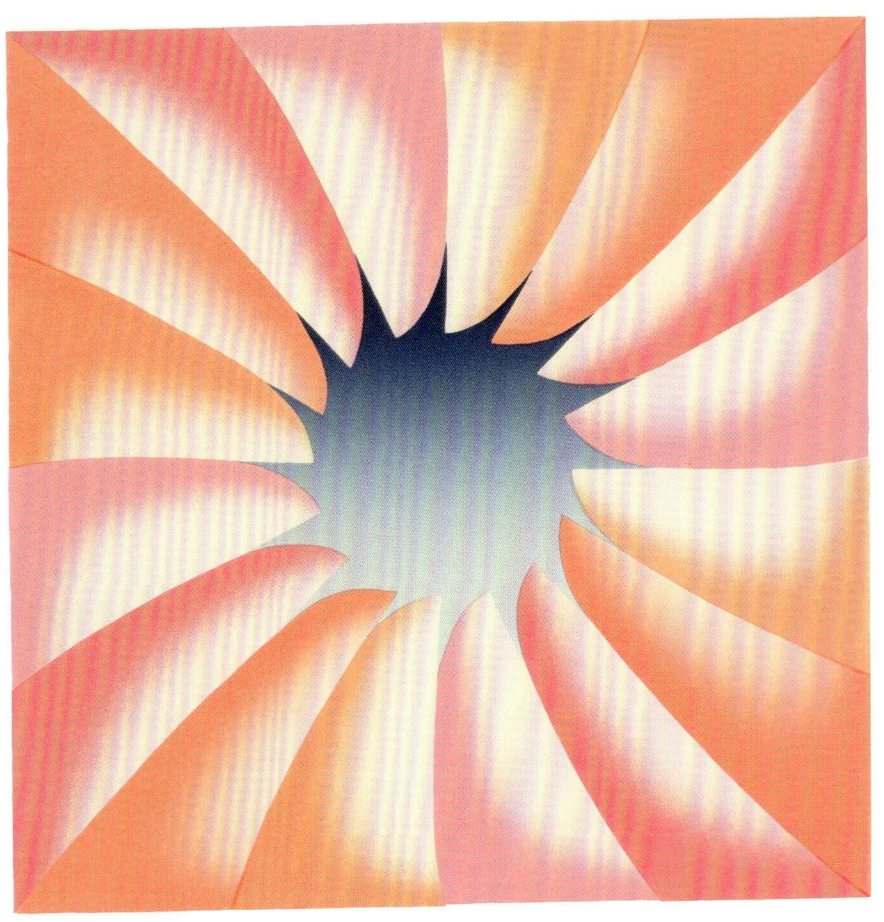

Judy Chicago
(American, b. 1939)
Through the Flower 3,
edition AP 1/1, 1972
lithograph
22 × 22 in. (55.9 × 55.9 cm)

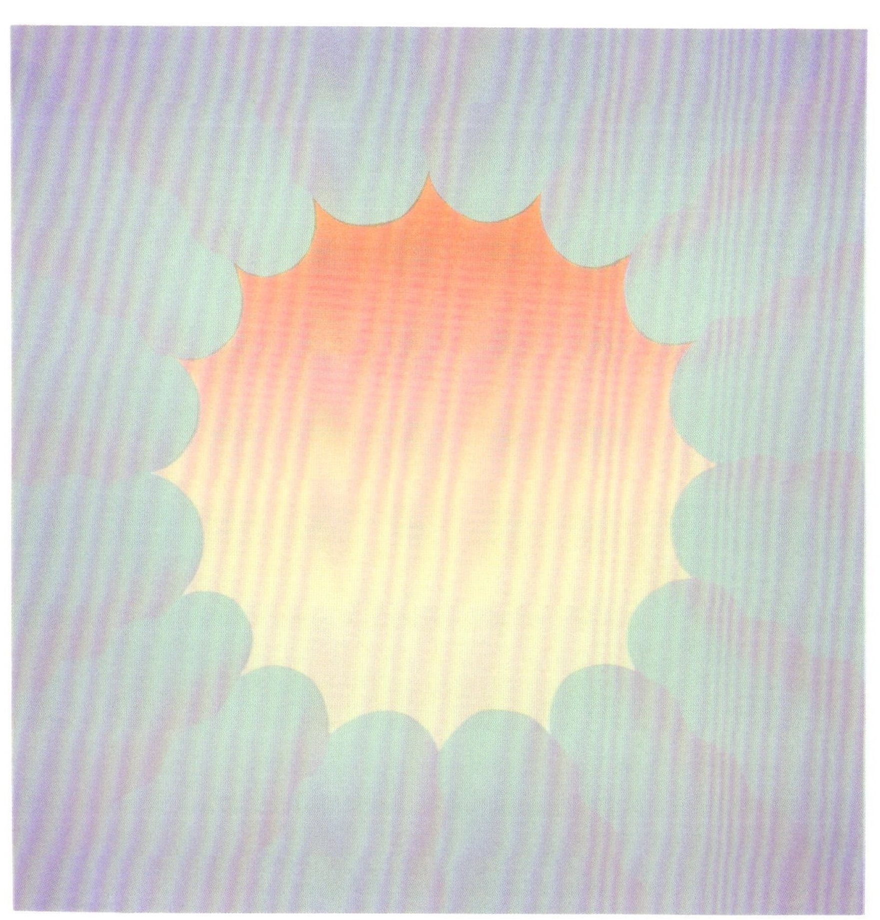

Judy Chicago
(American, b. 1939)
Through the Flower 4,
edition 8/10, 1972
lithograph
22 × 22 in. (55.9 × 55.9 cm)

Judy Chicago
(American, b. 1939)
Through the Flower Twice,
edition 6/10, 1972
lithograph
22 × 44 in. (55.9 × 111.8 cm)

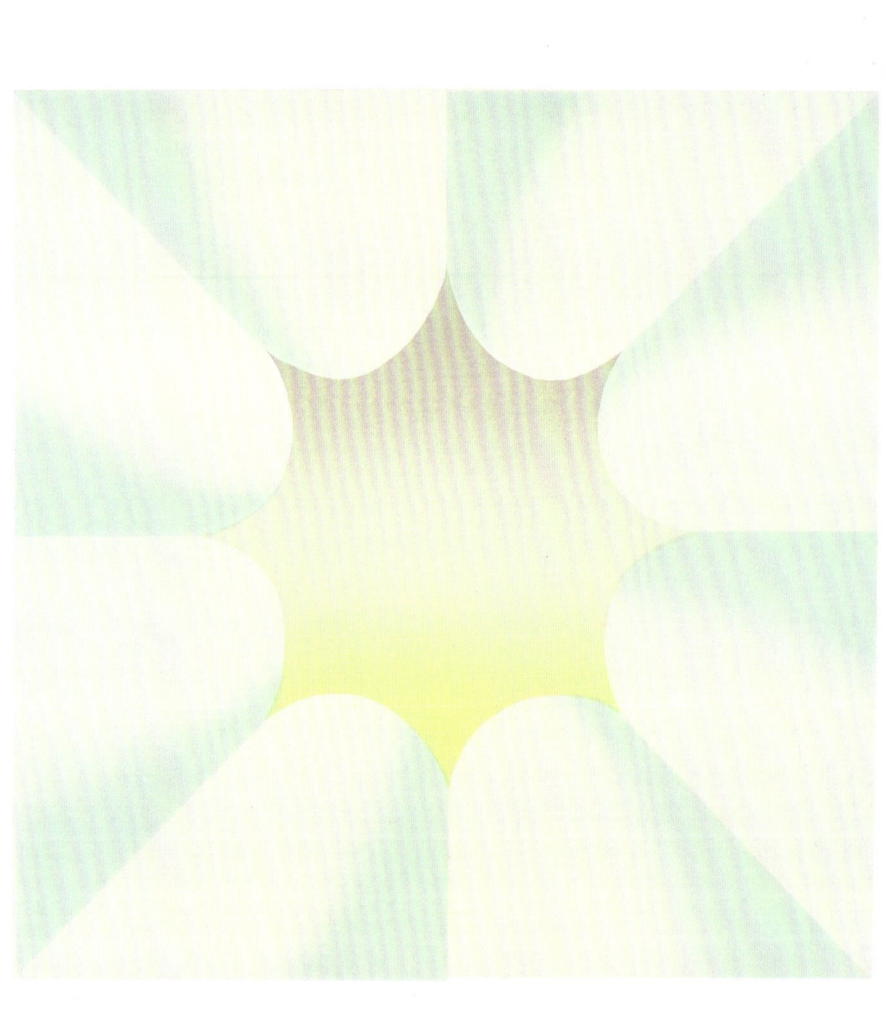

Nicole Eisenman

Nicole Eisenman (b. 1965) playfully confronts the legacy of modernism in their figurative paintings, sculpture, and prints. As the title suggests, the *Picabia Filter* suite, which comprises four intaglio prints created at 10 Grand Press in Brooklyn, engages with the legacy of the painter and dadaist Francis Picabia (1879–1953). Active in Paris in the early twentieth century, Picabia and others in Parisian avant-garde circles ushered in a new era of abstraction, promoting new technologies like photography, elevating low-brow cultural phenomena, and shocking the art world through pastiche and social satire. Ironically, after the First World War disintegrated the avant-garde community in Europe, many of those artists returned to representational painting, including Picabia, who most notably began creating figurative portraiture, including self-portraiture, in the late 1920s.

In their *Picabia Filter* suite, Eisenman conflates the posturing of high modernist sensibilities with those of the present day. At 10 Grand Press, Eisenman transferred a photographic self-portrait to the plate and then etched directly onto their image. Incising and obscuring their face, Eisenman created geometric eyes, polygonal noses, and fluid lines reminiscent of Picabia's later portraiture. Despite the hand-hewn nature of this type of etching, at the bottom of each print, a series of symbols similar to those found on Snapchat or Instagram liken the print to a digital screen, a tongue-in-cheek gesture paralleling the self-altering qualities of a social media filter with the inherent layering qualities of the printmaking media. This is further complicated through the invocation in the title of Picabia's own dialectic legacy as both a politically minded innovator early in his career and a solitary painter returning to an outmoded representational style later on. By "wearing" Picabia, Eisenman places themself within, and thereby "queers," a Euro-American male-dominated historical narrative about the development of twentieth-century modernism. But more specifically, by referencing the singular artist, Eisenman, whose work is often allegorical and represents versions of history interwoven with their own autobiographical details, presents the ever-changing self, one whose public image is reinscribed daily through social media, historically exemplified by Picabia's own unconventional arc as a creative producer. —SD

Nicole Eisenman
(American, b. 1965)

Picabia Filter I,
edition 10/15, 2018
intaglio with drypoint
22½ × 15 in. (57.2 × 38.1 cm)

Picabia Filter II,
edition 10/15, 2018
intaglio with drypoint
22½ × 15 in. (57.2 × 38.1 cm)

Picabia Filter III,
edition 10/15, 2018
intaglio with drypoint
22½ × 15 in. (57.2 × 38.1 cm)

Picabia Filter IV,
edition 10/15, 2018
intaglio with drypoint
22½ × 15 in. (57.2 × 38.1 cm)

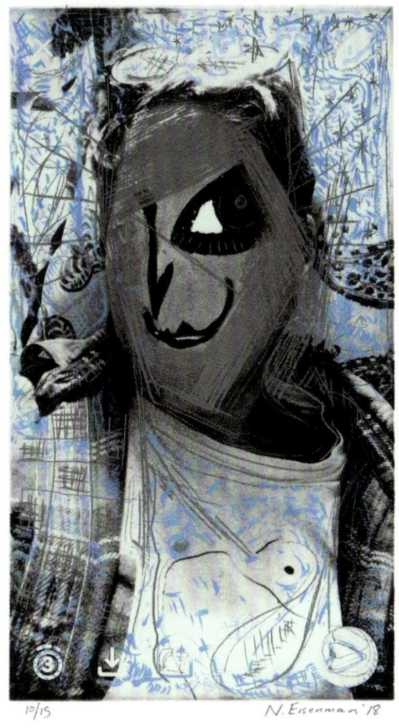

10/15 N. Eisenman '18

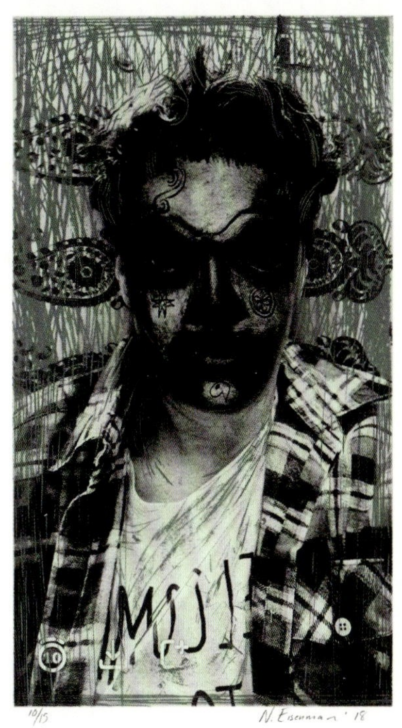

10/15 N. Eisenman '18

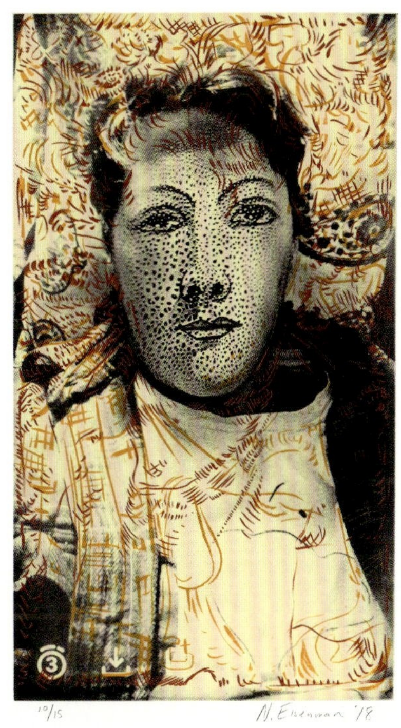

10/15 N. Eisenman '18

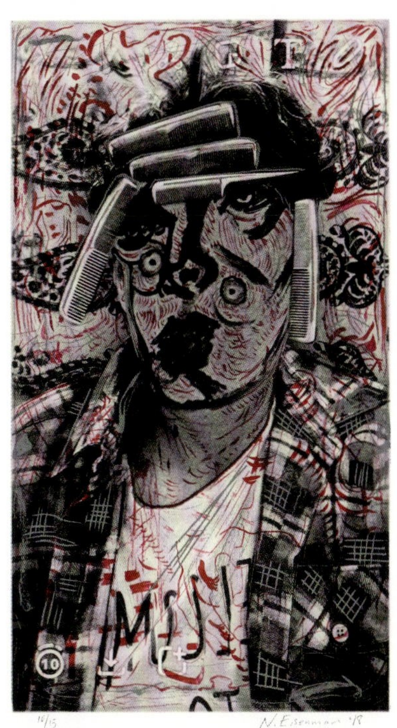

10/15 N. Eisenman '18

Ellen Gallagher

The American artist Ellen Gallagher (b. 1965) works in and across print, painting, drawing, collage, and film to explore issues of racial-cultural identity and representation. Her monumental print project *DeLuxe* (2004–5) embodies her characteristic visual language of repetition, accrual, and revision. It is composed of a grid of sixty prints, stacked five high by twelve wide and executed in a variety of printmaking techniques—ranging from etching and lithography to tattoo-machine engraving. With a particular interest in their grid-like structures, Gallagher collected and reworked wig advertisements from magazines spanning 1939 to the early 1970s and geared toward a Black readership, such as *Our World*, *Sepia*, and *Ebony*. The artist describes the sense of both loss and excitement she felt in reading certain more radical magazines from before 1960, as documents of a bygone Black world;[1] at the same time, she discusses the figures as "conscripts from another time and place, liberated from the 'race' magazines of the past. I have transformed them, here on the pages that once held them captive."[2]

Gallagher created her plates in many layers; to the finished prints, she then applied additional materials, such as yellow Plasticine, toy eyes, and gold leaf. Her working process in reconceiving the advertisements entailed a complex collaboration with master printmakers at the New York–based Two Palms Press. With each of the sixty prints existing in an edition of twenty, the project amounted to twelve hundred individual prints. Gallagher notes that this required her to structure artistic impulses that would otherwise have been improvisational, so that the printers could complete the editioning. The artist likens this working dynamic to call-and-response, noting that "it was exciting to see, repeated as a language, something that was usually a one-to-one-experience."[3] In its openness to a range of media, materials, and techniques, as well as the line it walks in relying upon yet dismantling tradition, *DeLuxe* has been seen as signaling a next step in twenty-first-century printmaking.[4] —JO

(following pages)
Ellen Gallagher
(American, b. 1965)
DeLuxe
2004–5
Edition 5/20
Grid of 60 photogravure, etching, aquatint, and drypoints with lithography, screenprint, embossing, tattoo-machine engraving, laser cutting, and chine collé; some with additions of Plasticine, paper collage, enamel, varnish, gouache, pencil, oil, polymer, watercolor, pomade, velvet, glitter, crystals, foil paper, gold leaf, toy eyeballs, and imitation ice cubes
13 × 10⅜ in. (33 × 26.5 cm) each
15⅜ × 12⅞ × 1¾ in. (39 × 32.6 × 4.6 cm) framed
84¾ × 176 in. (215.3 × 447 cm) overall

Courtesy the artist and Hauser & Wirth

---

1 Ellen Gallagher, "Interview: *eXelento* and *DeLuxe*," Art21, https://art21.org/read/ellen-gallagher-exelento-and-deluxe/.
2 Ellen Gallagher quoted in Suzanne P. Hudson, "Ellen Gallagher Talks About Pomp-Bang, 2003," *Artforum* 42, no. 8 (April 2004): 131.
3 Gallagher, "Interview."
4 Sarah Suzuki, "Print People: A Brief Taxonomy of Contemporary Printmaking," *Art Journal* 70, no. 4 (Winter 2011): 24–25.

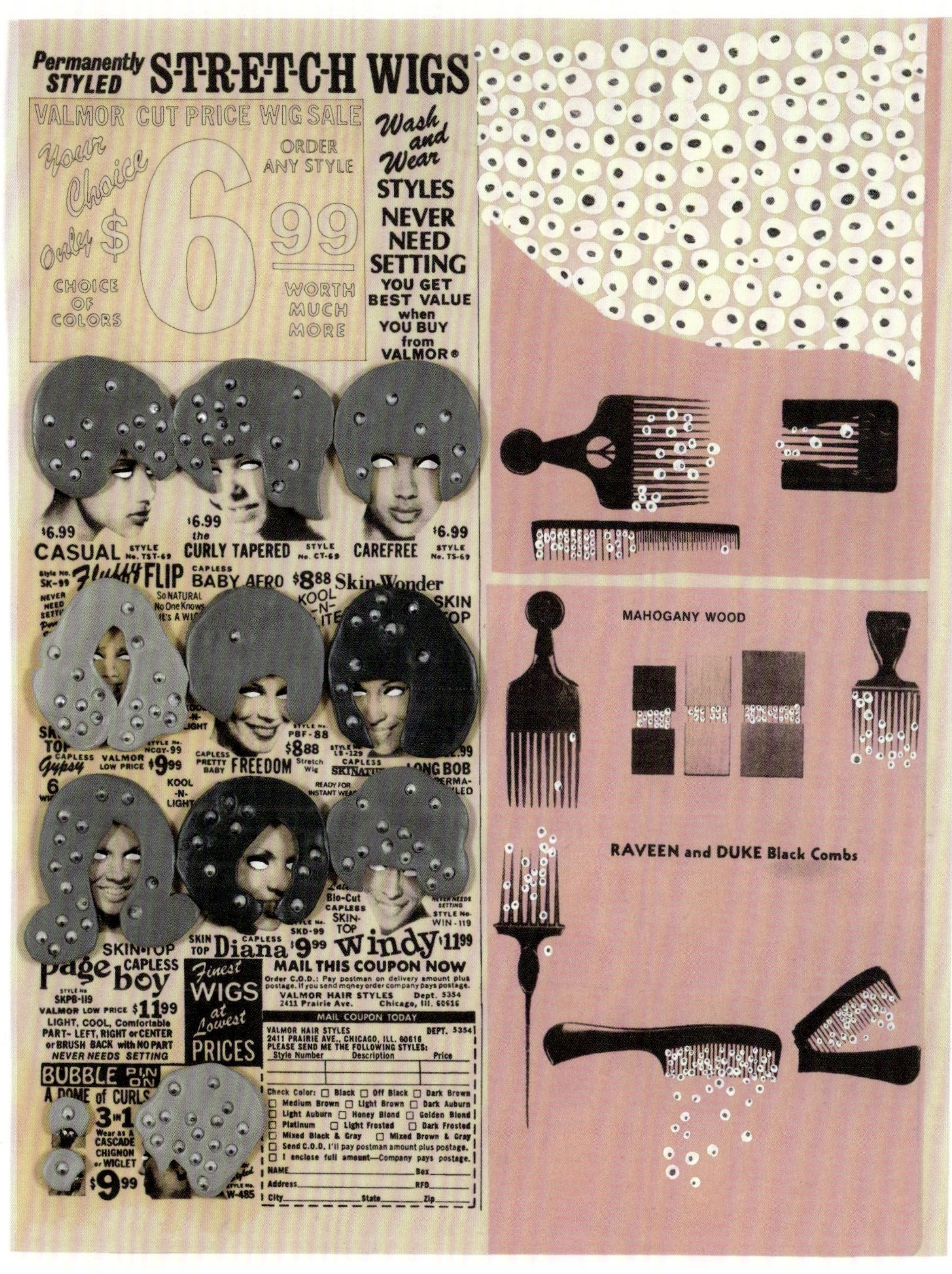
Permanently STYLED
S-T-R-E-T-C-H WIGS
VALMOR CUT PRICE WIG SALE
Your Choice Only $6.99
ORDER ANY STYLE
CHOICE OF COLORS
WORTH MUCH MORE
Wash and Wear STYLES
NEVER NEED SETTING
YOU GET BEST VALUE when YOU BUY from VALMOR®
$6.99 CASUAL
$6.99 the CURLY TAPERED
CAREFREE $6.99
BABY AFRO
$8.88 Skin-Wonder
FREEDOM
LONG BOB
Diana $9.99
Windy $11.99
page boy
VALMOR LOW PRICE $11.99
LIGHT, COOL, Comfortable
PART- LEFT, RIGHT or CENTER or BRUSH BACK with NO PART
NEVER NEEDS SETTING
Finest WIGS at Lowest PRICES
MAIL THIS COUPON NOW
MAIL COUPON TODAY
BUBBLE PIN ON
A DOME of CURLS
$9.99
MAHOGANY WOOD
RAVEEN and DUKE Black Combs

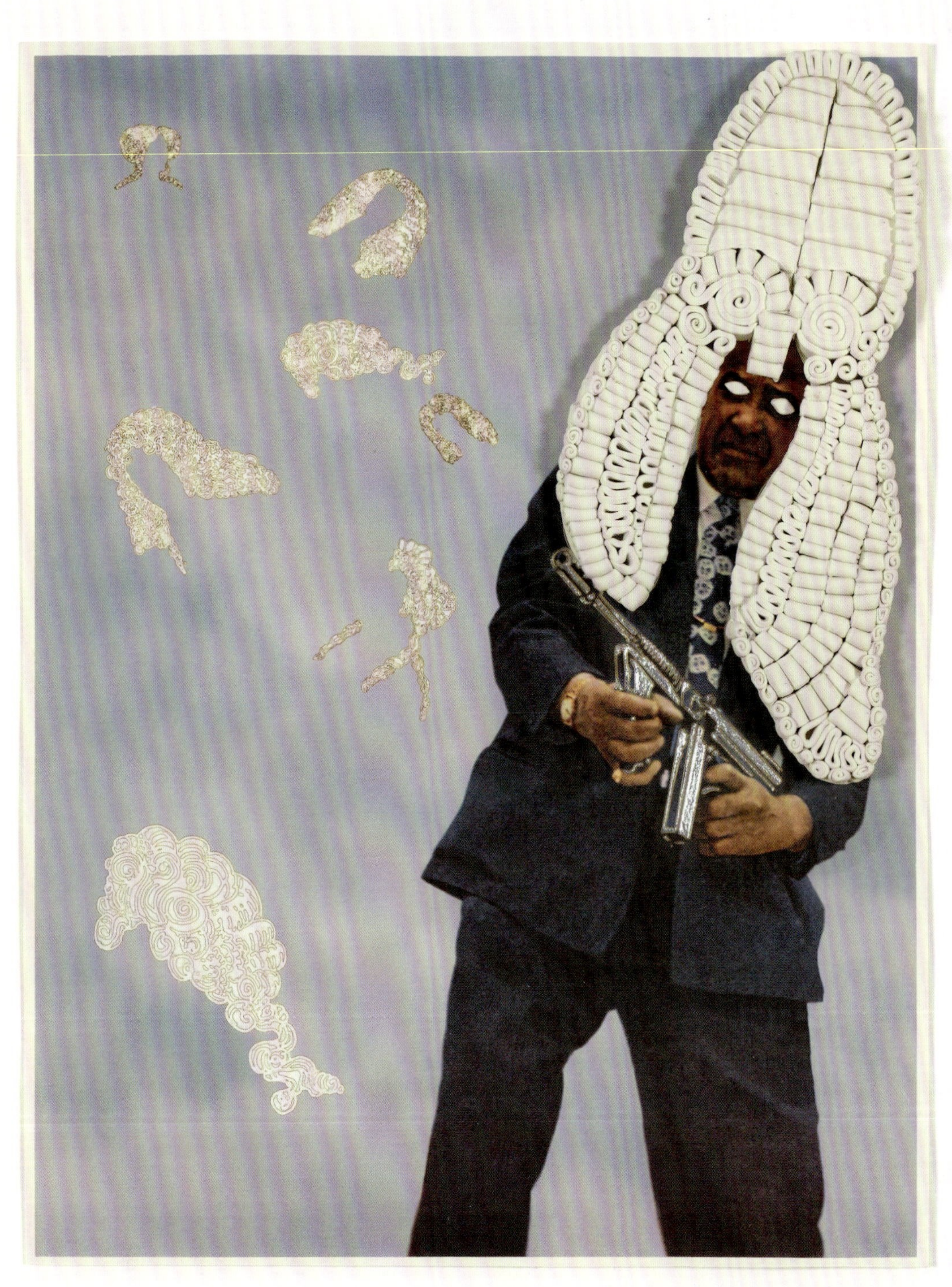

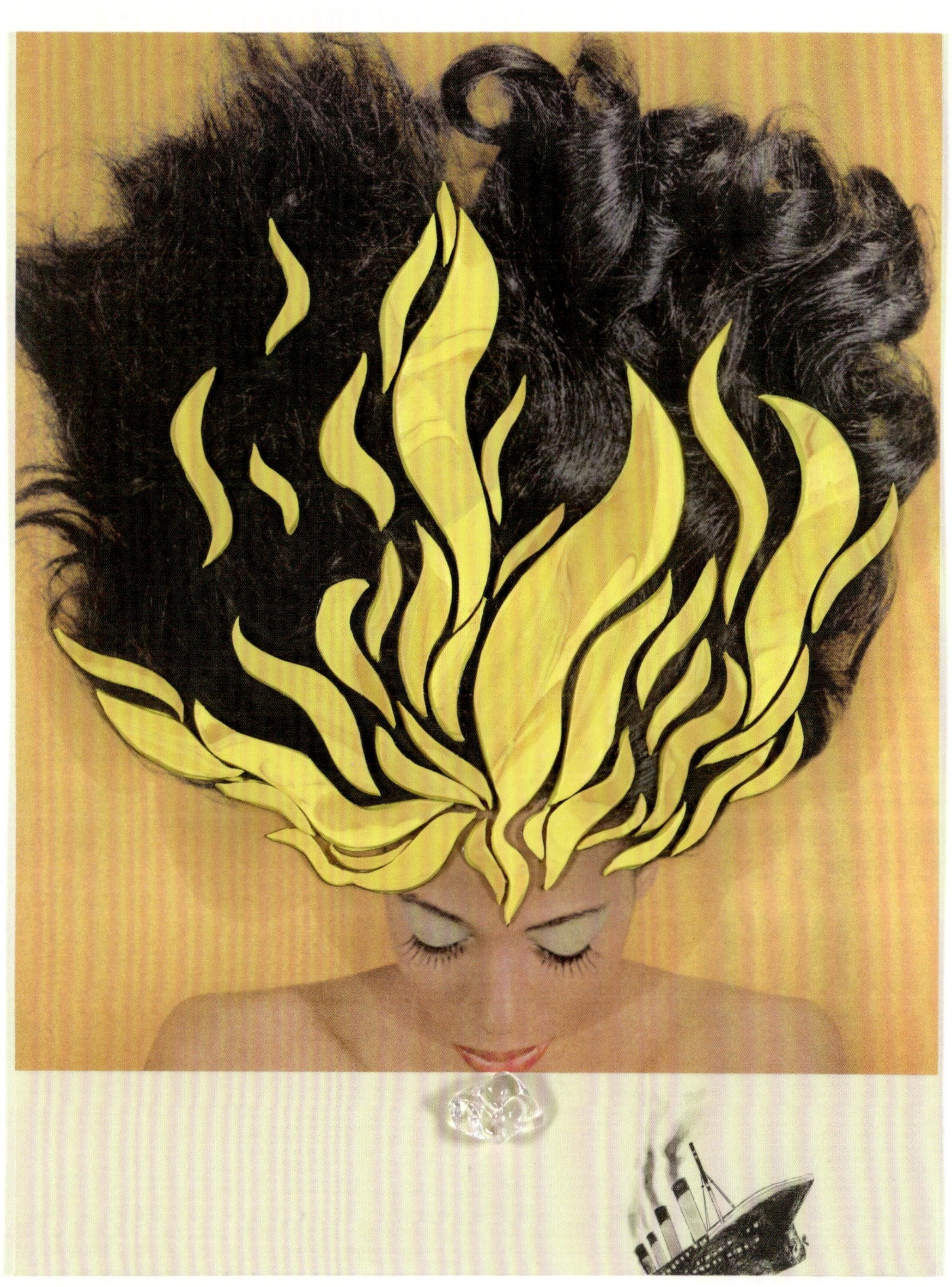

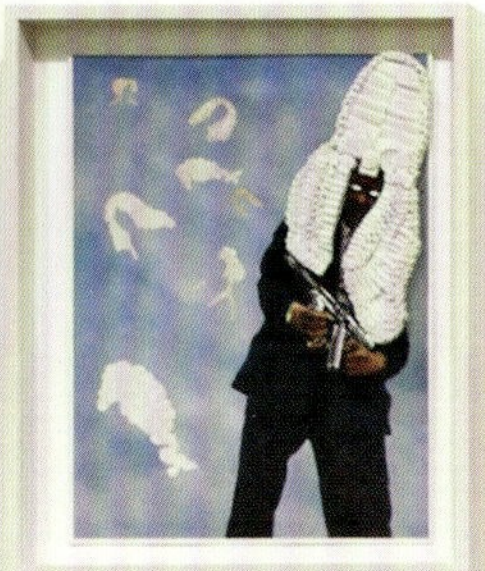
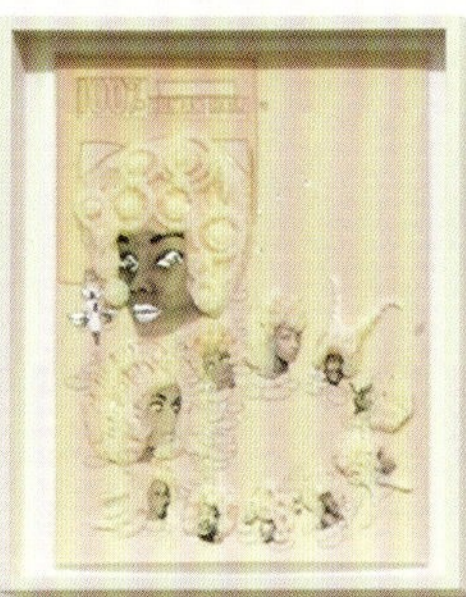
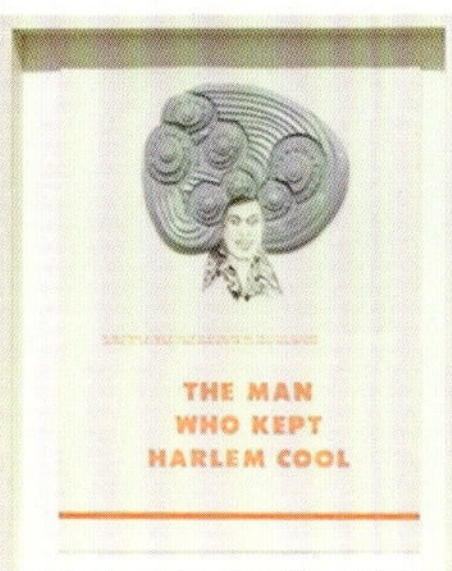
THE MAN
WHO KEPT
HARLEM COOL
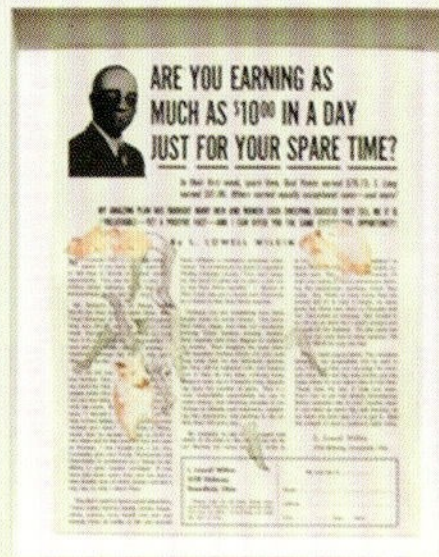
ARE YOU EARNING AS
JUST FOR YOUR SPARE TIME?
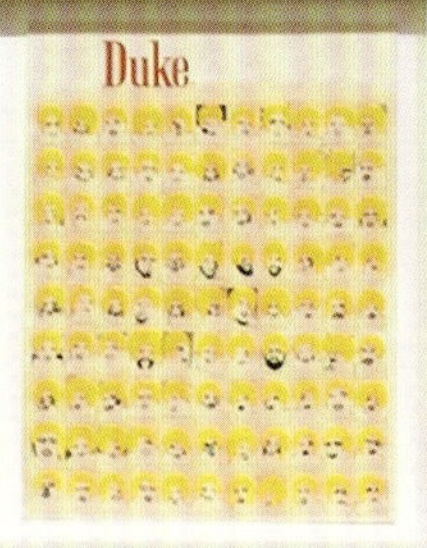
Duke
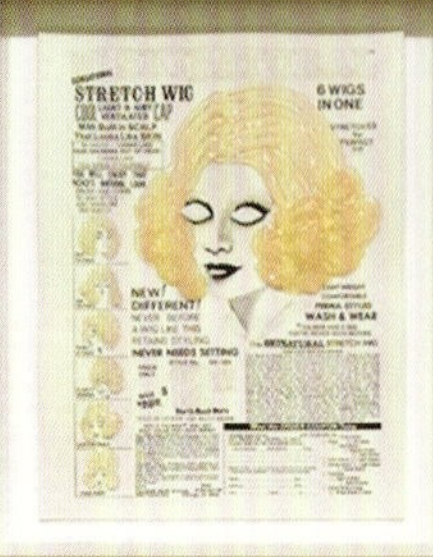
STRETCH WIG
6 WIGS IN ONE
WASH & WEAR
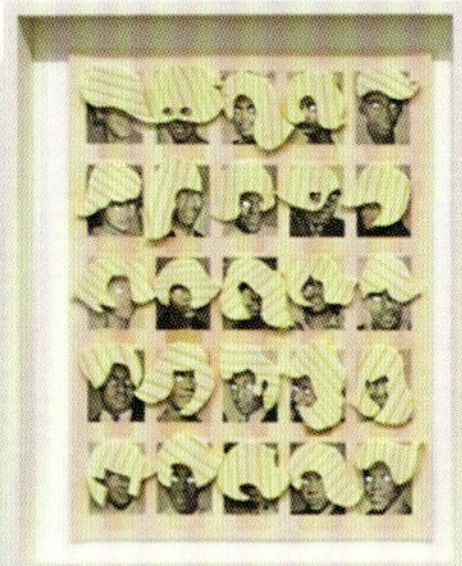
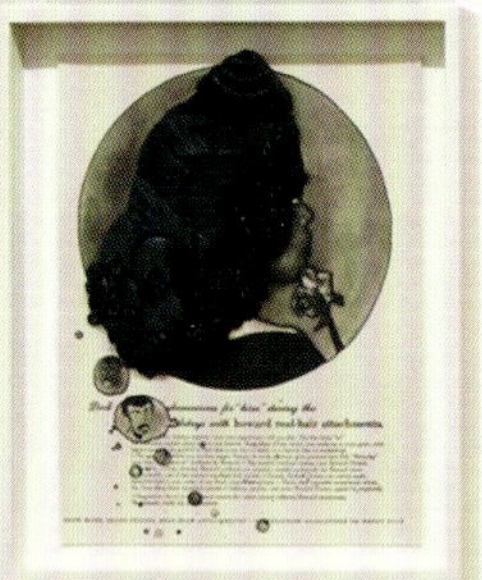
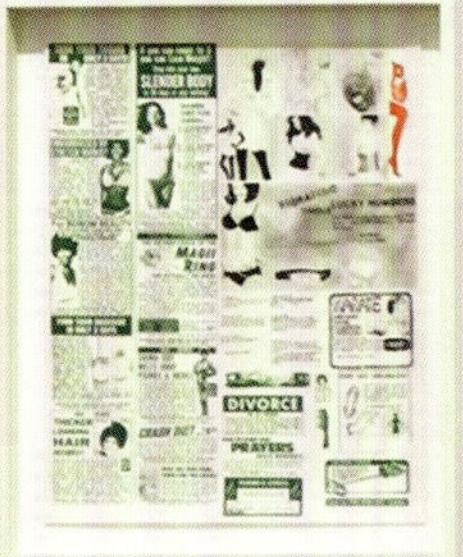
SLENDER BODY
DIVORCE
PRAYERS
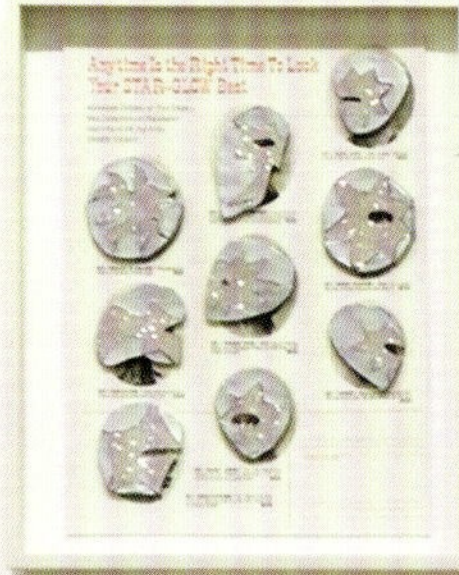
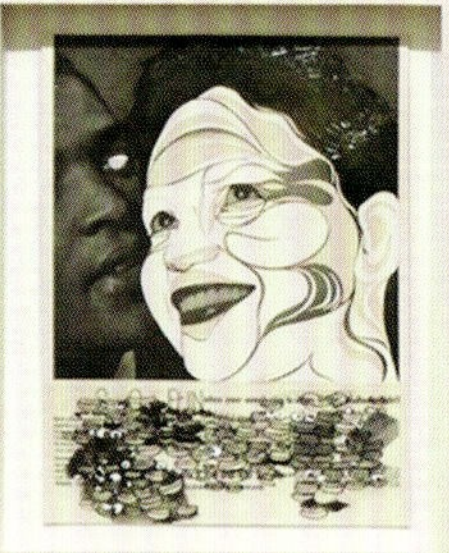
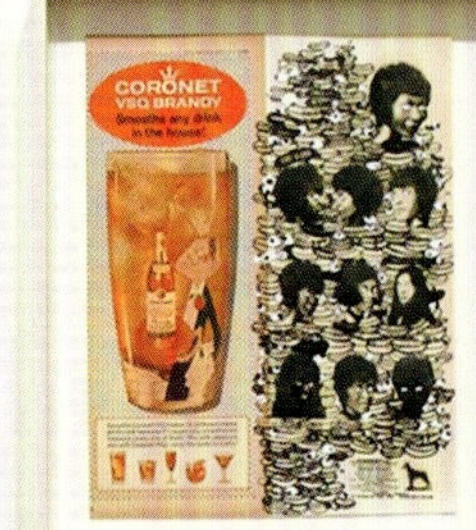
CORONET
VSQ BRANDY
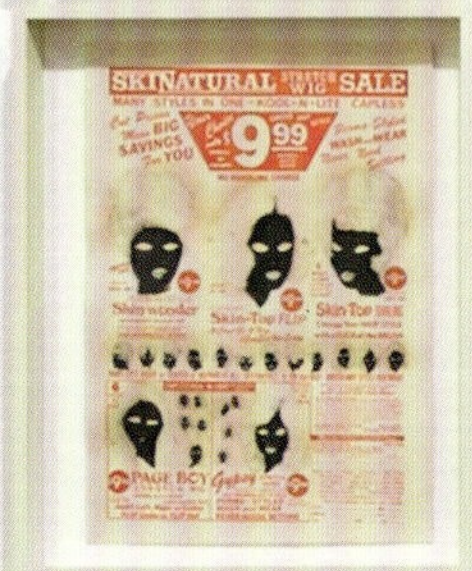
SKINATURAL
SALE
9.99
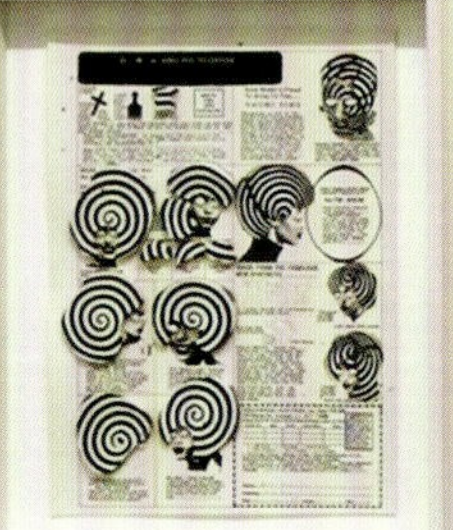
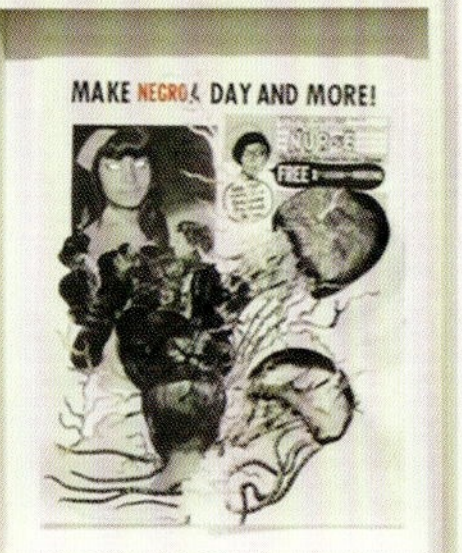
DAY AND MORE!
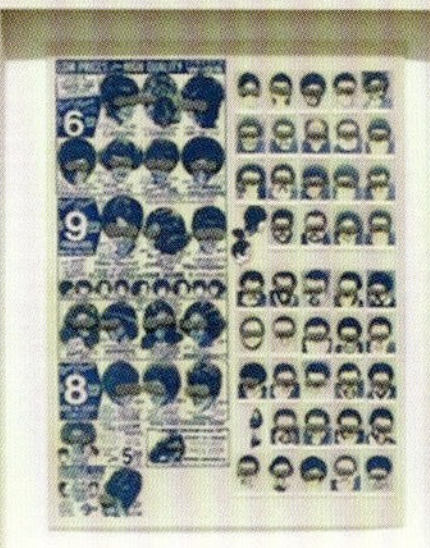
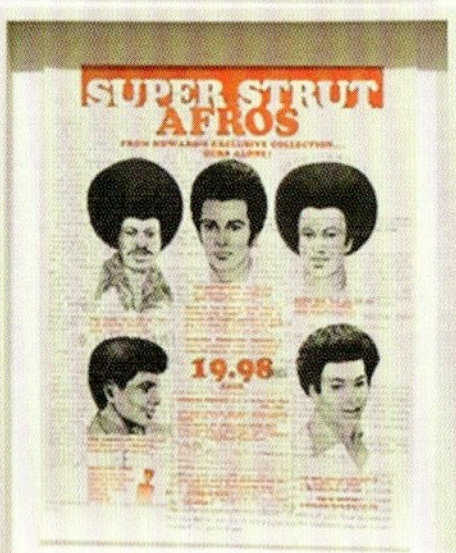
SUPER STRUT
AFROS
19.98
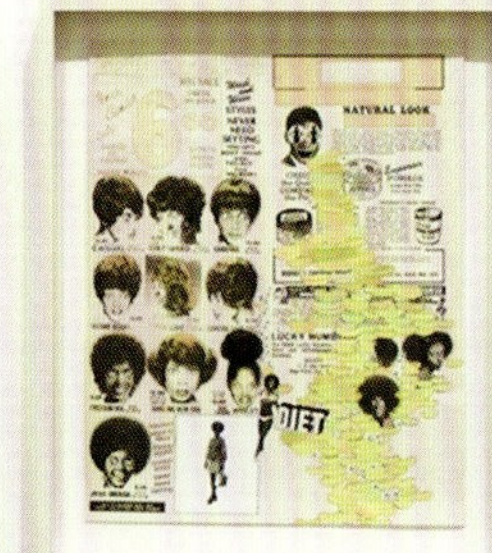
NATURAL LOOK
DIET
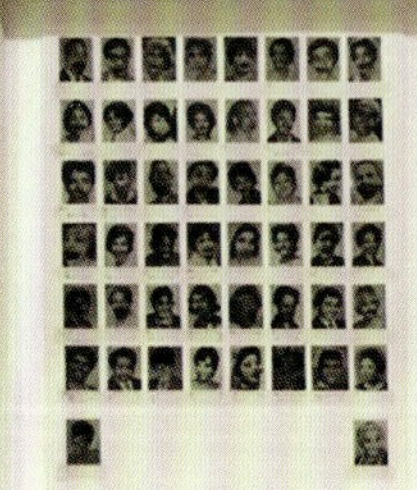
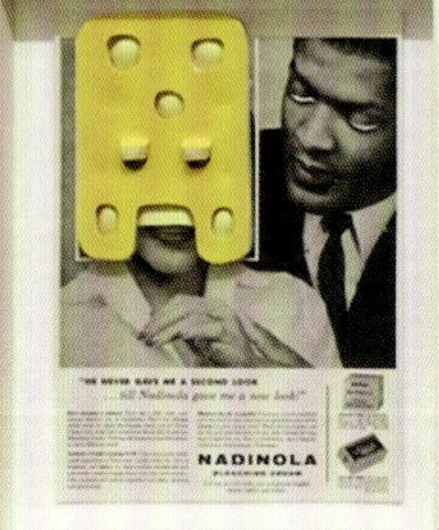
NADINOLA
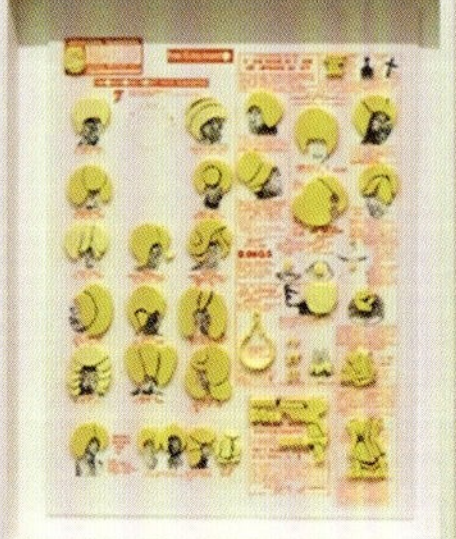
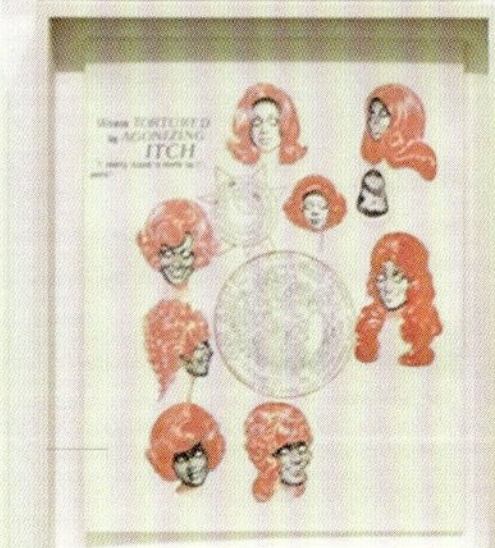
ITCH
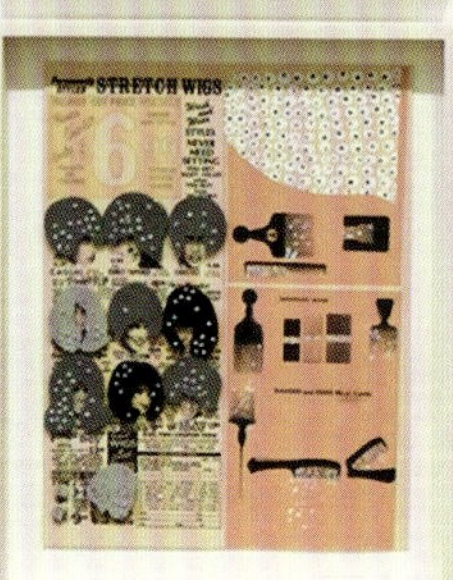
STRETCH WIGS
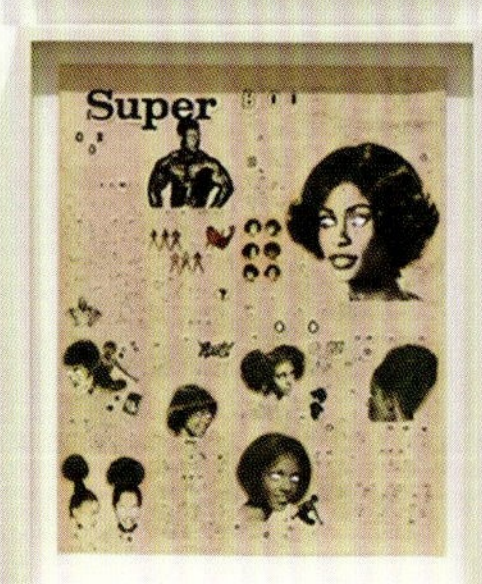
Super
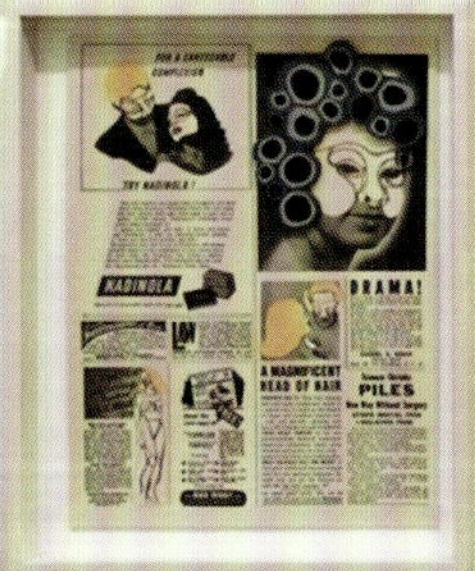
NADINOLA
DRAMA!
A MAGNIFICENT
HEAD OF HAIR
PILES
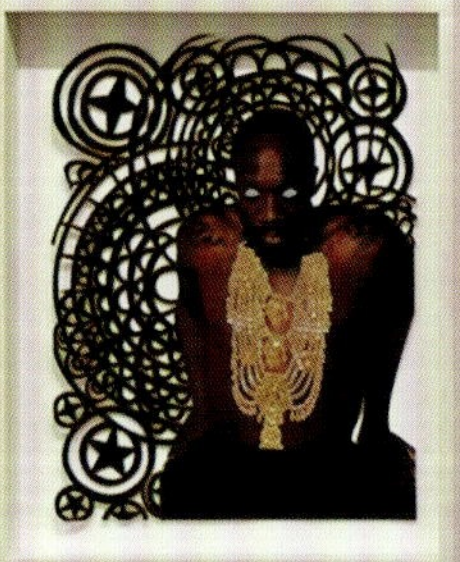
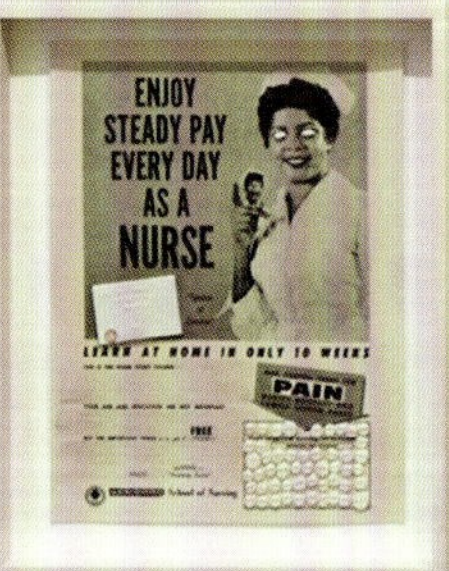
ENJOY
STEADY PAY
EVERY DAY
AS A
NURSE
LEARN AT HOME IN ONLY 10 WEEKS
PAIN
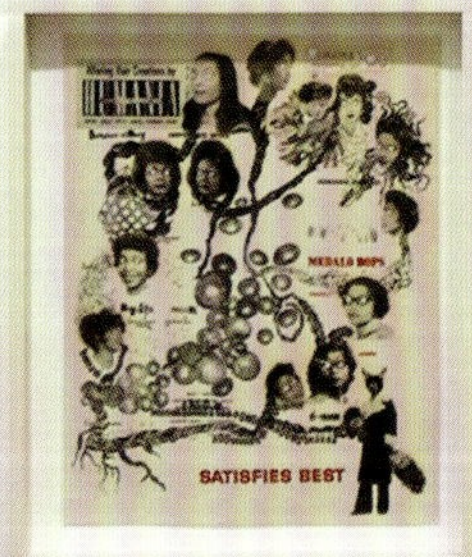
SATISFIES BEST
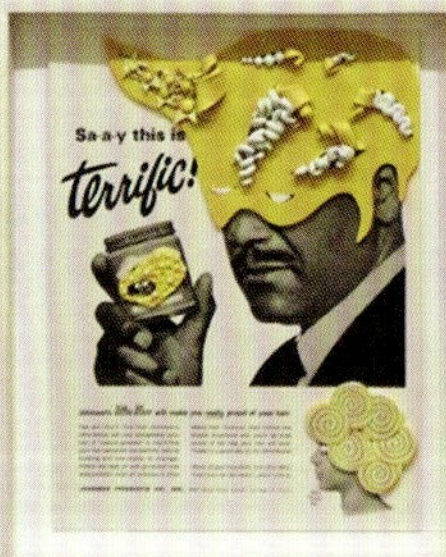
Sa-a-y this is
terrific!
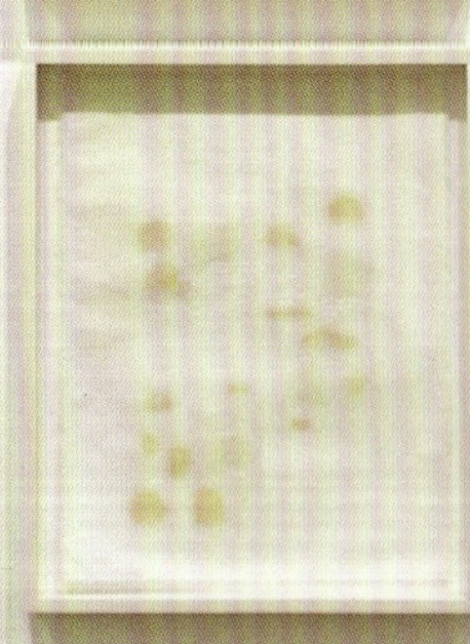

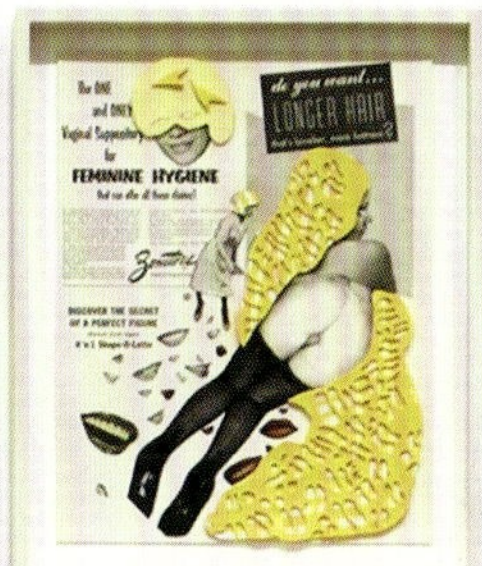
do you want...
LONGER HAIR
FEMININE HYGIENE
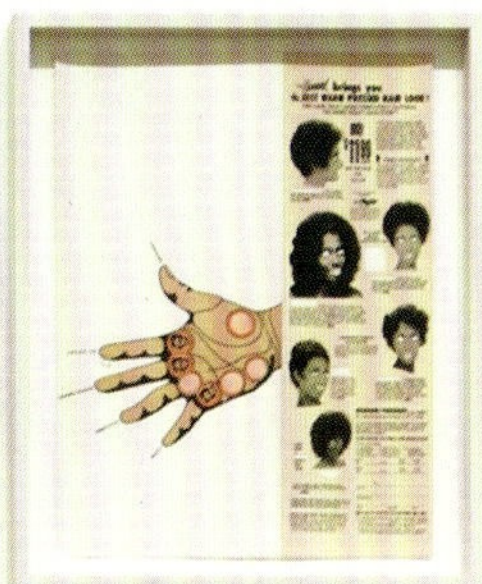
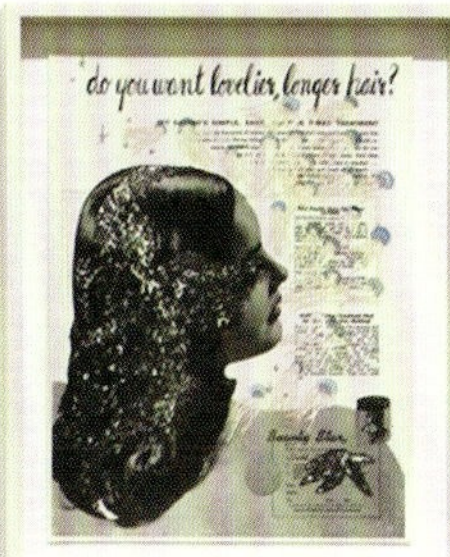
do you want lovelier, longer hair?
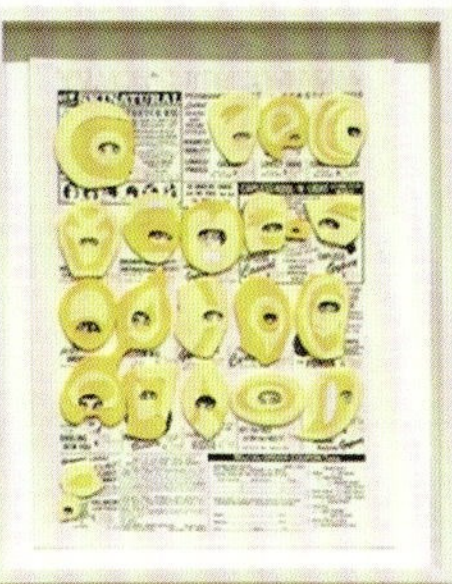
SKINATURAL
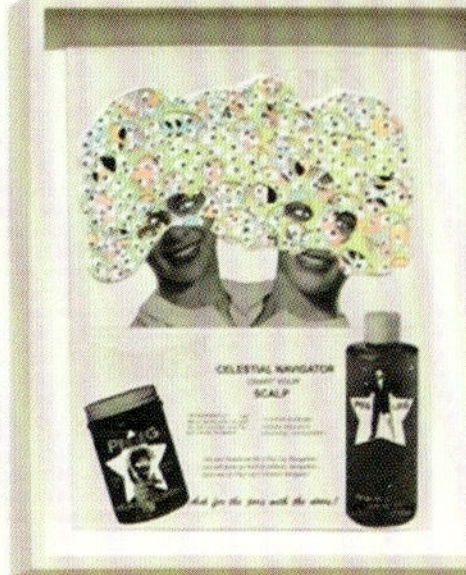
CELESTIAL NAVIGATOR
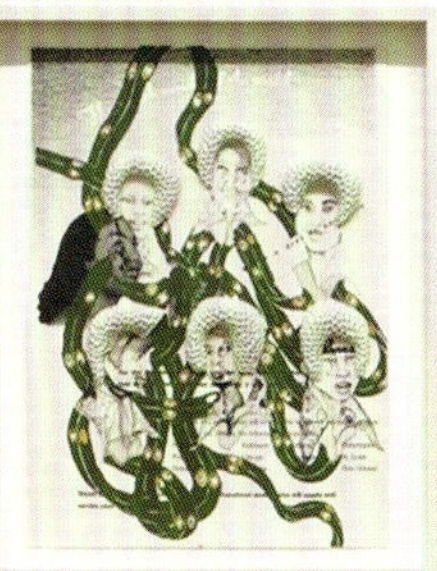
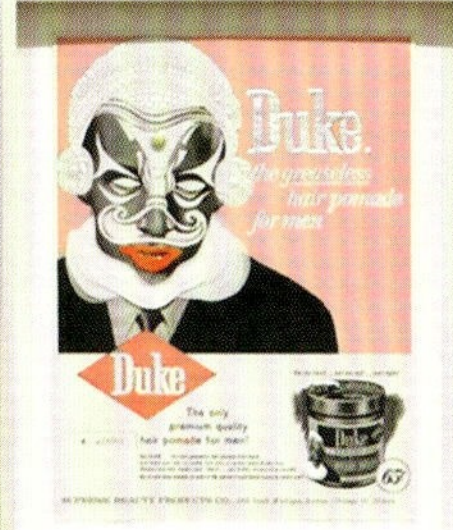
Duke
Duke
The only premium quality hair pomade for men
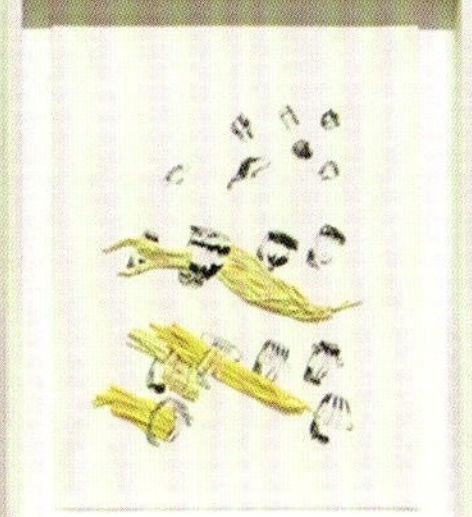
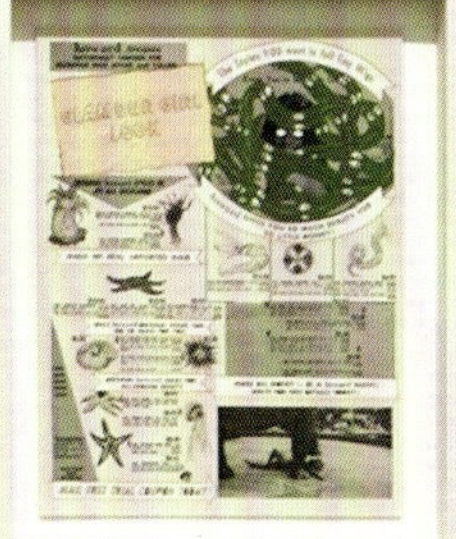
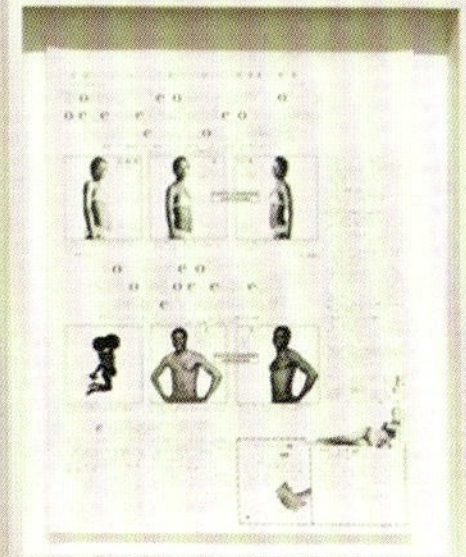
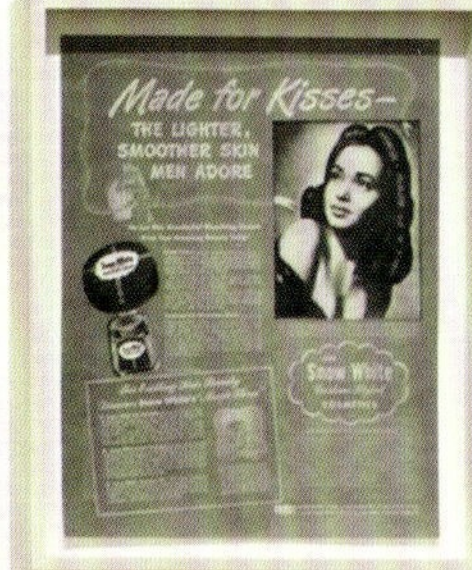
Made for Kisses—
THE LIGHTER, SMOOTHER SKIN MEN ADORE
Snow White
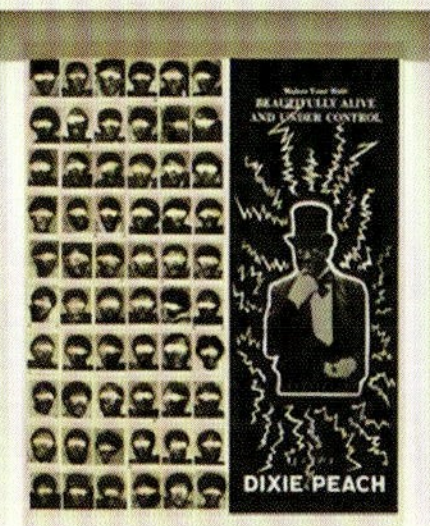
BEAUTIFULLY ALIVE AND UNDER CONTROL
DIXIE PEACH
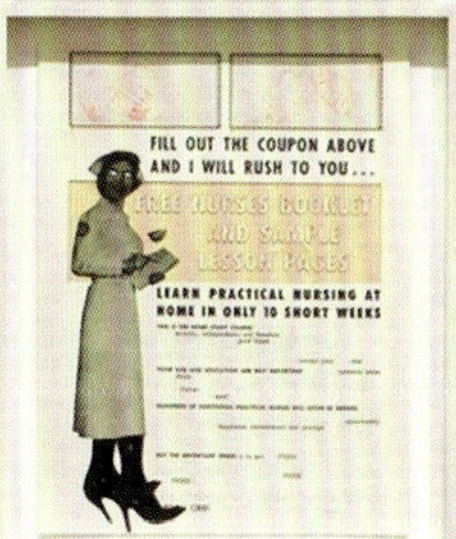
FILL OUT THE COUPON ABOVE AND I WILL RUSH TO YOU...
LEARN PRACTICAL NURSING AT HOME IN ONLY 10 SHORT WEEKS
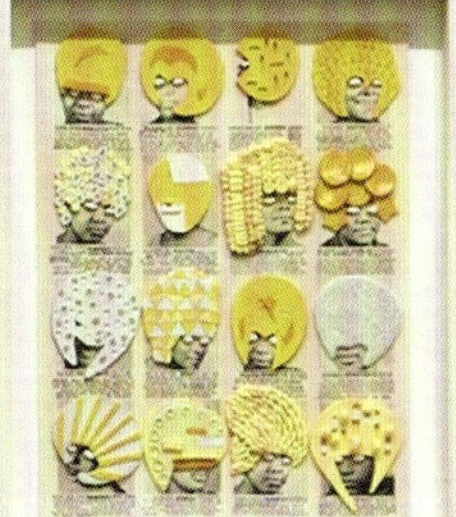
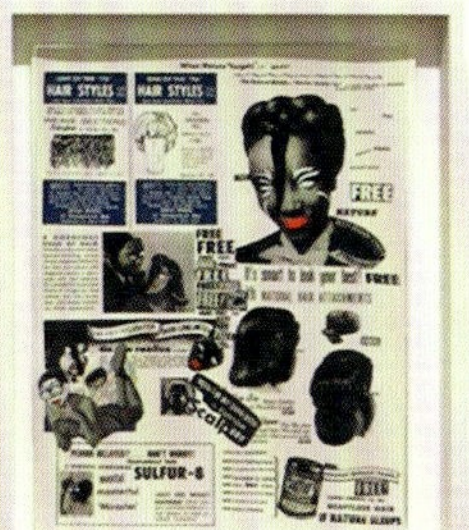
HAIR STYLES
SULFUR-8
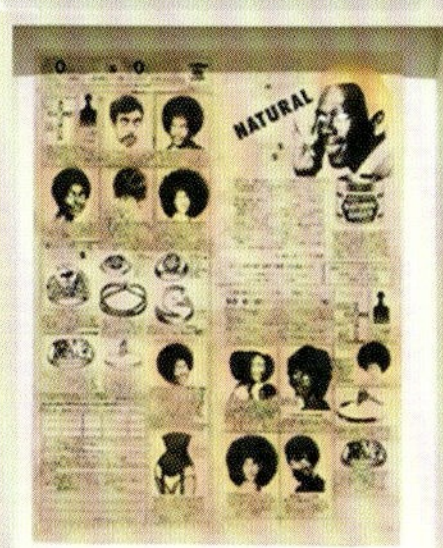
NATURAL
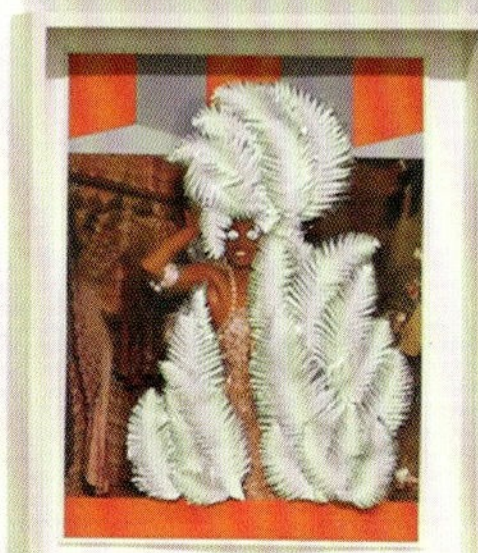
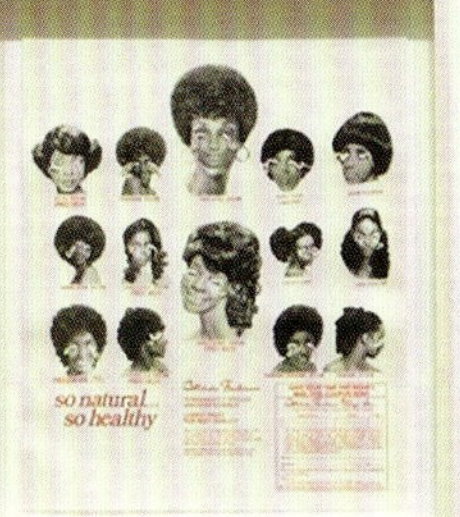
so natural
so healthy
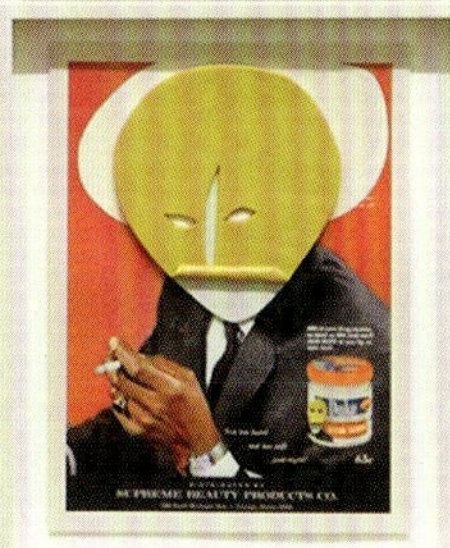
SUPREME BEAUTY PRODUCTS CO.
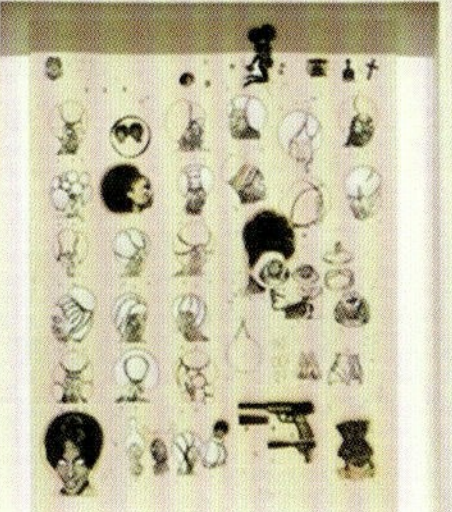
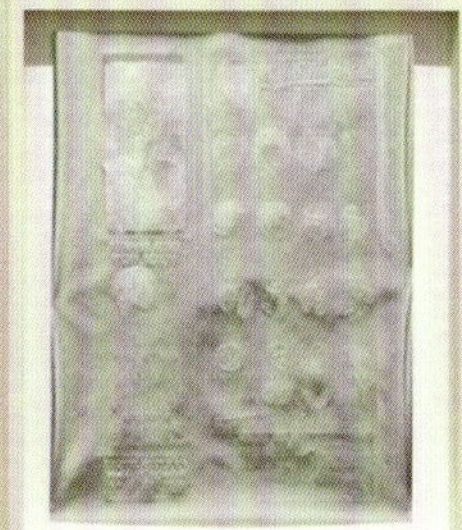
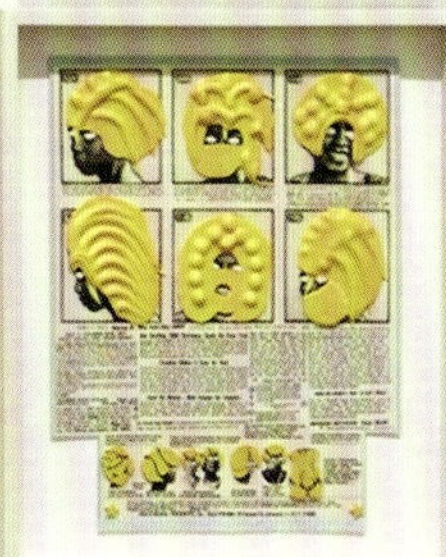
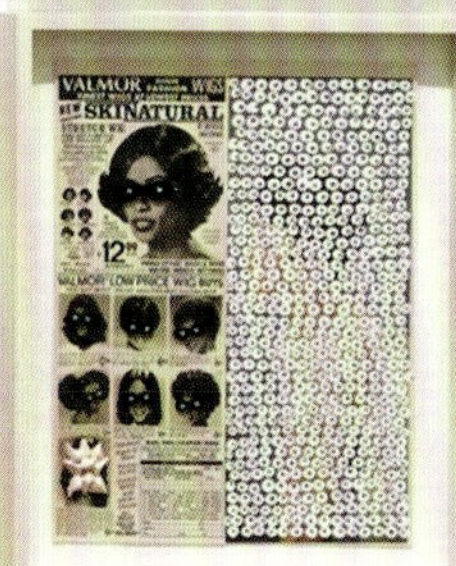
VALMOR
SKINATURAL
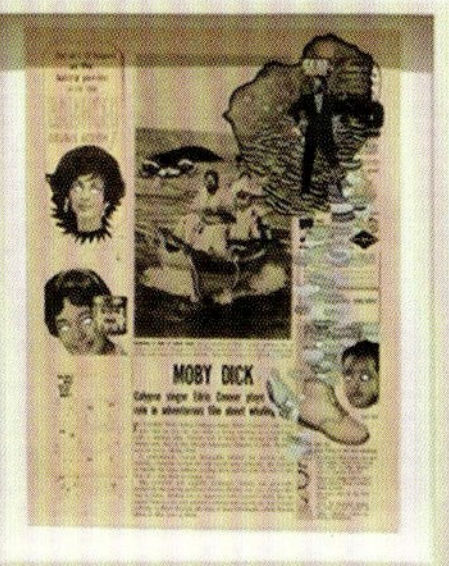
MOBY DICK
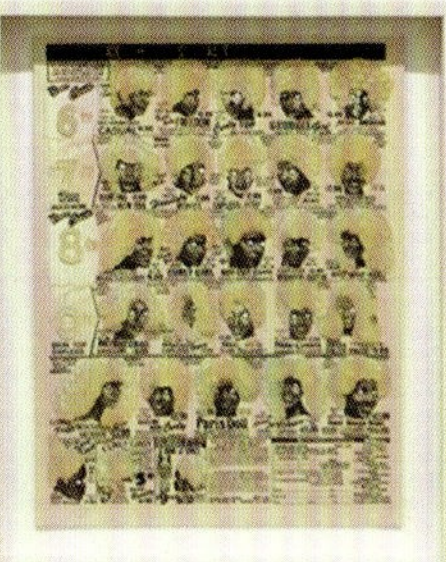
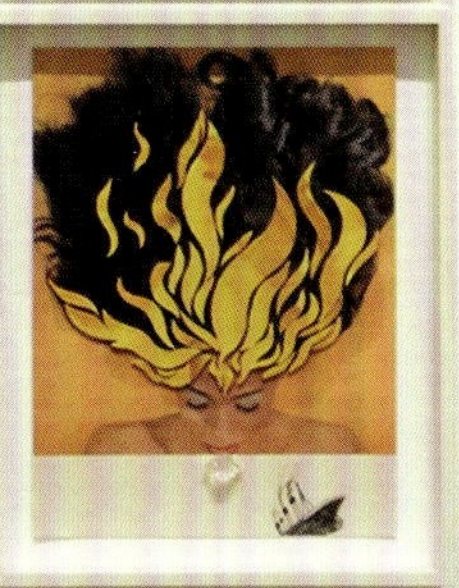
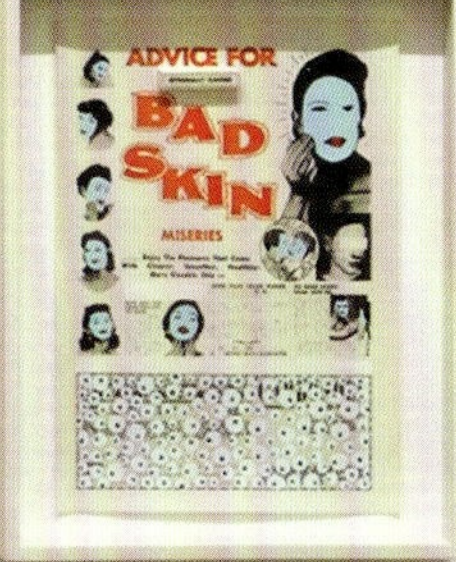
ADVICE FOR
BAD SKIN
MISERIES
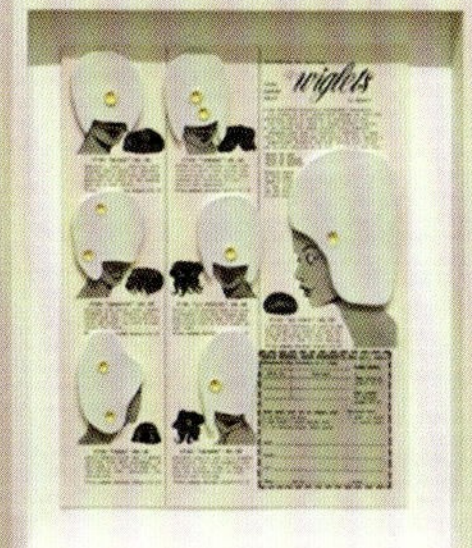
wiglets
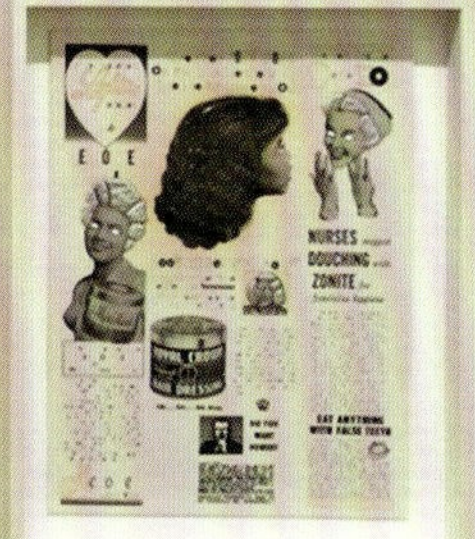
NURSES
DOUCHING
ZONITE
EAT ANYTHING WITH FALSE TEETH

Jenny Holzer

In 1979, the artist Jenny Holzer (American, b. 1950), now best known for her large-scale public installations, was an art student at the Whitney Independent Study Program in New York City. The readings in her classes from provocative and politically oriented authors like Mao Zedong, Vladimir Lenin, Emma Goldman, Adolf Hitler, and Leon Trotsky incited Holzer to create her memorable series *Inflammatory Essays*. For Holzer, the critical commentary on everyday life that she encountered in her classes seemed removed from the general public that the readings directly referenced. Piecing together fragments of the language she found in these texts, Holzer created one-hundred-word "essays" of twenty lines each that mimicked a generalized persuasive voice of a political theorist. Originally, Holzer printed dozens of copies of these essays on cheap paper and wheat-pasted them all over New York City at night, to avoid the authorities. While the original prints would have deteriorated within in a matter of days, the posters exist today as offset lithographs.

Posting these messages in public settings—subway stations, telephone poles, street-facing buildings—removed any barrier to entry for audiences to experience the work, creating an egalitarian environment for viewing art where passersby could even take out a pen and underline, circle, or scratch out phrases in response. By choosing to inexpensively affix her essays in this manner, Holzer draws upon a long history of broadsides, public announcements printed on cheap paper and displayed in common spaces. This form of public communication can be dated back to the earliest prints in history, around the time of the Gutenberg press in 1454, but public proclamations have a deep-seated place in American public life as well, and they played a critical role in disseminating information and ideas during the American independence movement and beyond. The *Inflammatory Essays* laid the groundwork for Holzer's later engagement with other public-facing media, like billboard signage and electric screens. As she commented in a 1989 interview: "I want to make art that's understandable, has some relevance and importance to almost anyone. And once I've made the stuff, the idea is get it out to the people. I want them to encounter it in different ways, find it on the street, in electric signs and so forth."[1] —SD

(following pages)
Jenny Holzer
(American, b. 1950)
Inflammatory Essays, 1979–82
offset prints on colored paper
17 × 17 in.
(43.2 × 43.2 cm) each

1 Grace Glueck, "And Now, a Few Words from Jenny Holzer," *New York Times*, December 3, 1989, https://www.nytimes.com/1989/12/03/magazine/and-now-a-few-words-from-jenny-holzer.html.

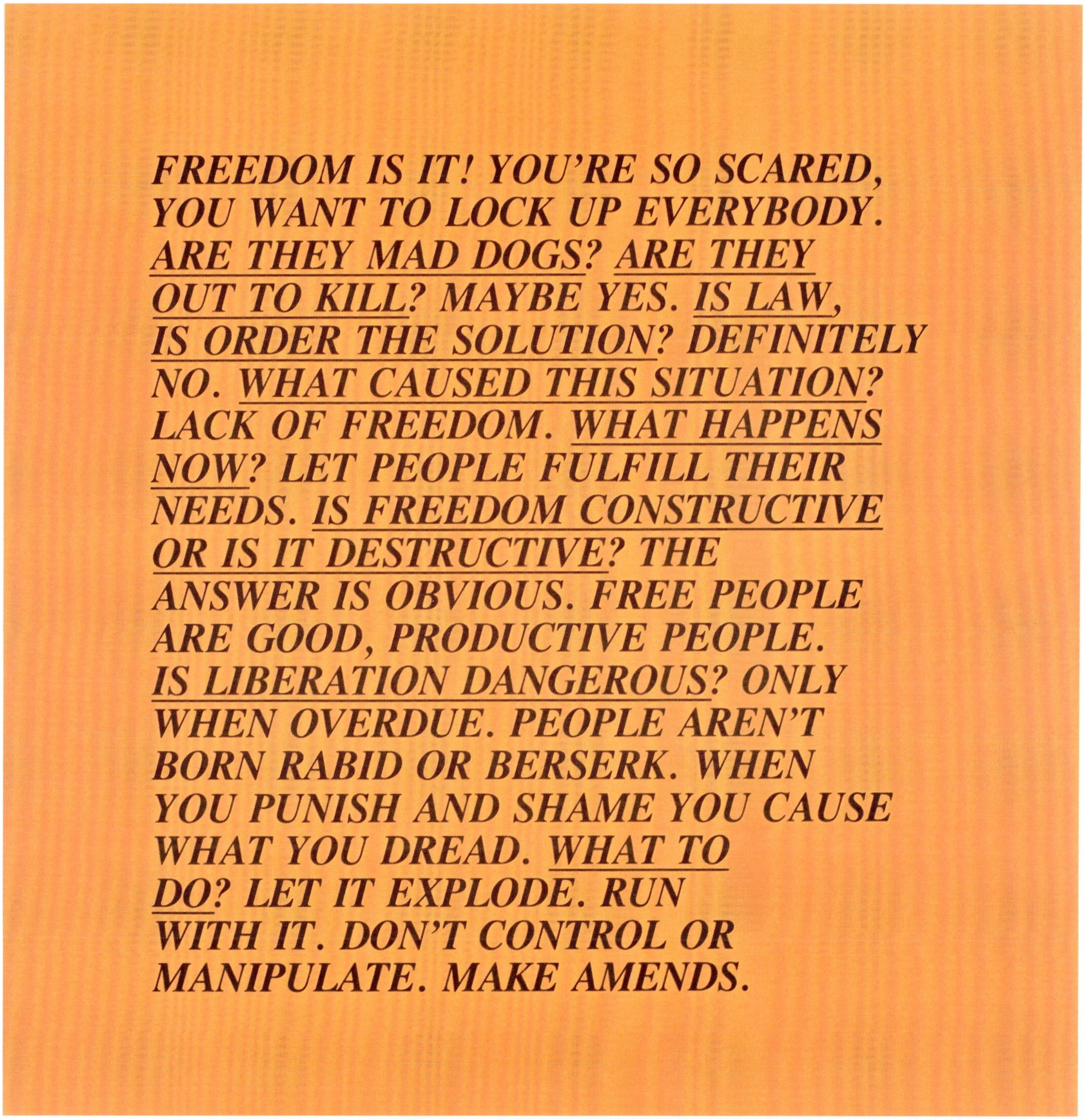

FREEDOM IS IT! YOU'RE SO SCARED, YOU WANT TO LOCK UP EVERYBODY. ARE THEY MAD DOGS? ARE THEY OUT TO KILL? MAYBE YES. IS LAW, IS ORDER THE SOLUTION? DEFINITELY NO. WHAT CAUSED THIS SITUATION? LACK OF FREEDOM. WHAT HAPPENS NOW? LET PEOPLE FULFILL THEIR NEEDS. IS FREEDOM CONSTRUCTIVE OR IS IT DESTRUCTIVE? THE ANSWER IS OBVIOUS. FREE PEOPLE ARE GOOD, PRODUCTIVE PEOPLE. IS LIBERATION DANGEROUS? ONLY WHEN OVERDUE. PEOPLE AREN'T BORN RABID OR BERSERK. WHEN YOU PUNISH AND SHAME YOU CAUSE WHAT YOU DREAD. WHAT TO DO? LET IT EXPLODE. RUN WITH IT. DON'T CONTROL OR MANIPULATE. MAKE AMENDS.

Jenny Holzer
(American, b. 1950)
Inflammatory Essays: Freedom Is It!..., 1979–82
offset prints on colored paper
17 × 17 in. (43.2 × 43.2 cm)

THOU ART THAT KIND OF PRIVILEGED WOMAN WHO IS REALLY REALLY SURE THAT NOTHING WILL EVER HAPPEN TO THEE. THOU IMAGINE THAT THOU ART SACRED, THAT THY BODY IS A TEMPLE WHERE NONE BUT THE ANOINTED MAY ENTER. SURPRISE! THY TEMPLE GATES ARE ABOUT TO BE OPENED. BEFORE THOU CAN SHIVER, EVERYONE WILL BE EXPLORING THY SECRET ALTAR. FREE ADMISSION! THOU WILL BE COMMON PROPERTY, EVERYONE'S WHORE, BEFORE THOU ART USED-UP, MESSED-UP AND THROWN IN A PILE WITH OTHER JUNK THAT USED TO LOOK GOOD BUT IS USELESS. IT IS THINE OWN FAULT. THOU THOUGHT THOU WERE BETTER THAN US.

CHANGE IS THE BASIS OF ALL HISTORY, THE PROOF OF VIGOR. THE OLD IS SOILED AND DISGUSTING BY NATURE. STALE FOOD IS REPELLENT, MONOGAMOUS LOVE BREEDS CONTEMPT, SENILITY CRIPPLES THE GOVERNMENT THAT IS TOO POWERFUL TOO LONG. UPHEAVAL IS DESIRABLE BECAUSE FRESH, UNTAINTED GROUPS SEIZE OPPORTUNITY. VIOLENT OVERTHROW IS APPROPRIATE WHEN THE SITUATION IS INTOLERABLE. SLOW MODIFICATION CAN BE EFFECTIVE; MEN CHANGE BEFORE THEY NOTICE AND RESIST. THE DECADENT AND THE POWERFUL CHAMPION CONTINUITY. "NOTHING ESSENTIAL CHANGES." THAT IS A MYTH. IT WILL BE REFUTED. THE NECESSARY BIRTH CONVULSIONS WILL BE TRIGGERED. ACTION WILL BRING THE EVIDENCE TO YOUR DOORSTEP.

FOOD WON'T GO DOWN WHEN YOU KNOW YOUR MOTHER DIDN'T WANT YOU, NEVER LIKED TO FEED YOU, ALWAYS HATED YOU IN HER ROOMS. YOU WERE WRONG TO CLUTCH AND SWALLOW AND MOVE YOUR MOUTH. YOU MUST NOT BE FLUSHED, LAYERED IN FAT OR RIPE FROM MEAT OR SHE WILL DESPISE YOUR SIGHT. YOUR SKELETON CRIES, "I MAKE NO DEMANDS, I AM ASHAMED OF MY NEEDS, I AM UNWORTHY. I'M AWARE OF THOSE MORE DESERVING, THOSE WITH PRIOR AND URGENT CLAIMS TO FOOD." SKELETON SAYS, "MY SAFETY IS IN SLIGHTNESS, MY PRIDE IS DENIAL. MY VICTORY IS NO GLUTTONY, NO GUILT."

MONDAY, *SOMEONE DIED BECAUSE HE HURT ME SO I CUT HIM WITHOUT THINKING.* TUESDAY, *SOME ANIMAL DIED BECAUSE HE WAS TOO DANGEROUS TO BE FREE.* WEDNESDAY, *A THIEF DIED SO EVERYONE WILL KNOW TO RESPECT PRIVATE PROPERTY.* THURSDAY, *SOME POLITICO DIED BECAUSE HIS IDEAS WERE CRAZY AND TOO CONTAGIOUS.* FRIDAY, *SOME RAPIST DIED BECAUSE HE LEFT HIS VICTIM WISHING SHE WAS DEAD. HE HAD TO DIE WISHING HE WAS ALIVE.* SATURDAY, *I KILLED A CONDEMNED MAN SO NO ONE ELSE WOULD GET BLOOD ON THEIR HANDS.* SUNDAY, *I RESTED.* MONDAY, *SIX PEOPLE JUMPED ME SO I CUT THEM WITHOUT THINKING.*

OH LORD WHEN YOU ARE ALONE AND DO NOT WANT TO BE, YOU LIE IN BED WITH YOUR OWN SHOULDER WRAPPED AROUND AND BENEATH YOURSELF SO THAT THE SURGES OF PAIN KEEP YOU COMPANY. THIS IS HURTFUL BUT IT IS SO MUCH BETTER THAN NO NERVES FIRING AT ALL. THE WORST IS WHEN THERE'S NO ONE NEAR TO PRESS ON YOU AND MAKE DENTS IN YOUR SKIN WITH THEIR FINGER NAILS. YOU ARE LEFT RUNNING YOUR HANDS ALL OVER YOURSELF, BITING TRYING AND EXPERIMENTING TO CREATE SENSATIONS. THE ENORMOUS FEELINGS YOU MAKE PROVE TO YOURSELF THAT YOU CREATE GREAT EXCITEMENT.

DESTROY SUPERABUNDANCE. STARVE THE FLESH, SHAVE THE HAIR, EXPOSE THE BONE, CLARIFY THE MIND, DEFINE THE WILL, RESTRAIN THE SENSES, LEAVE THE FAMILY, FLEE THE CHURCH, KILL THE VERMIN, VOMIT THE HEART, FORGET THE DEAD. LIMIT TIME, FORGO AMUSEMENT, DENY NATURE, REJECT ACQUAINTANCES, DISCARD OBJECTS, FORGET TRUTHS, DISSECT MYTH, STOP MOTION, BLOCK IMPULSE, CHOKE SOBS, SWALLOW CHATTER. SCORN JOY, SCORN TOUCH, SCORN TRAGEDY, SCORN LIBERTY, SCORN CONSTANCY, SCORN HOPE, SCORN EXALTATION, SCORN REPRODUCTION, SCORN VARIETY, SCORN EMBELLISHMENT, SCORN RELEASE, SCORN REST, SCORN SWEETNESS, SCORN LIGHT. IT'S A QUESTION OF FORM AS MUCH AS FUNCTION. IT IS A MATTER OF REVULSION.

A REAL TORTURE WOULD BE TO BUILD A SPARKLING CAGE WITH 2-WAY MIRRORS AND STEEL BARS. IN THERE WOULD BE GOOD-LOOKING AND YOUNG GIRLS WHO'LL THINK THEY'RE IN A REGULAR MOTEL ROOM SO THEY'LL TAKE THEIR CLOTHES OFF AND DO THE DELICATE THINGS THAT GIRLS DO WHEN THEY'RE SURE THEY'RE ALONE. EVERYONE WHO WATCHES WILL GO CRAZY BECAUSE THEY WON'T BE BELIEVING WHAT THEY'RE SEEING BUT THEY'LL SEE THE BARS AND KNOW THEY CAN'T GET IN. AND, THEY'LL BE AFRAID TO MAKE A MOVE BECAUSE THEY DON'T WANT TO SCARE THE GIRLS AWAY FROM DOING THE DELICIOUS THINGS THEY'RE DOING.

WHAT SCARES PEASANTS IS THINKING THEIR BODIES WILL BE THROWN OUT IN PUBLIC AND LEFT TO ROT. THEY FEEL SHAME— AS IF IT MATTERS WHAT POSITION THEIR LEGS ARE IN WHEN THEY'RE DEAD. LUCKY THEY'RE SUPERSTITIOUS BECAUSE THEY'RE EASIER TO MANAGE. MAKE AN EXAMPLE OF 2 OR 3 REBELS, DROP THEIR BODIES BY A ROAD, GET THEM FLAT AND DRY SO BONES SHOW AND THE GRASS WEARS THE CLOTHES. SHOOT THE FINGERS OFF ANYONE WHO COMES TO COLLECT THE REMAINS. THOSE BODIES STAY AS A SIGN OF ABSOLUTE AUTHORITY. IF PEASANTS THINK THEIR SOULS CAN'T REST, SO MUCH THE BETTER.

SENTIMENTALITY DELAYS THE REMOVAL OF THE POLITICALLY BACKWARD AND THE ORGANICALLY UNSOUND. RIGOROUS SELECTION IS MANDATORY IN SOCIAL AND GENETIC ENGINEERING. INCORRECT MERCIFUL IMPULSES POSTPONE THE CLEANSING THAT PRECEDES REFORM. SHORT-TERM NICETIES MUST YIELD TO LONG-RANGE NECESSITY. MORALS WILL BE REVISED TO MEET THE REQUIREMENTS OF TODAY. MEANINGLESS PLATITUDES WILL BE PULLED FROM TONGUES AND MINDS. WORDS LIKE "PURGE" AND "EUTHANASIA" DESERVE NEW CONNOTATIONS. THEY SHOULD BE RECOGNIZED AS THE RATIONAL PUBLIC POLICIES THEY ARE. THE GREATEST DANGER IS NOT EXCESSIVE ZEAL BUT UNDUE HESITATION. WE WILL LEARN TO IMITATE NATURE. HER KILLS NOURISH STRONG LIFE. SQUEAMISHNESS IS THE CRIME.

A CRUEL BUT ANCIENT LAW DEMANDS AN EYE FOR AN EYE. MURDER MUST BE ANSWERED BY EXECUTION. ONLY GOD HAS THE RIGHT TO TAKE A LIFE AND WHEN SOMEONE BREAKS THIS LAW HE WILL BE PUNISHED. JUSTICE MUST COME SWIFTLY. IT DOESN'T HELP ANYONE TO STALL. THE VICTIM'S FAMILY CRIES OUT FOR SATISFACTION, THE COMMUNITY BEGS FOR PROTECTION AND THE DEPARTED CRAVES VENGEANCE SO HE CAN REST. THE KILLER KNEW IN ADVANCE THERE WAS NO EXCUSE FOR HIS ACT, TRULY HE HAS TAKEN HIS OWN LIFE. HE, NOT SOCIETY, IS RESPONSIBLE FOR HIS FATE. HE ALONE STANDS GUILTY AND DAMNED.

FEAR IS THE MOST ELEGANT WEAPON, YOUR HANDS ARE NEVER MESSY. THREATENING BODILY HARM IS CRUDE. WORK INSTEAD ON MINDS AND BELIEFS, PLAY INSECURITIES LIKE A PIANO. BE CREATIVE IN APPROACH. FORCE ANXIETY TO EXCRUCIATING LEVELS OR GENTLY UNDERMINE THE PUBLIC CONFIDENCE. PANIC DRIVES HUMAN HERDS OVER CLIFFS; AN ALTERNATIVE IS TERROR-INDUCED IMMOBILIZATION. FEAR FEEDS ON FEAR. PUT THIS EFFICIENT PROCESS IN MOTION. MANIPULATION IS NOT LIMITED TO PEOPLE. ECONOMIC, SOCIAL AND DEMOCRATIC INSTITUTIONS CAN BE SHAKEN. IT WILL BE DEMONSTRATED THAT NOTHING IS SAFE, SACRED OR SANE. THERE IS NO RESPITE FROM HORROR. ABSOLUTES ARE QUICKSILVER. RESULTS ARE SPECTACULAR.

BECAUSE THERE IS NO GOD SOMEONE MUST TAKE RESPONSIBILITY FOR MEN. A CHARISMATIC LEADER IS IMPERATIVE. HE CAN SUBORDINATE THE SMALL WILLS TO THE GREAT ONE. HIS STRENGTH AND HIS VISION REDEEM MEN. HIS PERFECTION MAKES THEM GRATEFUL. LIFE ITSELF IS NOT SACRED, THERE IS NO DIGNITY IN THE FLESH. UNDIRECTED MEN ARE CONTENT WITH RANDOM, SQUALID, POINTLESS LIVES. THE LEADER GIVES DIRECTION AND PURPOSE. THE LEADER FORCES GREAT ACCOMPLISHMENTS, MANDATES PEACE AND REPELS OUTSIDE AGGRESSORS. HE IS THE ARCHITECT OF DESTINY. HE DEMANDS ABSOLUTE LOYALTY. HE MERITS UNQUESTIONING DEVOTION. HE ASKS THE SUPREME SACRIFICE. HE IS THE ONLY HOPE.

Nicola López

With an MFA in printmaking, the American artist Nicola López (b. 1975) combines various techniques of the medium, and sometimes also installation, collage, and drawing, to build up dense compositions that evoke urban landscapes in flux. Her *Urban Transformation* series (2009) was produced through a combination of etching, lithography, and woodcut, resulting in remarkably textured surfaces thematizing accretion. Here, the remnants of urban industry appear to collapse in on themselves and, at the same time, to explode outward. Their remnants and tentacles ostensibly spill over the borders of the paper and onto the white mounting—in a clever trompe l'oeil move that plays on the way works on paper are traditionally fixed to a mount before framing. As Charles Schultz notes, this animated quality of López's compositions renders them an anthropomorphic industrial saga, one rooted not in narrative but in the "creaturely."[1]

Though López's active period predates the mainstream attunement to the global-warming crisis, many have seen in the artist's work a strong engagement with the excesses of the Anthropocene.[2] *The Babel Cycle* (2014) makes this explicit in its rhythmic animation of the assembling and collapsing of built worlds. —JO

Nicola López
(American, b. 1975)
Urban Transformation #1
(detail), edition 8/12, 2009
etching, lithography, and
woodcut with Mylar elements
30 × 30 in. (76.2 × 76.2 cm)

1 Charles Schultz, "Nicola López: Structural Detours," *Art in Print* 1, no. 2 (July–August 2011): 33–34.

2 "Trevor Paglen on Nicola López," *BOMB* 100 (Summer 2007): 72–73.

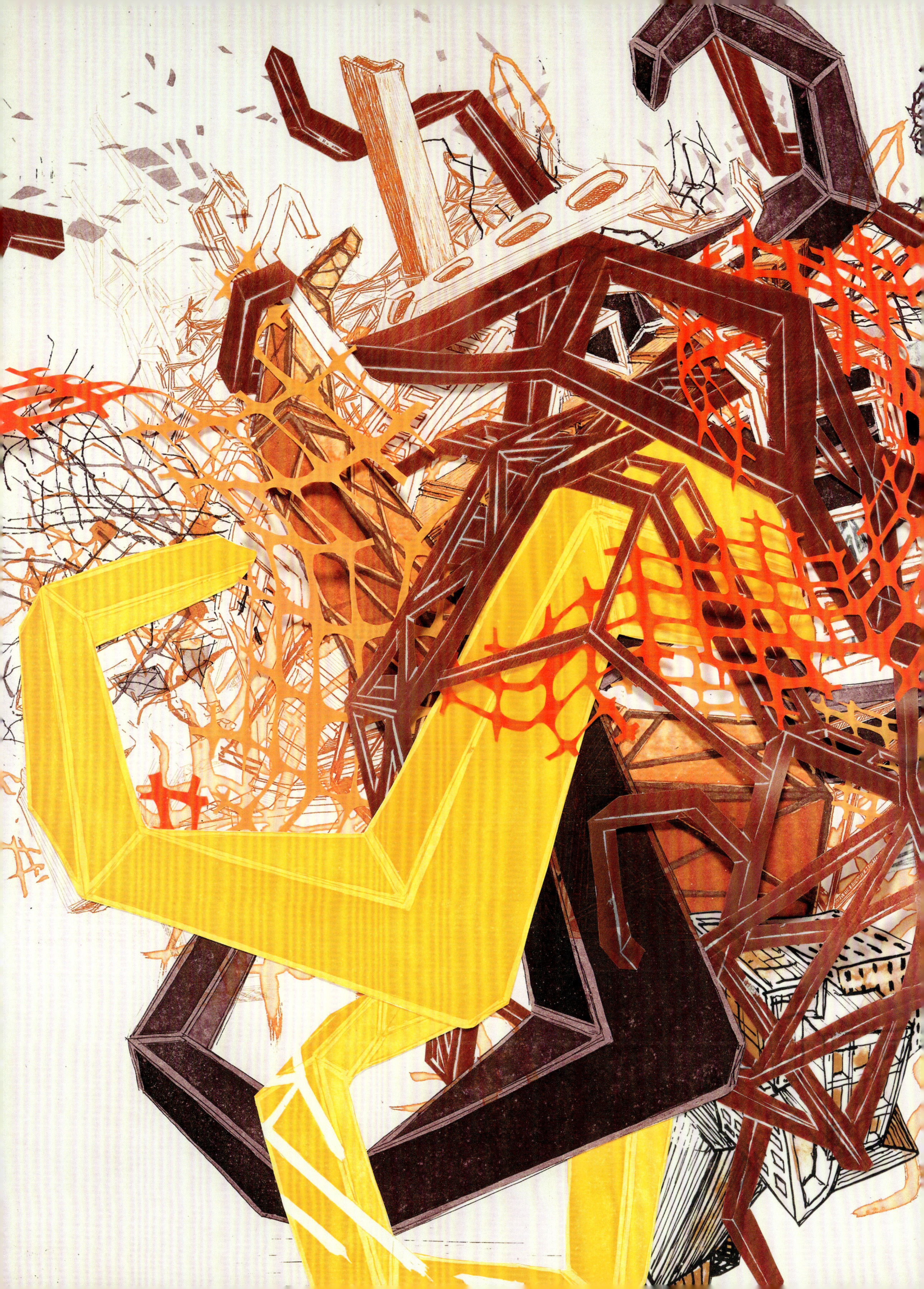

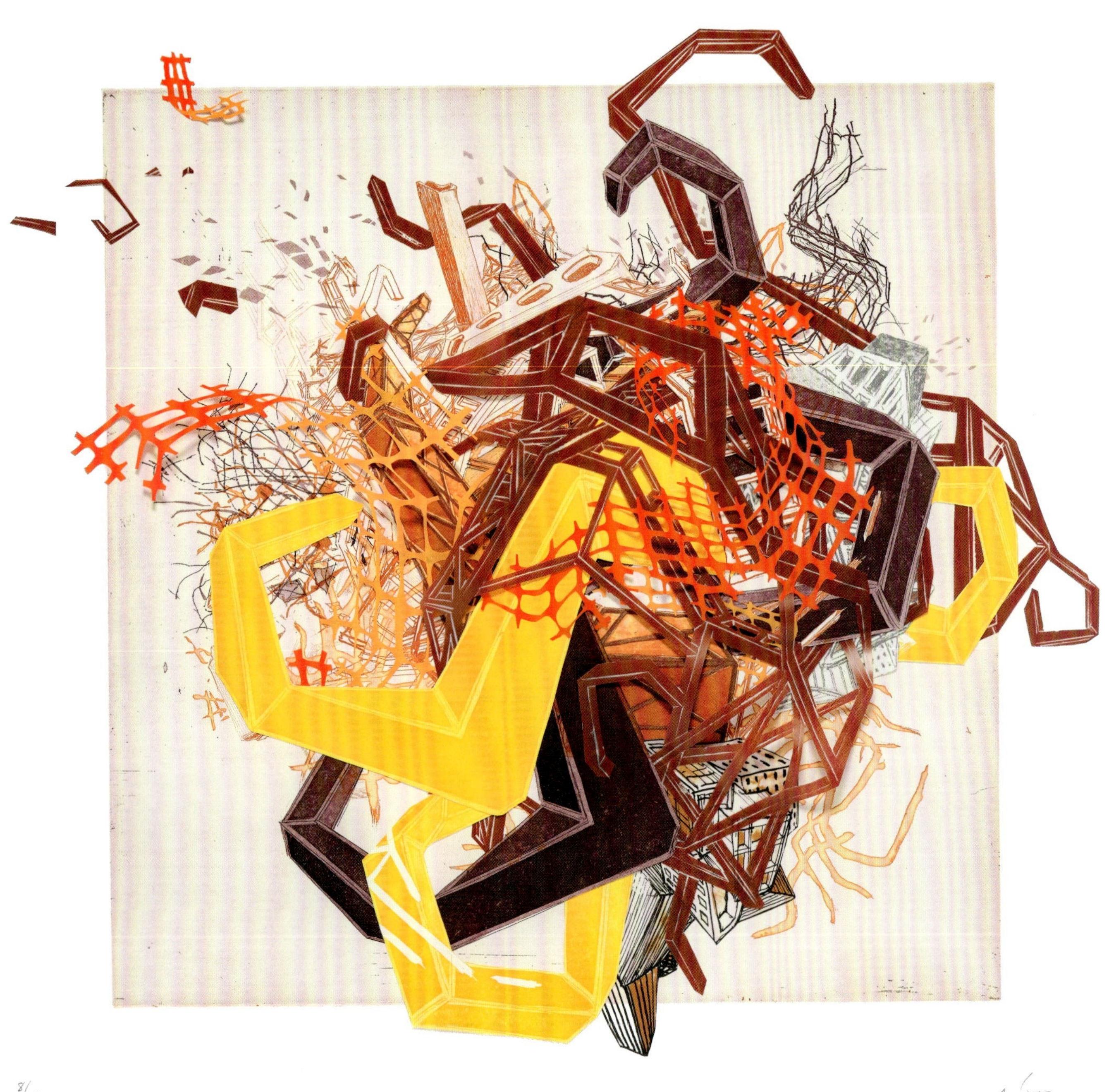

Nicola López
(American, b. 1975)
Urban Transformation #1,
edition 8/12, 2009
etching, lithography, and
woodcut with Mylar elements
30 × 30 in. (76.2 × 76.2 cm)

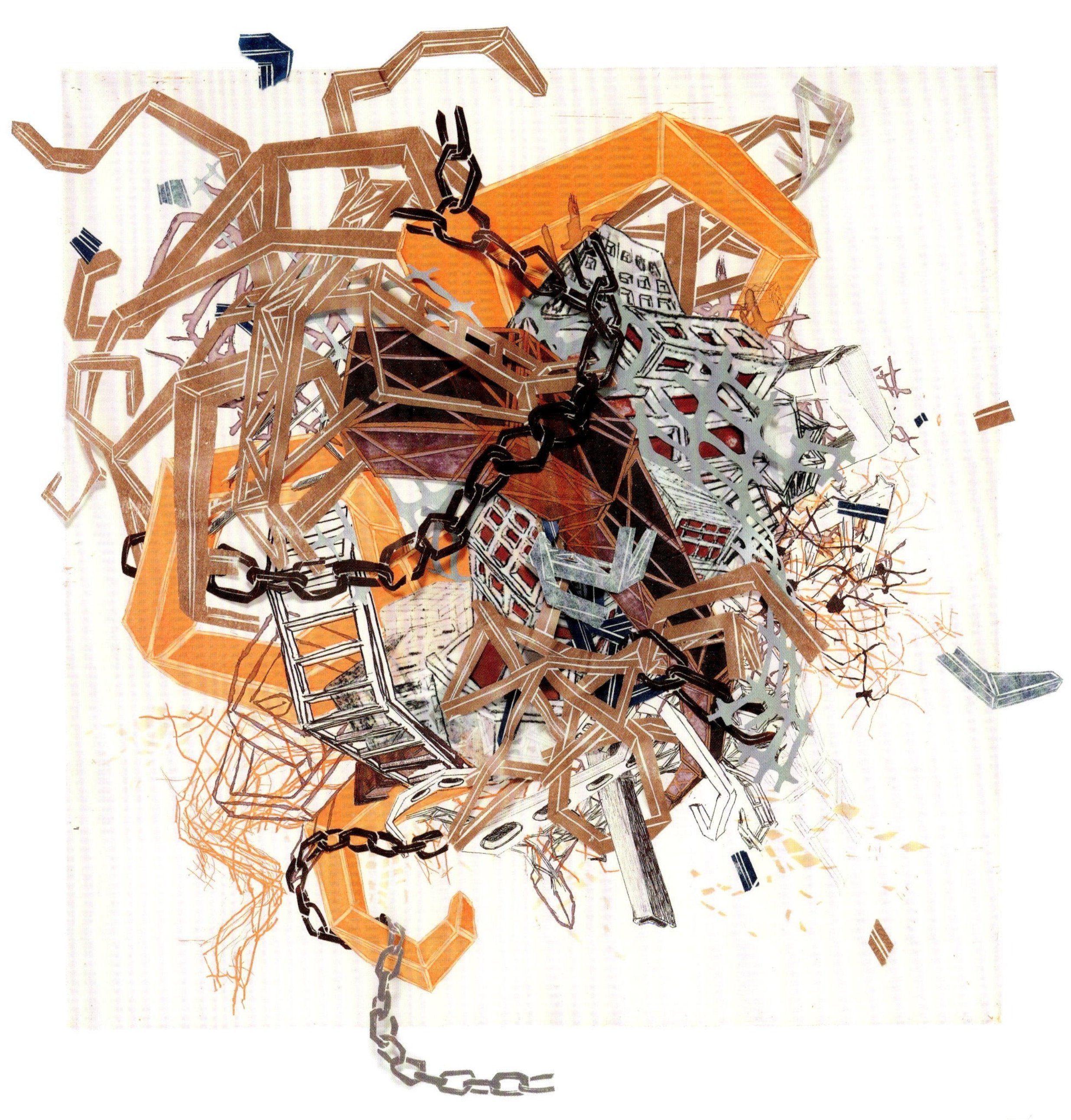

Nicola López
(American, b. 1975)
Urban Transformation #2,
edition 8/12, 2009
etching, lithography, and
woodcut with Mylar elements
30 × 30 in. (76.2 × 76.2 cm)

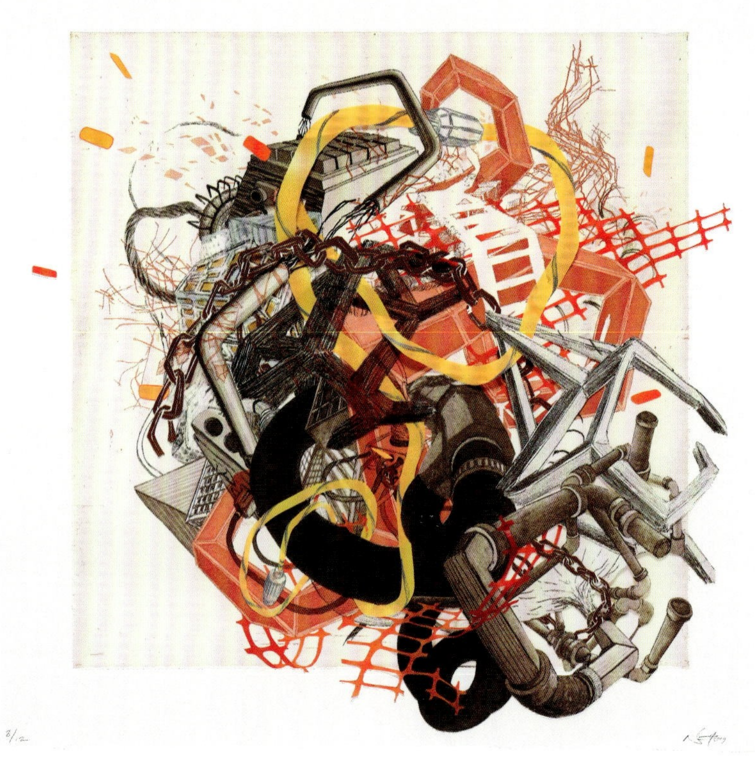

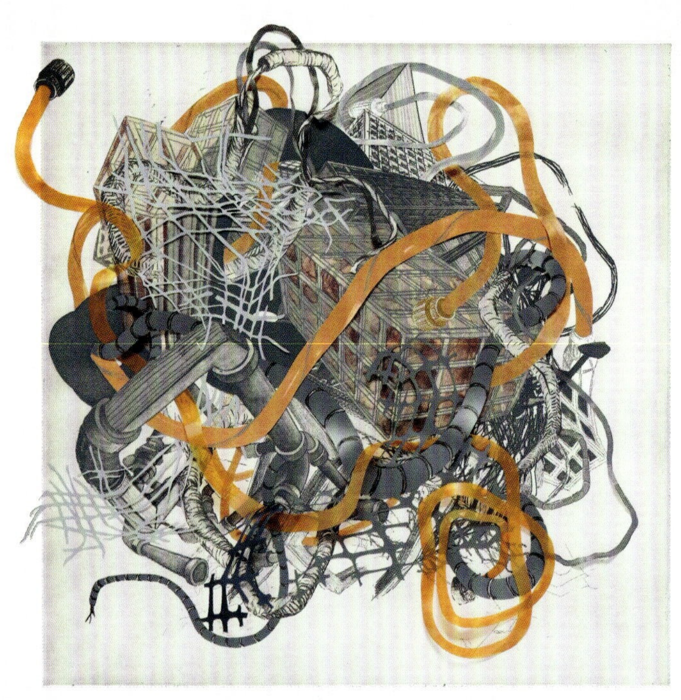

Nicola López
(American, b. 1975)
Urban Transformation #3,
edition 8/12, 2009
etching, lithography, and
woodcut with Mylar elements
30 × 30 in. (76.2 × 76.2 cm)

Urban Transformation #4,
edition 8/12, 2009
etching, lithography, and
woodcut with Mylar elements
30 × 30 in. (76.2 × 76.2 cm)

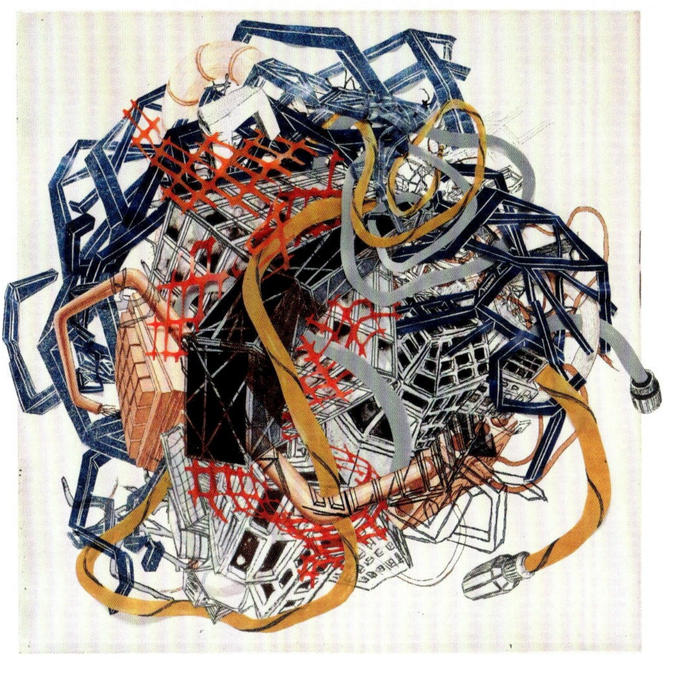

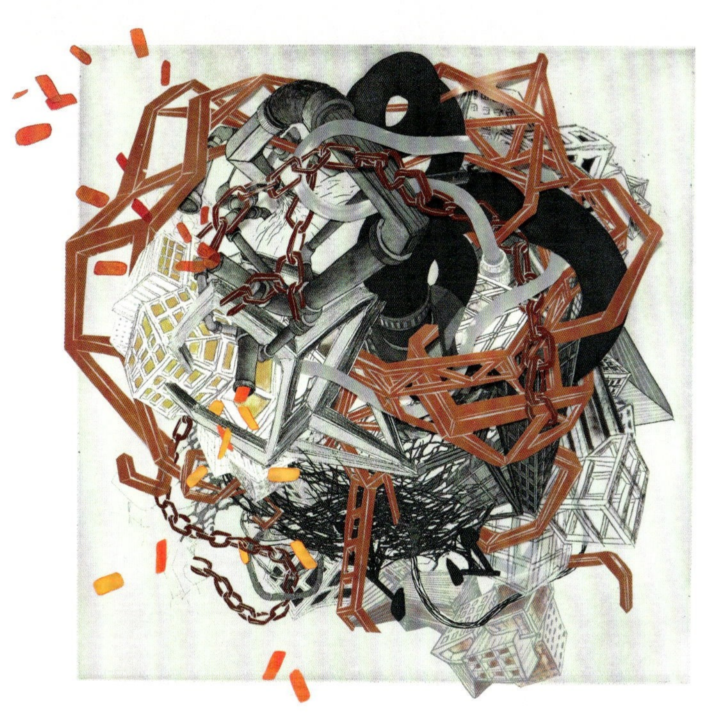

Urban Transformation #5,
edition 8/12, 2009
etching, lithography, and
woodcut with Mylar elements
30 × 30 in. (76.2 × 76.2 cm)

Urban Transformation #6,
edition 8/12, 2009
etching, lithography, and
woodcut with Mylar elements
30 × 30 in. (76.2 × 76.2 cm)

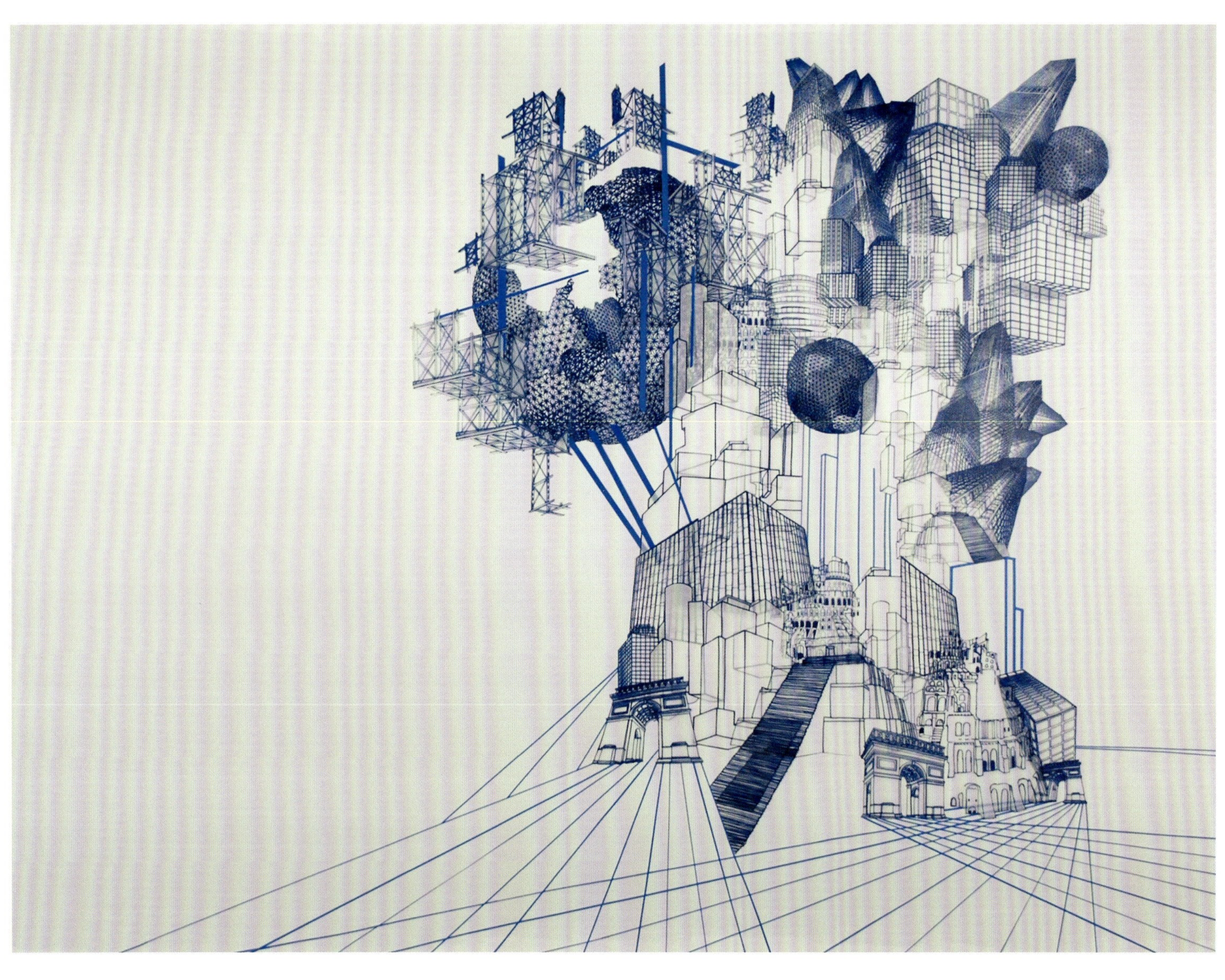

Nicola López
(American, b. 1975)
Stills from *The Babel Cycle*,
2014
Single-channel digital
stop-frame animation using
silkscreen-printed elements
and blue tape
8 minutes, 27 seconds

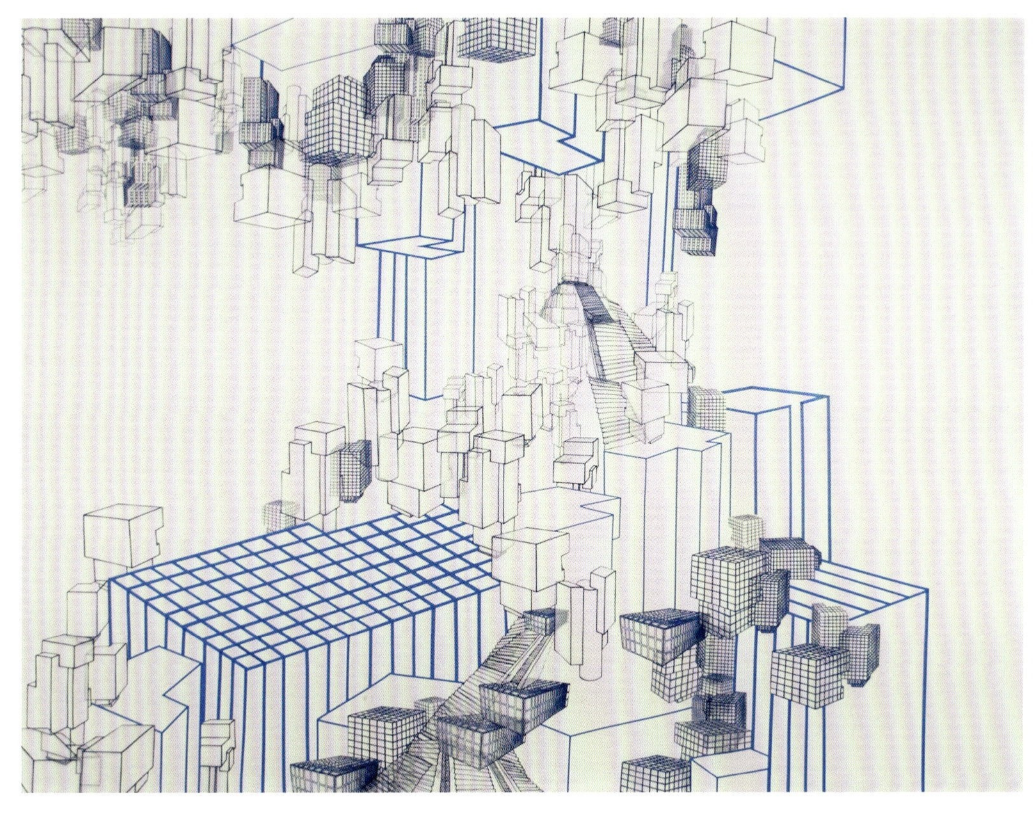

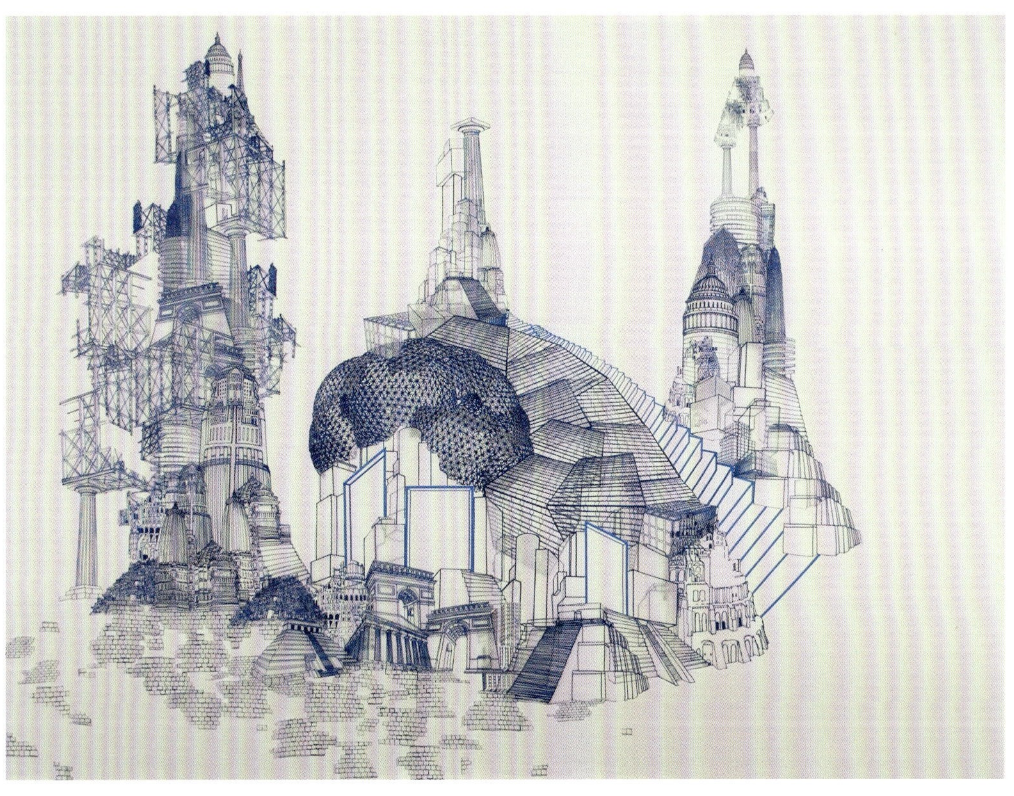

Julie Mehretu

The Ethiopian-born artist Julie Mehretu (b. 1970) is known for her large-format abstract works layering drawing and acrylic paint to capture "riotous geographies,"[1] informed by architectural drawings and cartography, among other sources. For her *Six Bardos* series of aquatints (2018), Mehretu employed a technique more akin to painting than to traditional intaglio printing. Rather than isolating each color and printing in meticulously aligned layers, the artist and her collaborators at Gemini G.E.L., Los Angeles, hand-applied the various colored inks to the single copper etching plate using rounded balls of cloth—a method known as *à la poupée*, or "with the doll"[2]—before passing the paper through the press just once. The result is a visual field featuring the tonal qualities that distinguish aquatint but with added tonality and gradation in the colors and forms themselves. The effect encapsulates the concepts of liminality and passage that Mehretu sought to explore in the project, evident in the subtitles of the two prints, *Transmutation* and *Transmigration.* These terms refer to the stages of the soul between death and reincarnation in Buddhism. To begin to unpack the complex compositions of Mehretu's *Six Bardos*, we might look to the artist's own comparison of her works to Chinese calligraphy paintings and specifically their "desire to describe the cosmos in a certain way, with marks that are signifiers, towards the cosmos as a system."[3] —JO

Julie Mehretu
(American, b. Ethiopia, 1970)
Six Bardos: Transmutation,
edition 23/45, 2018
aquatint
50½ × 61¼ in.
(128.3 × 155.6 cm)
All works © 2018
Julie Mehretu and
Gemini G.E.L. LLC

---

1 Daniella Brito, "Julie Mehretu Reminds Us That Borders Are Meant to Be Trespassed," *Hyperallergic*, May 3, 2021, https://hyperallergic.com/642645/julie-mehretu-whitney-museum-survey/.

2 "Julie Mehretu at Gemini G.E.L.: Six Bardos," press release, n.d., https://geminigel-media-w2.s3-us-west-2.amazonaws.com/files/_U2mhTXbTiCzgPbk--kbWg.pdf.

3 Quoted in Catherine de Zegher, *Julie Mehretu: Drawings* (New York: Rizzoli, 2007), 25.

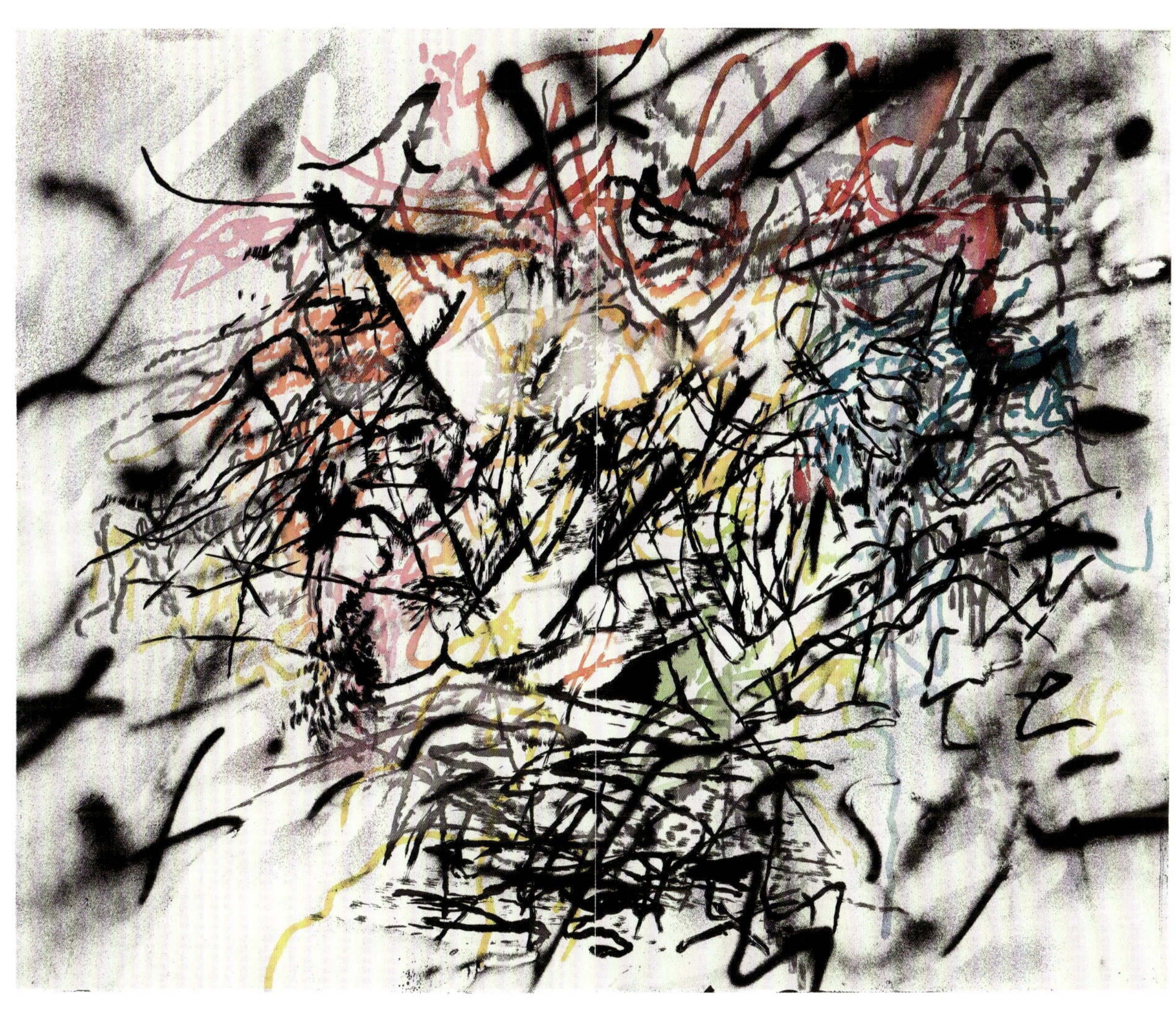

Julie Mehretu
(American, b. Ethiopia, 1970)
Six Bardos: Transmigration,
edition 23/25, 2018
aquatint
98 × 74 in. (248.9 × 188 cm)

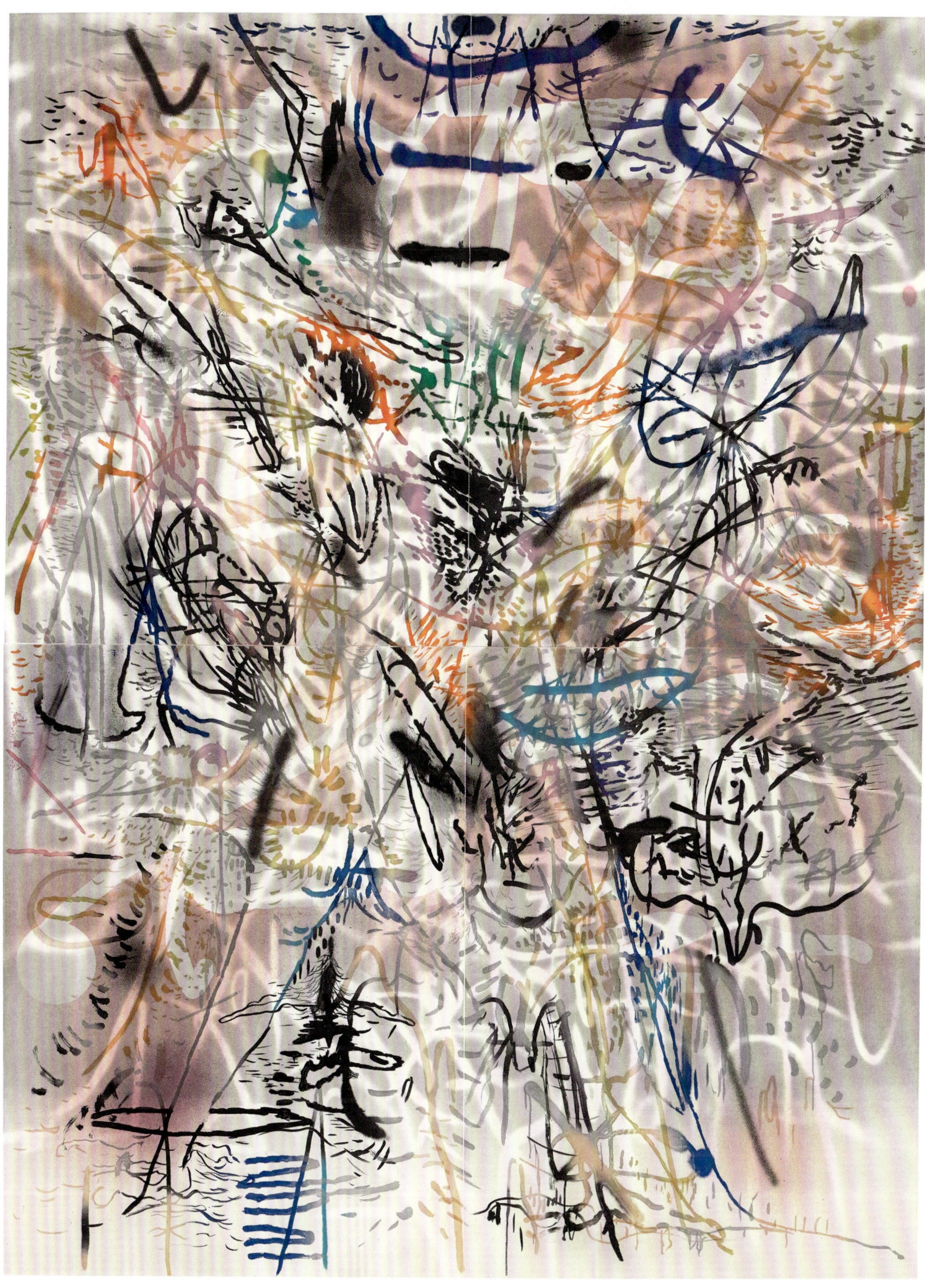

Sarah Morris

Sarah Morris (b. 1967) investigates urban architecture and built spaces in her abstract paintings and films. Her first-ever suite of prints, *Dulles (Capital)*, refers to Dulles International Airport in Washington, DC, designed in 1958 by the Finnish architect Eero Saarinen (1910–1961), who also designed the Gateway Arch in St. Louis and the TWA Terminal at Kennedy International Airport. Each of the nine square screenprints that make up the portfolio depicts a series of intersecting white lines that cut through a brightly colored background. When viewed together in a three-by-three grid, the panels appear to depict an off-center white latticework, whose perspective recedes into the background at an extreme angle in relation to the viewer's line of sight. Morris, whose paintings and films often draw from American cityscapes, worked from photographs of Dulles International Airport to create this series of prints as well as a number of paintings. Though they are not direct abstractions of the photographs, the individual prints flatten the play between the bisecting white lines and the colored background, a gesture toward the high modernist principles revered at the time Dulles airport was constructed. However, the receding white grid composed in the overall installation creates the illusion of space, as if the viewer is peering into the steel-beam-and-glass armature of the building itself. The simultaneous experience of flatness and depth achieved in *Dulles (Capital)* deconstructs the high modernist aesthetics of Saarinen's famous building. —SD

Sarah Morris
(American, b. Britain, 1967)
Dulles (Capital), 2001,
edition 32/45,
installation view
9 screenprints
29 × 29 in. (73.7 × 73.7 cm)
each panel

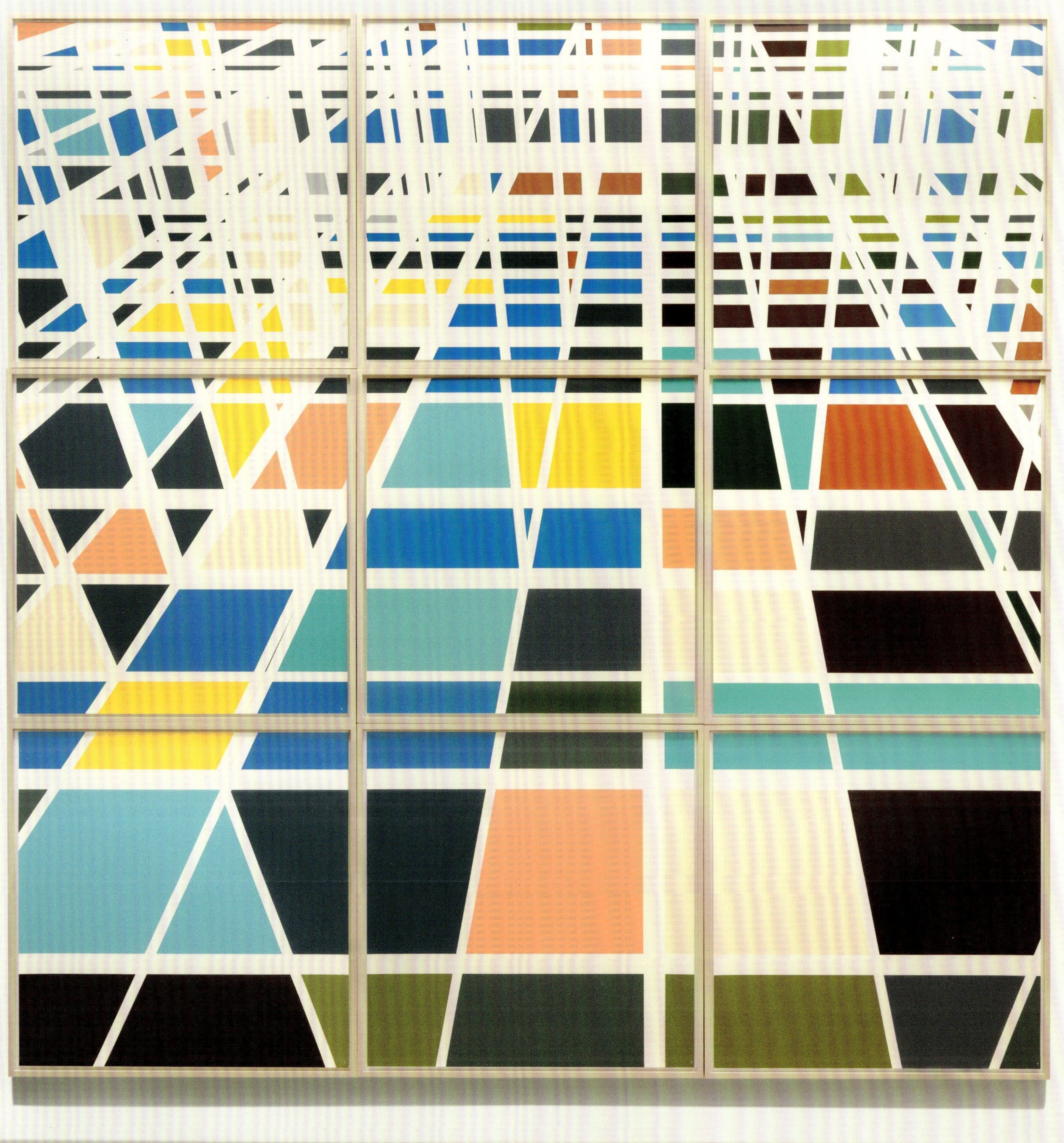

Wangechi Mutu

Born in Kenya and based in New York, Wangechi Mutu (b. 1972) is known for her collages of Black female hybrid figures. She draws her source material from publications from a range of cultural strata—whether pornographic, fashion, or motorcycle magazines, those exploring world cultures such as *National Geographic*, or medical publications. Mutu has expressed, "As a woman of color, how I'm represented in these publications is of absolute relevance and importance to me because it tells me where I stand in that particular culture."[1]

For her series of twelve prints *Histology of the Different Classes of Uterine Tumors* (2006), Mutu collaged onto the yellowed pages of Victorian-era medical illustrations of diseases of the female reproductive system to produce portrait busts of Black women, which she in turn embellished with hair, glitter, and/or rabbit fur. Some of the busts are shown in profile, but most of them address the viewer directly. By activating with these hybrid forms an interplay between repugnance and seduction, Mutu seeks to make visible and approachable inequities at the intersection of race and gender.[2] Elaborating on this double effect while also pointing to how these images of disfigured bodies relate to the histories of colonialism and slavery, the artist notes that the Black female body

> has been violated and revered in very specific ways by the outsider—Europeans, especially. The issues that pertain to race: pathologizing the black mind, exoticizing and fearing of the black body, objectifying the body as a specimen, or a sexual machine, or a work animal, or relating the black body to non-human species as a way to justify cruelty.... The body is put to work, devoured, tortured, broken, mutilated, and then prepared for display as an artifact, a totem, a specimen. Even in this state of containment and capture, our body is valued and worshipped—yet feared and reviled.[3]

The interplay between repulsion and attraction is particularly pronounced in Mutu's later series of printed-paper collages on postcard, *Bedroom Masks* (2011), which draws more explicitly upon portrayals of the Black female body in pornography. —JO

Wangechi Mutu
(Kenyan, b. 1972)
Bedroom Masks, 2011
printed paper collage
on postcard
16 × 12 in. (40.6 × 30.5 cm)
each
All works Courtesy of
the Artist.

---

1 Robert Enright, "Resonant Surgeries: The Collaged World of Wangechi Mutu," *Border Crossings*, no. 105 (February 2008), https://bordercrossingsmag.com/article/resonant-surgeries-the-collaged-world-of-wangechi-mutu.

2 Zoe Whitley, "International Geographic: Wangechi Mutu on Paper, Print, and Printmaking," *Art in Print* 4, no. 4 (November–December 2014): 11–15.

3 Deborah Willis, "Wangechi Mutu," *BOMB*, February 28, 2014, https://bombmagazine.org/articles/wangechi-mutu/.

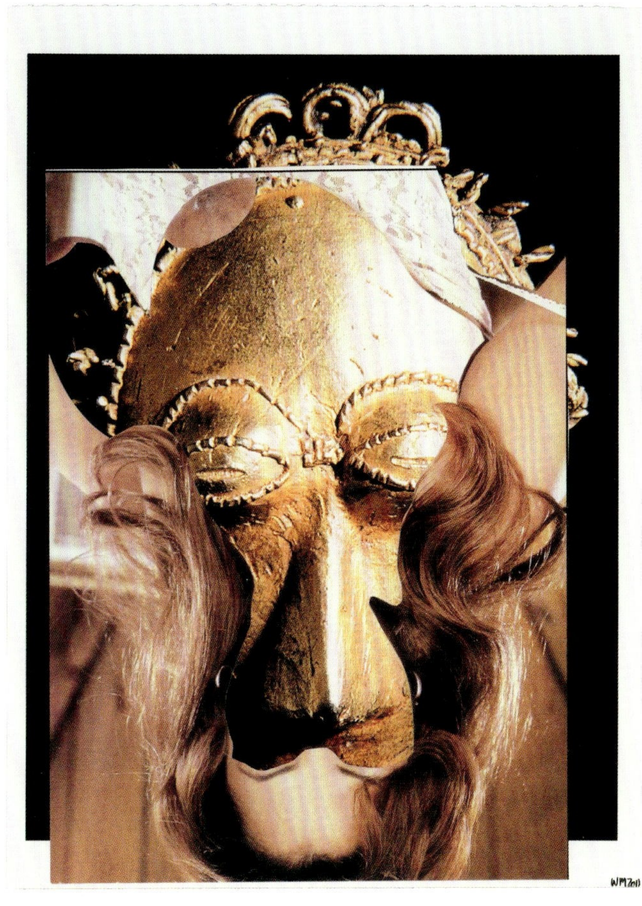
WM2011

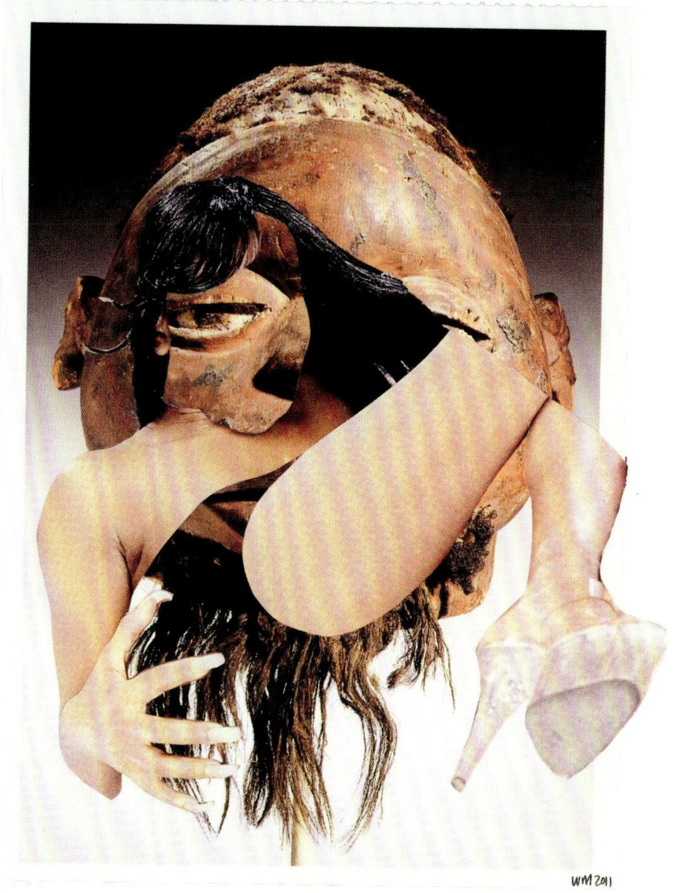
WM2011

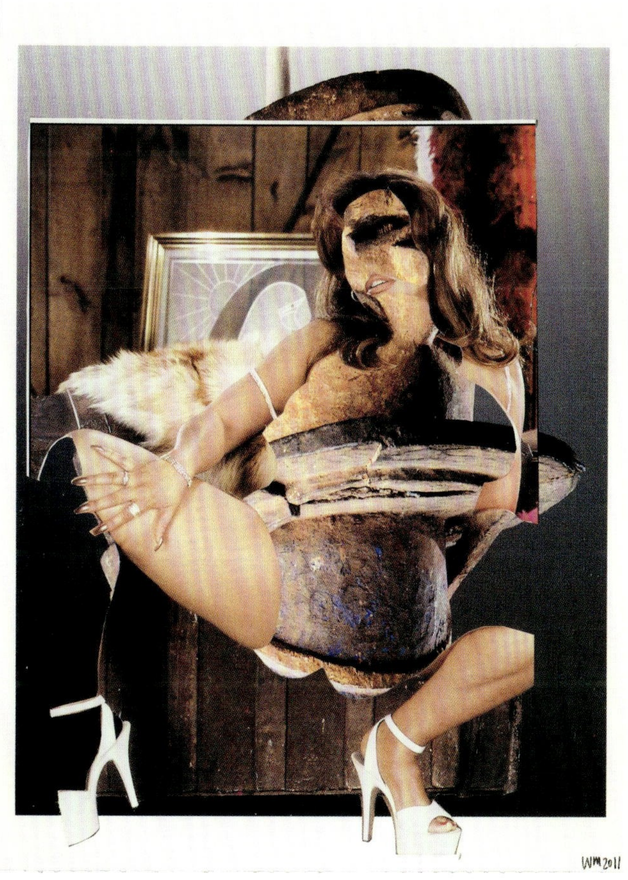
WM2011

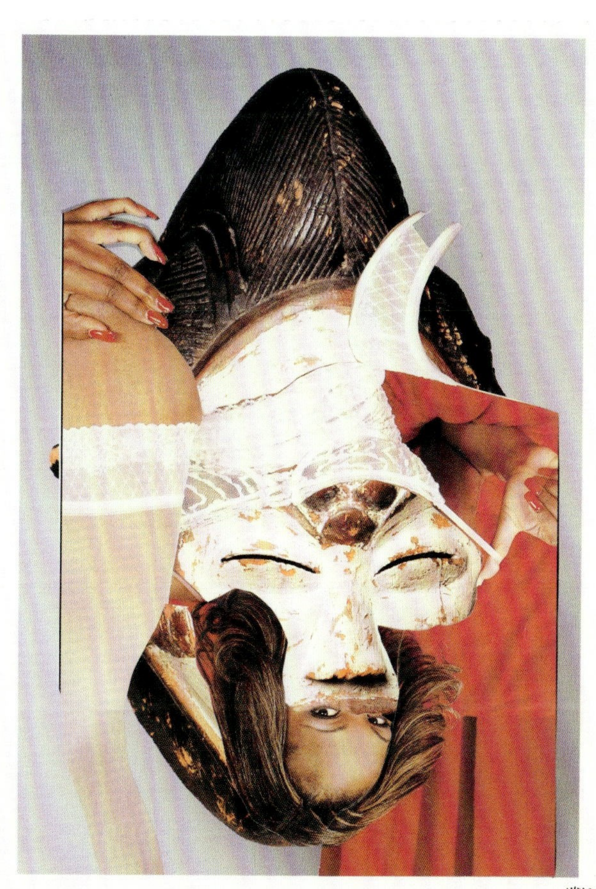
WM2011

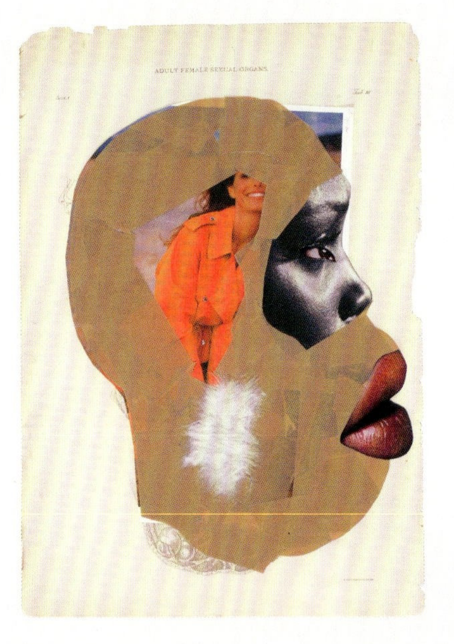

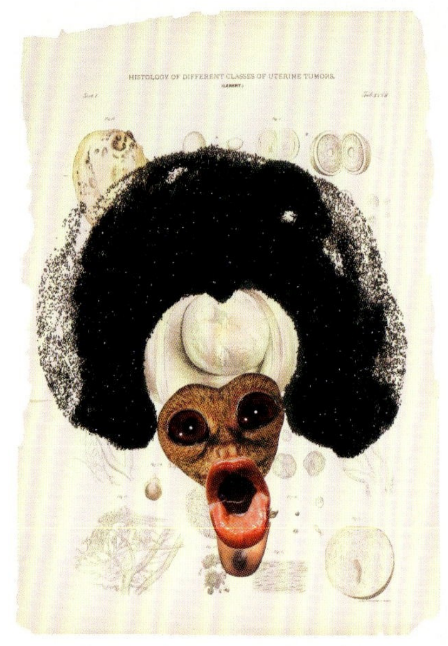

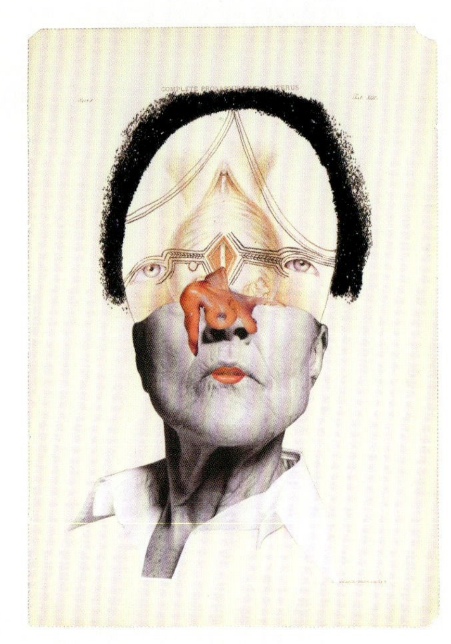

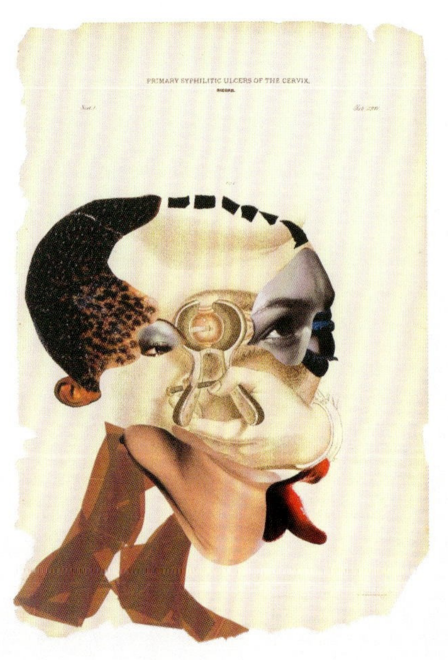

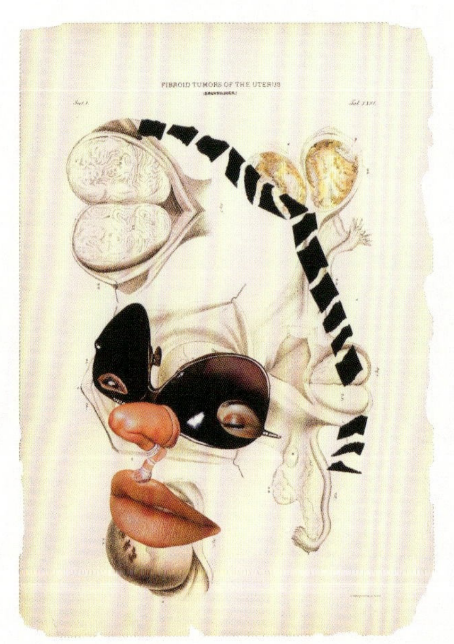

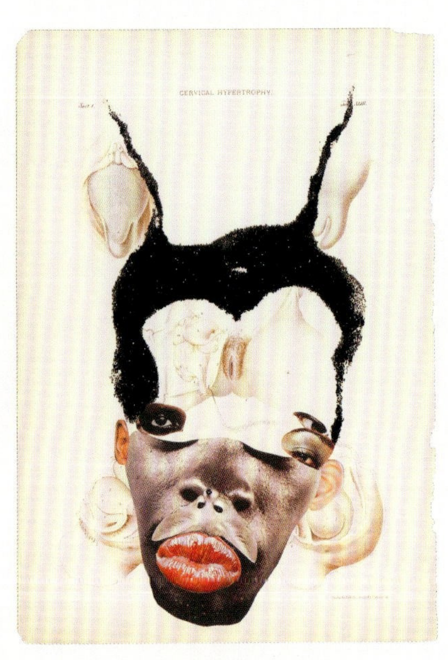

Wangechi Mutu
(Kenyan, b. 1972)
Histology of the Different Classes of Uterine Tumors,
edition 14/25, 2006
collage on found medical illustration paper
23 × 17 in. (58.4 × 43.2 cm) each

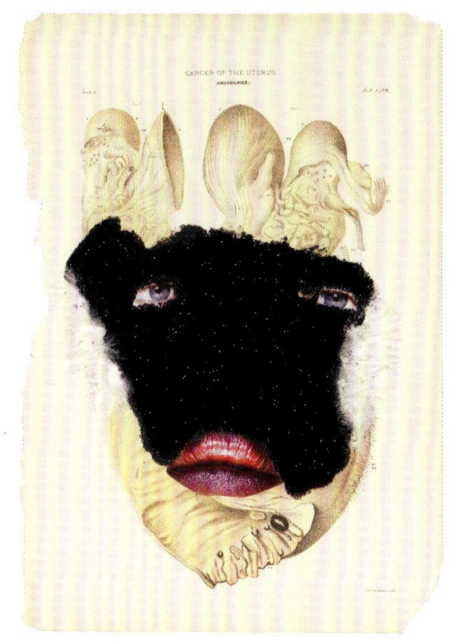

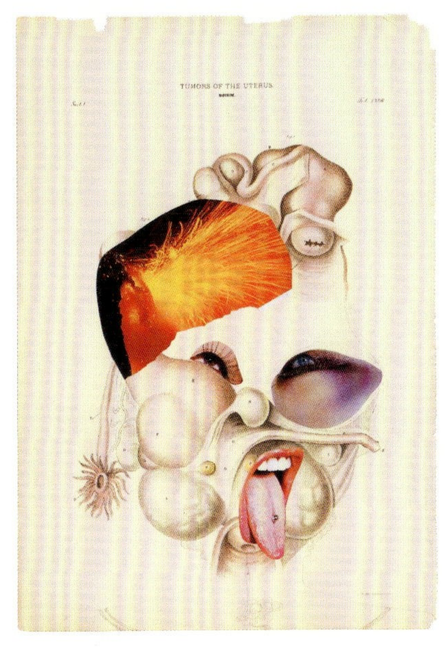

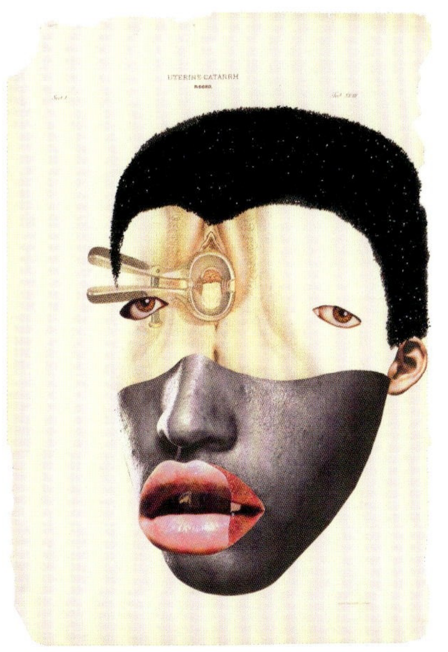

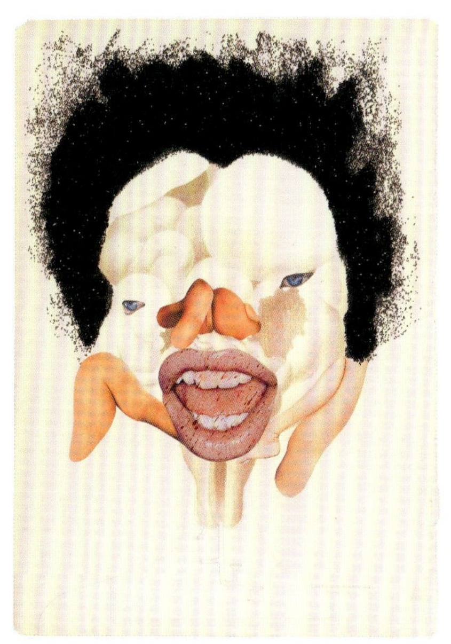

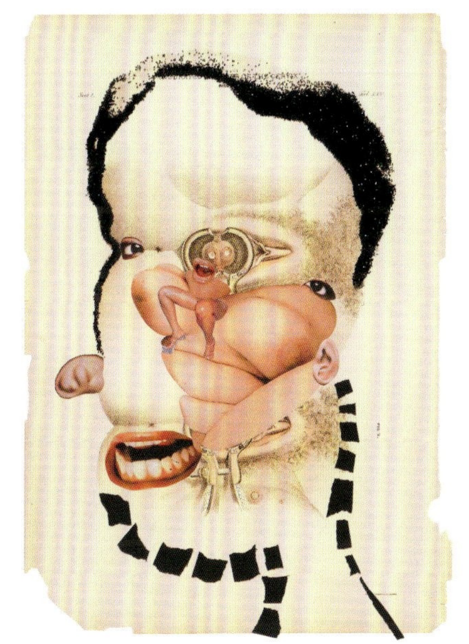

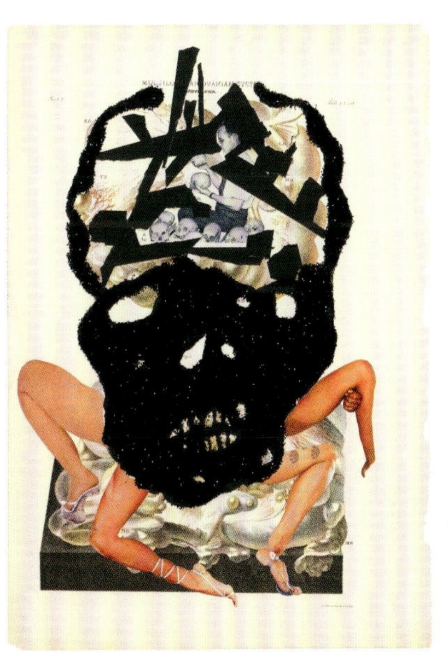

Judy Pfaff

Active since the early 1970s, the British-born American artist Judy Pfaff (b. 1946) has redefined installation art with her immersive, site-specific works. The complex relationship between two- and three-dimensionality posed by these installations is evident in descriptions of them as "paintings in space"[1] or "collages in space."[2] And inversely, this terminology provides a rubric for understanding Pfaff's prints, which manage to convey the multidimensionality of the environments they depict.

Untitled (target, garden, lily pad) (2000) is a stepped take on a triptych. The largest image of the three, on the right, takes as its source a nineteenth-century botanical illustration depicting the underside of a water lily—an orientation that implies the viewer's submersion beneath the surface of the water. This immersive relationship to the natural environment is further evoked by Pfaff's application of ripples of green dye across much of the surface of the finished print, as well as by her subsequent collaging of the print with tactile plant specimens. However, moving to the leftmost image, the viewer is ascribed the opposite viewpoint, with the green bullseye form suggesting the lily pad as seen from an aerial view. The middle image, finally, positions the viewer at perhaps the greatest remove from nature, namely looking out onto a carefully manicured Japanese garden as though from a window or balcony. *Til Skogen* (2000) and *a Venezia* (2002) likewise use a multipart format to afford the viewer a multidimensional experience of environments—respectively, a dense forested setting and the urban landscape of Venice. —JO

1 "About," Judy Pfaff Studio, https://www.judypfaffstudio.com/about.

2 The *New York Times* art critic Roberta Smith referred to Pfaff as a "collagist in space"; quoted in "Judy Pfaff: A Collagist in Space," Boston University Contemporary Perspectives Lecture Series, March 28, 2011, https://www.youtube.com/watch?v=wa3PhmOE1iY.

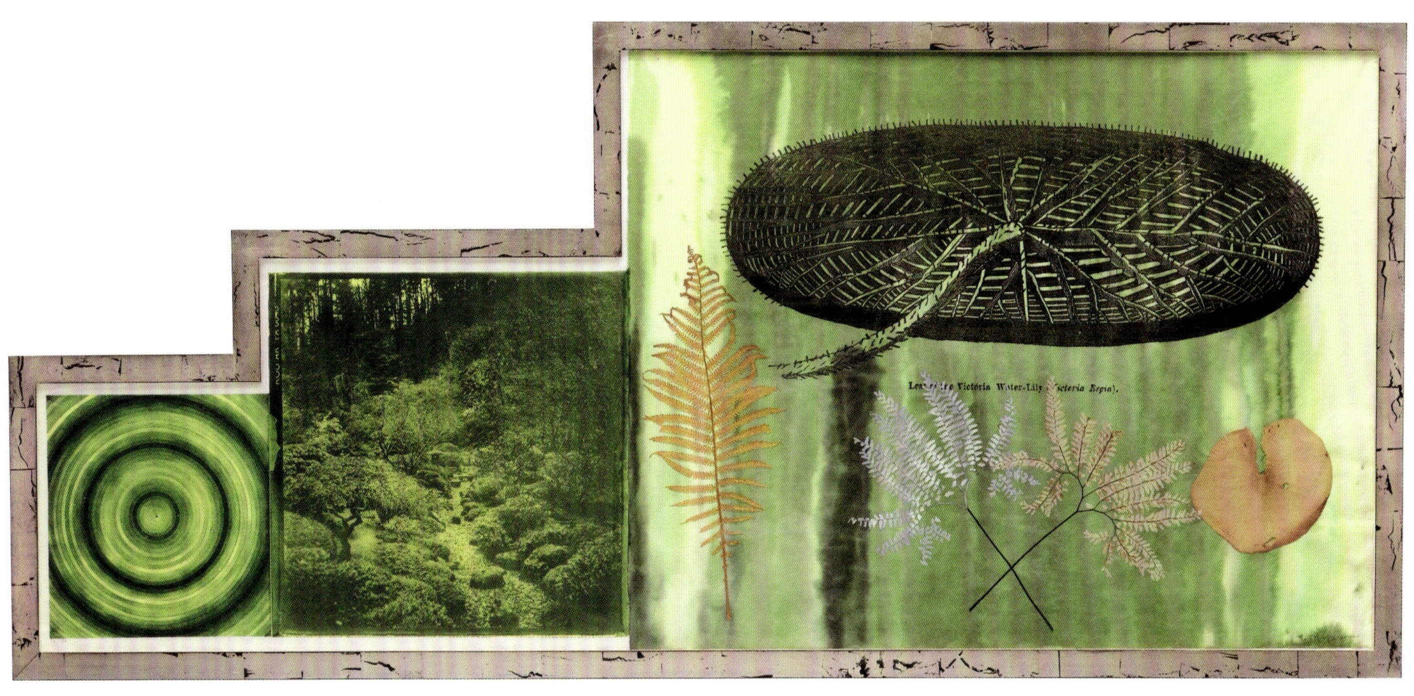

Judy Pfaff
(American, b. 1946)
Untitled (target, garden, lily pad), edition 16/30, 2000
photogravure, etching, lithograph, dye, applied leaves
37 × 84½ in. (94 × 214.6 cm)

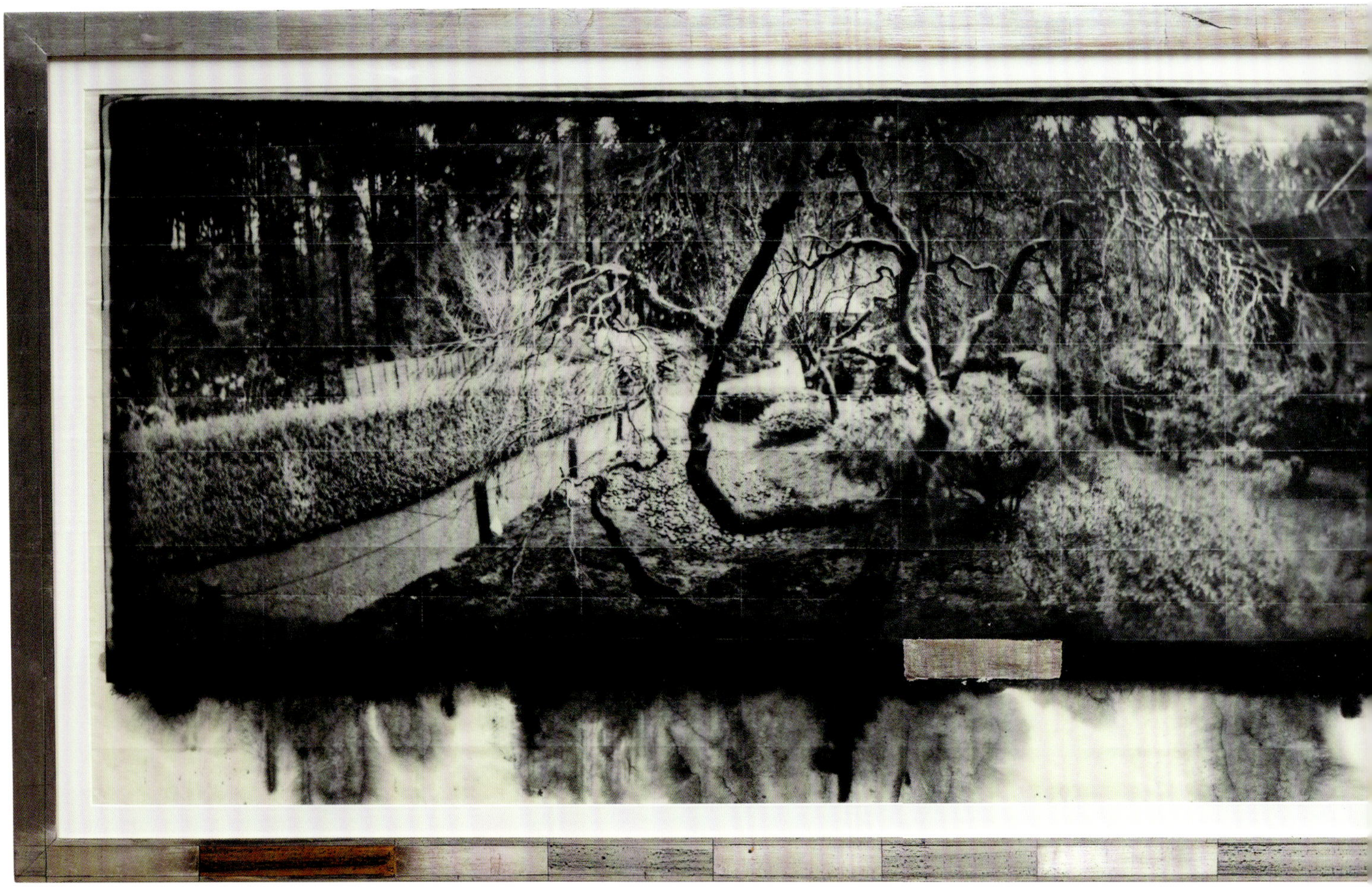

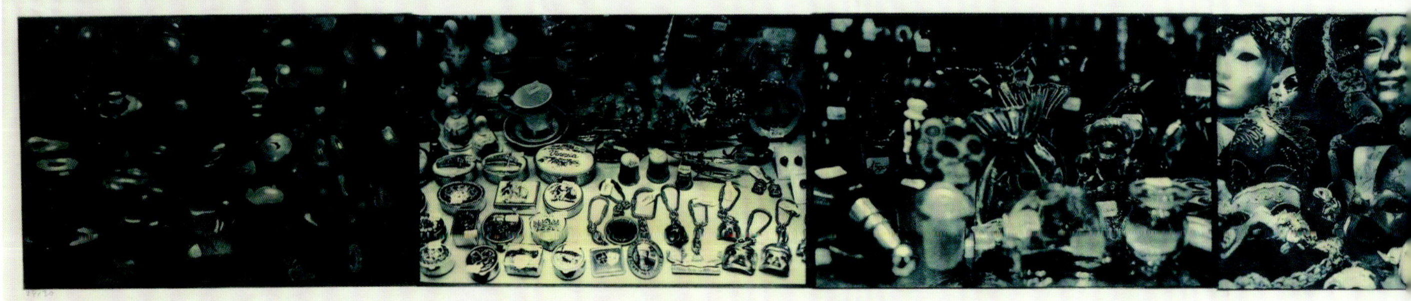

Judy Pfaff
(American, b. 1946)
Til Skogen, edition 22/30, 2000
photogravure, dye, beeswax
30 × 104½ in.
(76.2 × 265.4 cm)

a Venezia, edition 24/30, 2002
photogravure, spitbite, and
relief roll
12 × 95¾ in. (30.5 × 243.2 cm)

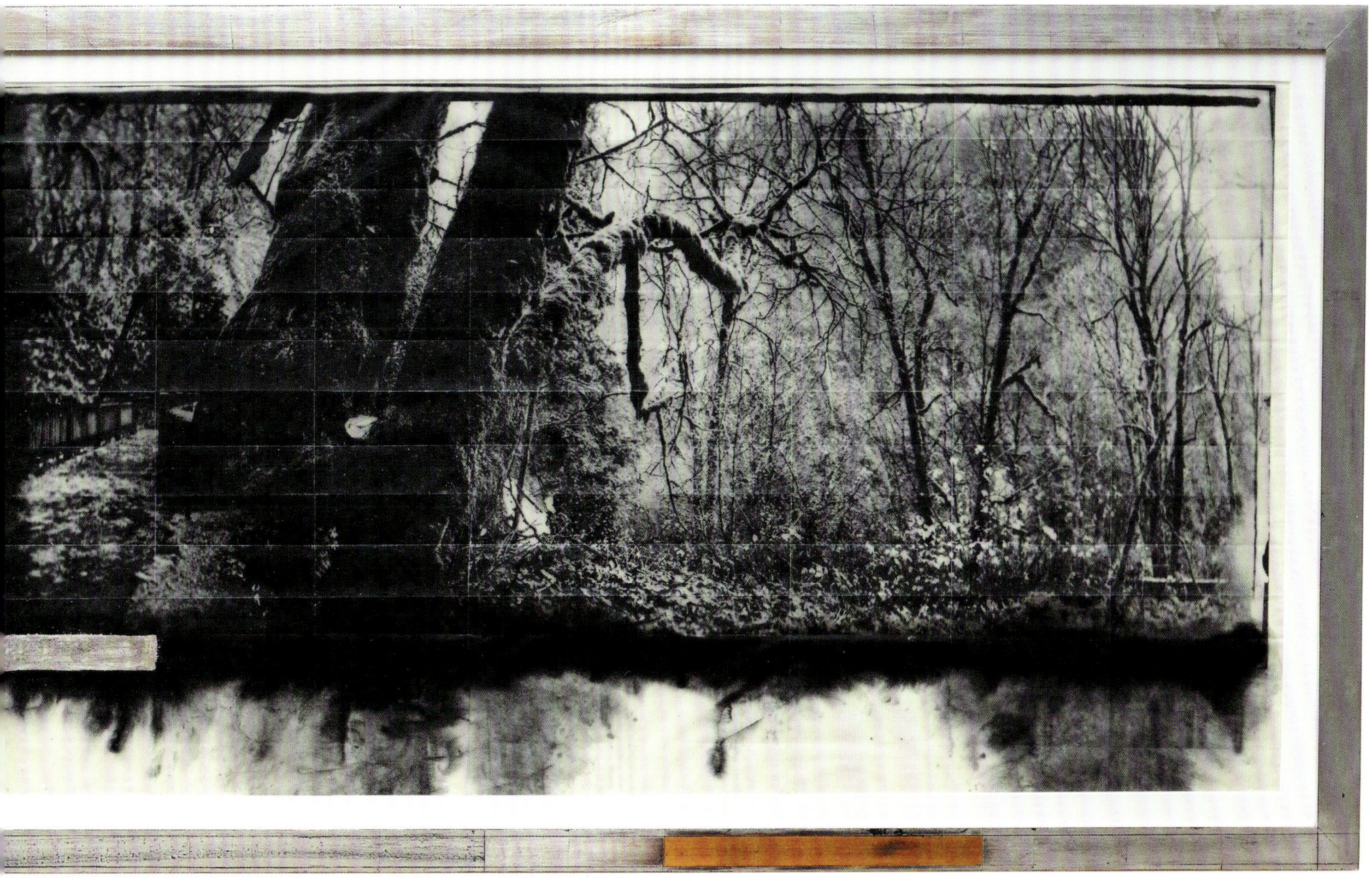

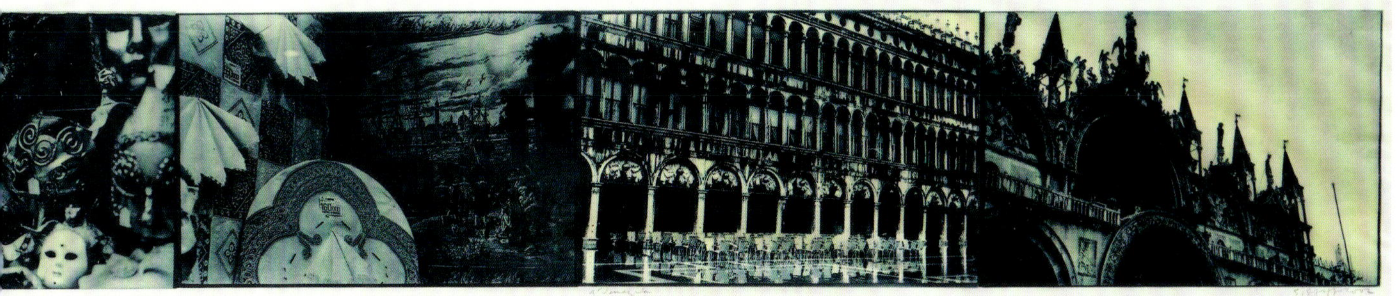

Wendy Red Star

A member of the Apsáalooke (Crow) tribe, Wendy Red Star (b. 1981) poetically layers her experience growing up on a reservation in Montana with in-depth historical research about Indigenous cultures in the United States to create works across a variety of media, including photography, sculpture, video, fiber arts, and performance. In 2015, Red Star created two prints at the revered Crow's Shadow Institute of the Arts, a print workshop that has provided creative resources and opportunities for Native American artists for more than twenty-five years.

In *Yakima or Yakama—Not For Me To Say* and *iilaalée = car (goes by itself) + ii = by means of which + dáanniili = we parade*, the artist layered photographs of the annual Crow Fair, a yearly gathering of the three distinct bands of the Crow/Apsáalooke people, over hand-drawn iterations of designs frequently woven into Pendleton Woolen Mills products. Pendleton has been using Native designs in its blankets since its establishment in 1863, and while profiting off the cultural heritage of those tribes, the company has since become an integral part of the economic prosperity and community identity in Pendleton, Oregon, close to the Confederated Tribes of the Umatilla Indian Reservation, where Crow's Shadow is located. Red Star uses the Pendleton blankets as a backdrop for inserting her personal history, overlaying reproductions of her father's photographs of the Crow Fair, where items of personal wealth, like parfleche bags and blankets, are displayed in a traditional procession. Though this type of parade was once performed on horseback, cars are now the contemporary equivalent.

Marrying the complex history of Pendleton with her own personal memories of her Apsáalooke upbringing, Red Star presents a complicated vision of cultural resilience in the face of modernization and the legacy of colonialism. As the titles of these works suggest, a re-appropriation and recouping of cultural signifiers—whether through language, blanket design, or parade—affirms sovereignty for Native people. —SD

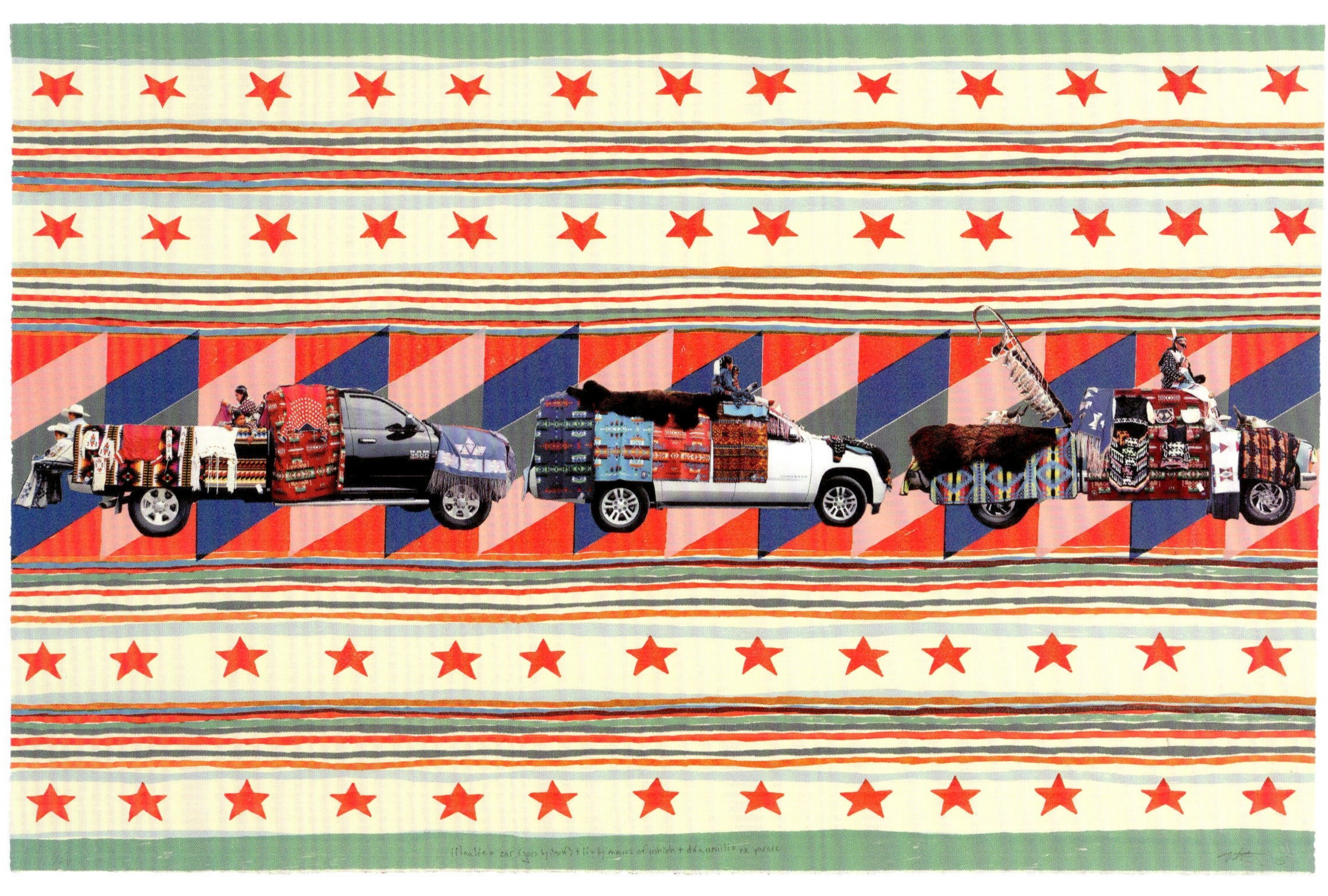

Wendy Red Star
(Apsáalooke [Crow], b. 1981)
iilaalée = car (goes by itself) + ii = by means of which + dáanniili = we parade, edition 1/20, 2015–16
lithograph with archival pigment ink photographs
24 × 38 in. (61 × 96.5 cm)

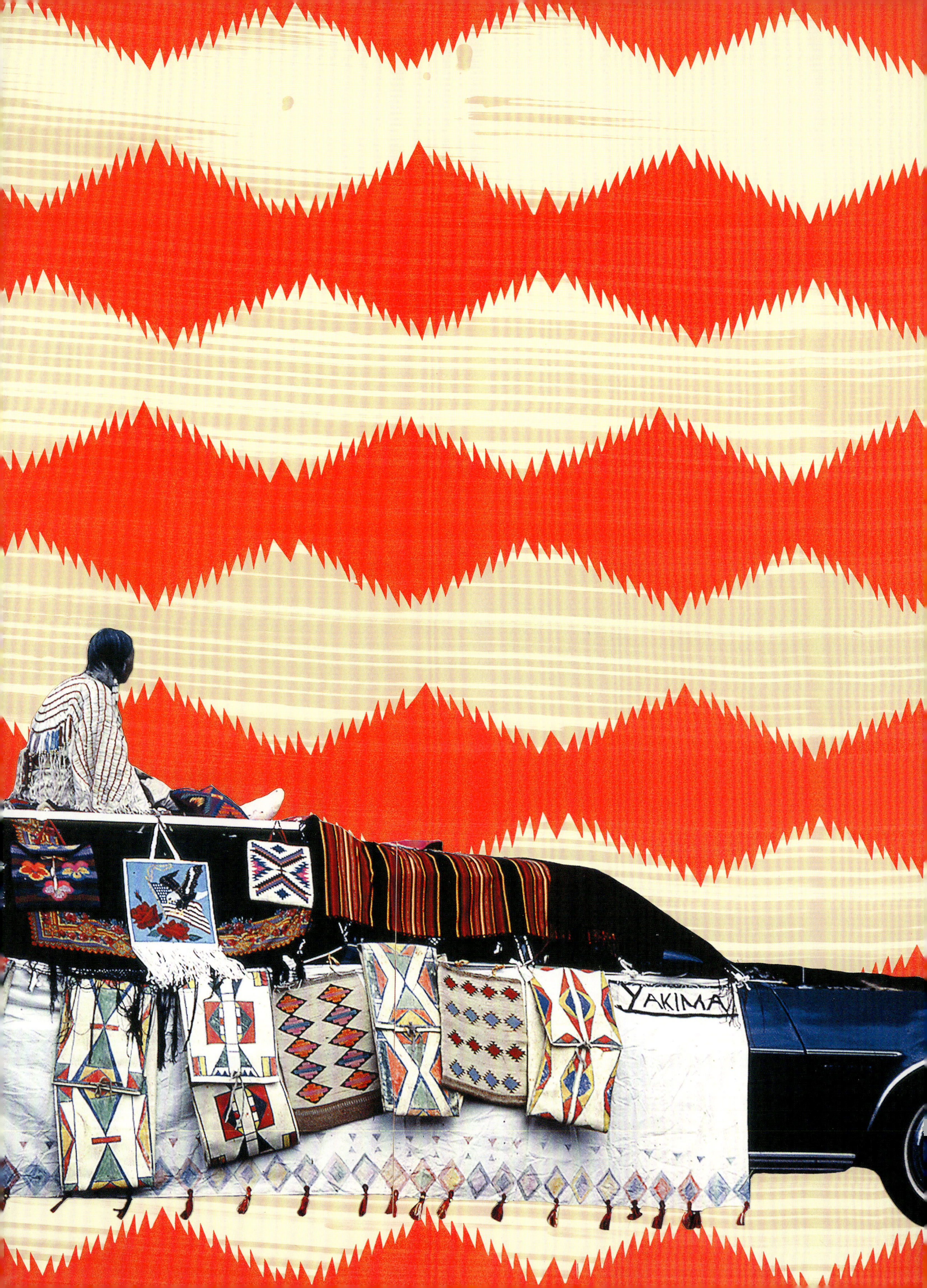
YAKIMA

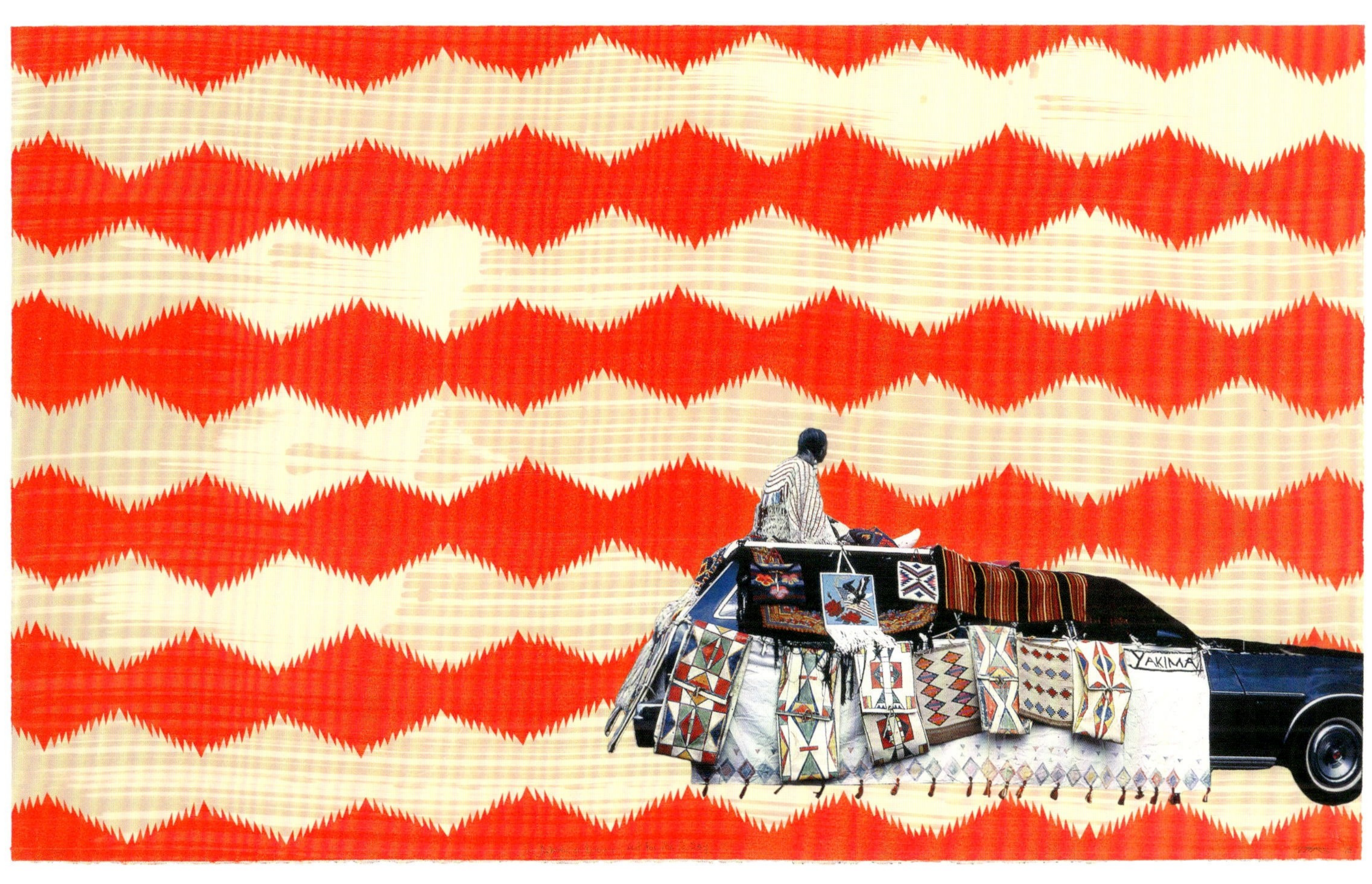

Wendy Red Star
(Apsáalooke [Crow], b. 1981)
Yakima or Yakama—Not For Me To Say, edition 2/20, 2015
lithograph with archival pigment ink photograph
24 × 40 in. (61 × 101.6 cm)

Lorna Simpson

Lorna Simpson (b. 1960) first became well known in the 1980s for her pioneering work in conceptual and large-scale photography. Her practice has since expanded to include painting, sculpture, collage, film, and drawings. In the mid-1990s, Simpson began creating suites of printed photographs that were displayed alongside text.

One such portfolio, *Wigs* (1994), features twenty-one images, each depicting a unique style of hair. Based in Brooklyn, Simpson frequented the Fulton Mall, where dozens of wig stores offer everything from real human hair to yak hair to turn-of-the-century doll wigs to French sixteenth-century merkins, or wigs placed around the genitals. Collecting and photographing a variety of wigs, the artist scaled and transferred these images via lithography onto felt in order to create a sense of human scale. When seen pinned to the wall as an arrangement alongside small snippets of text, the felt prints appear life-size, as if the viewer could select and wear each wig. Simpson was interested at the time in "eliminating the figure" in her work, while still alluding to but not representing the human body. By suggesting personhood in the arrangement of wigs on display, Simpson allows the viewer to construct a narrative around the possible identities each type of hair might signify while more broadly questioning stereotypes around race and gender.

Another suite of prints from the same time, *Details* (1996), similarly juxtaposes photographs and text to allow for a multivalence of interpretations. Each of the twenty-one photogravures in the series has a screenprinted caption, such as "acted in self defense," "in love and tried to stay out of trouble," and "carried a gun." The images show hands in action, lightly touching a purse or the back of a couch; they originate from found photographs, cropped to allow for an ambiguous interpretation of the subjects' gestures. These scenes, complicated by their fragmented, sometimes violent descriptions, create an urgent though incomplete narrative of gendered violence. The artist has stated she was interested exploring "the sites of public—yet unseen—sexual encounters."[1] Rather than representing a specific interpretation, the absence of the body invites an exploration of gender and race in contemporary society. —SD

Lorna Simpson
(American, b. 1960)
Counting, edition 13/60, 1991
photogravure with silkscreen
73 × 38 in. (185.4 × 96.5 cm)

1 "Lorna Simpson," Lorna Simpson BIO, https://lsimpsonstudio.com/bio.

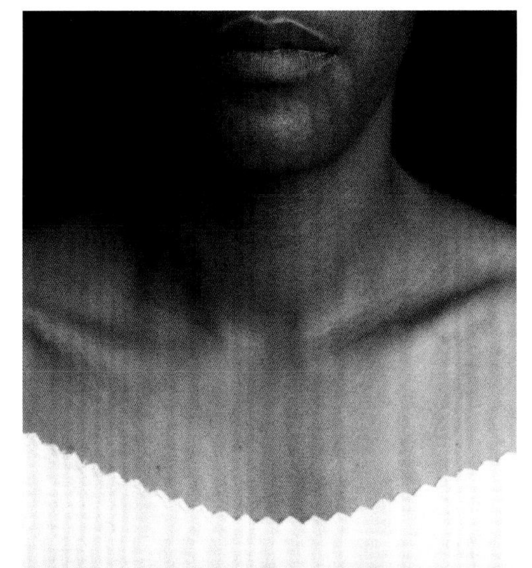

9am-1pm
2am-6pm
11pm-4am
8pm-10[pm
9am-11am

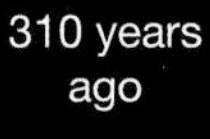

1575
bricks

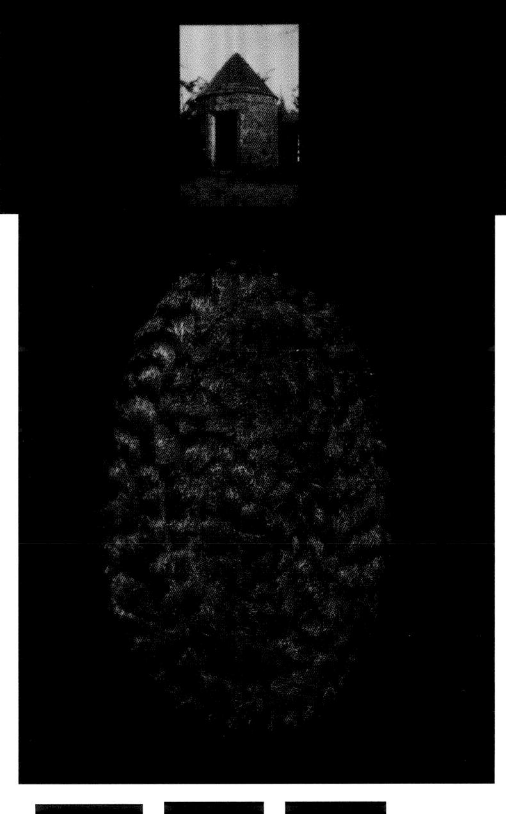

25 twists

70 braids

50 locks

Lorna Simpson
(American, b. 1960)
Details, edition 35/40, 1996
Portfolio of 21 photogravures with text
10 × 8 in. (25.4 × 20.3 cm) each

(following pages)
Wigs (Portfolio),
edition 13/15, 1994
waterless lithograph on felt, 38 panels, including 17 with text
72 × 162 in. (182.9 × 411.5 cm) overall

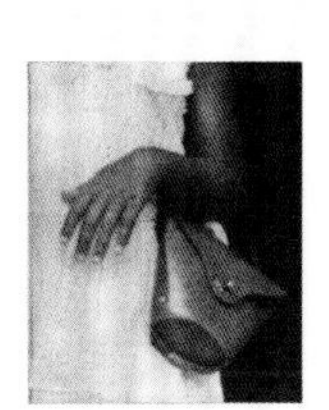

acted in self defense

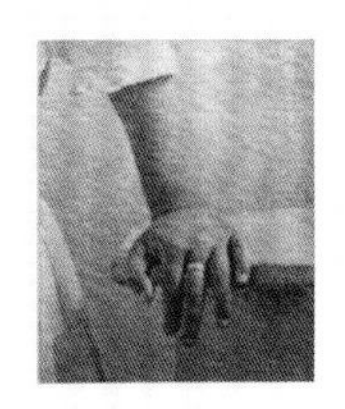

reckless

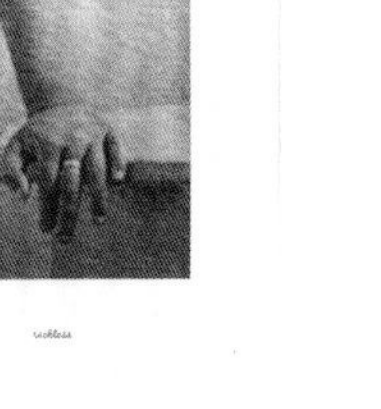

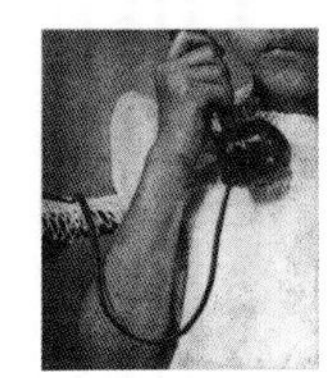

half learned

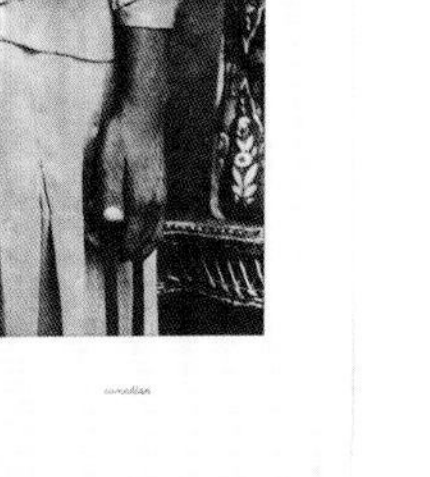

comedian

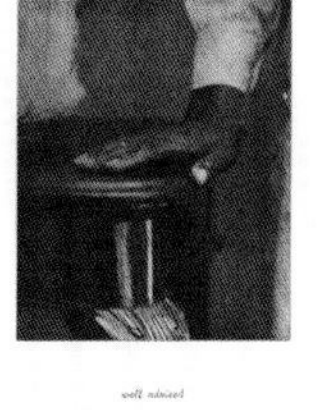

well advised

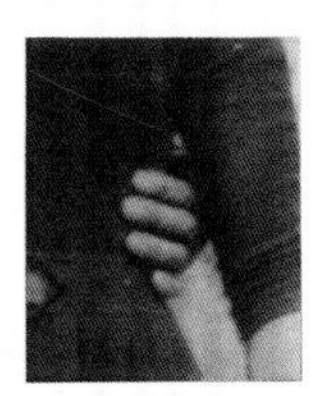

in love and tried to stay out of trouble

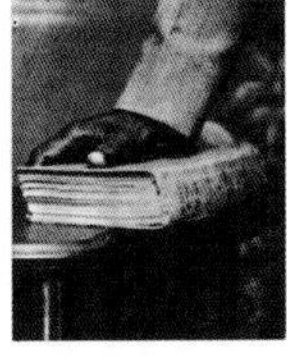

indifferent

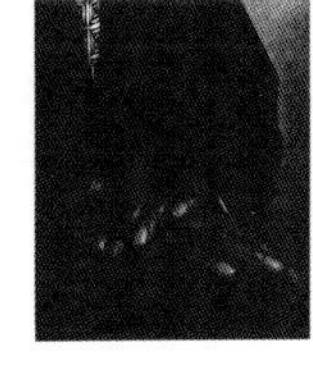

hit the nail on the head many a time

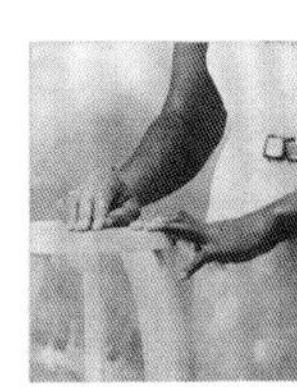

carried a gun

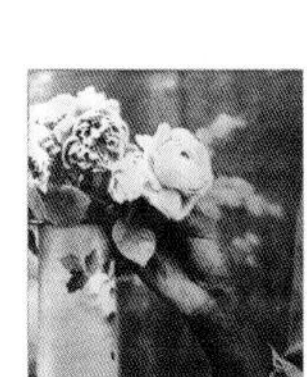

soulful

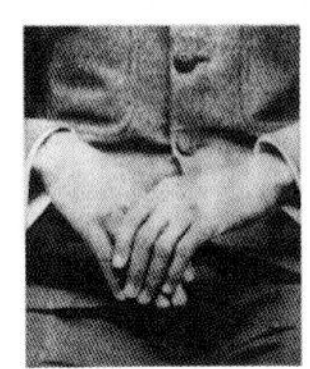

lived in the neighborhood

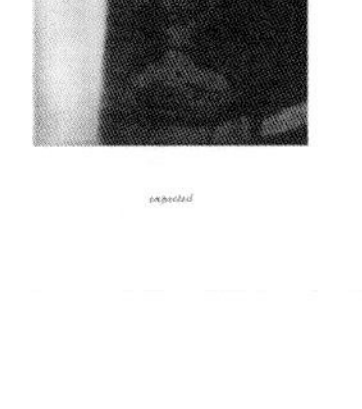

suspected

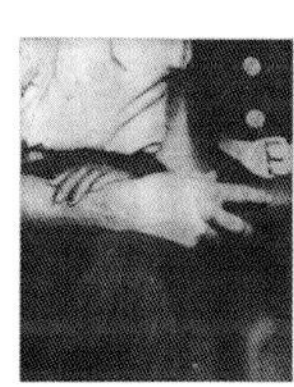

separated

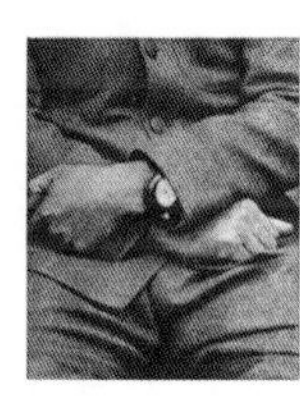

deathly

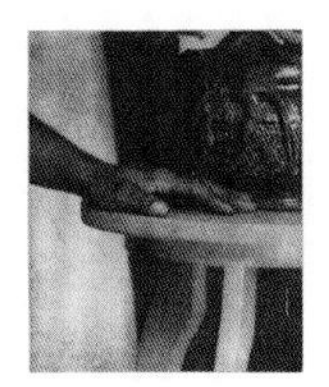

the worst had already come to pass

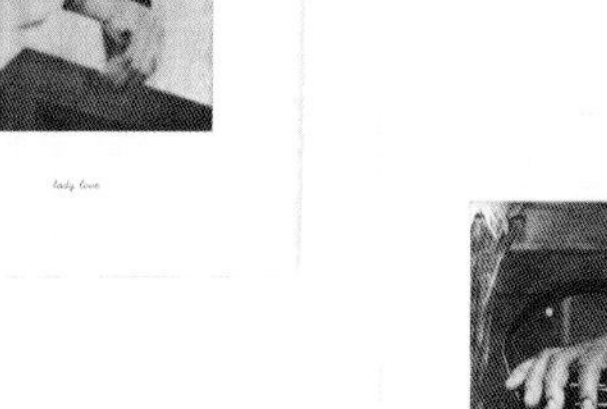

lady love

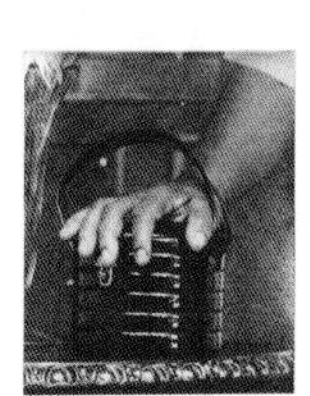

unattended

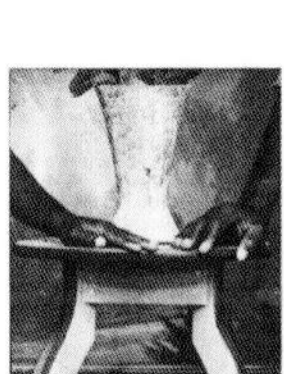

stopped speaking to each other

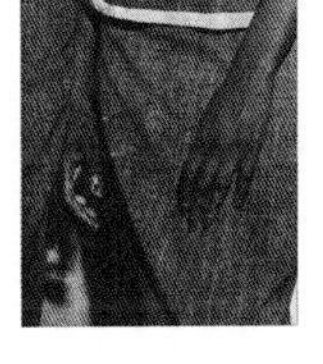

number

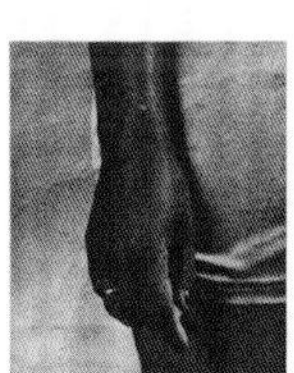

desired

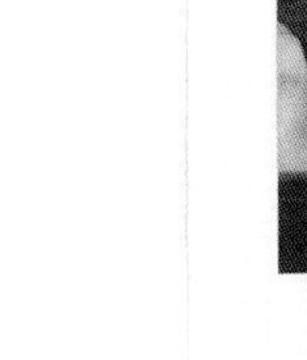

weighty

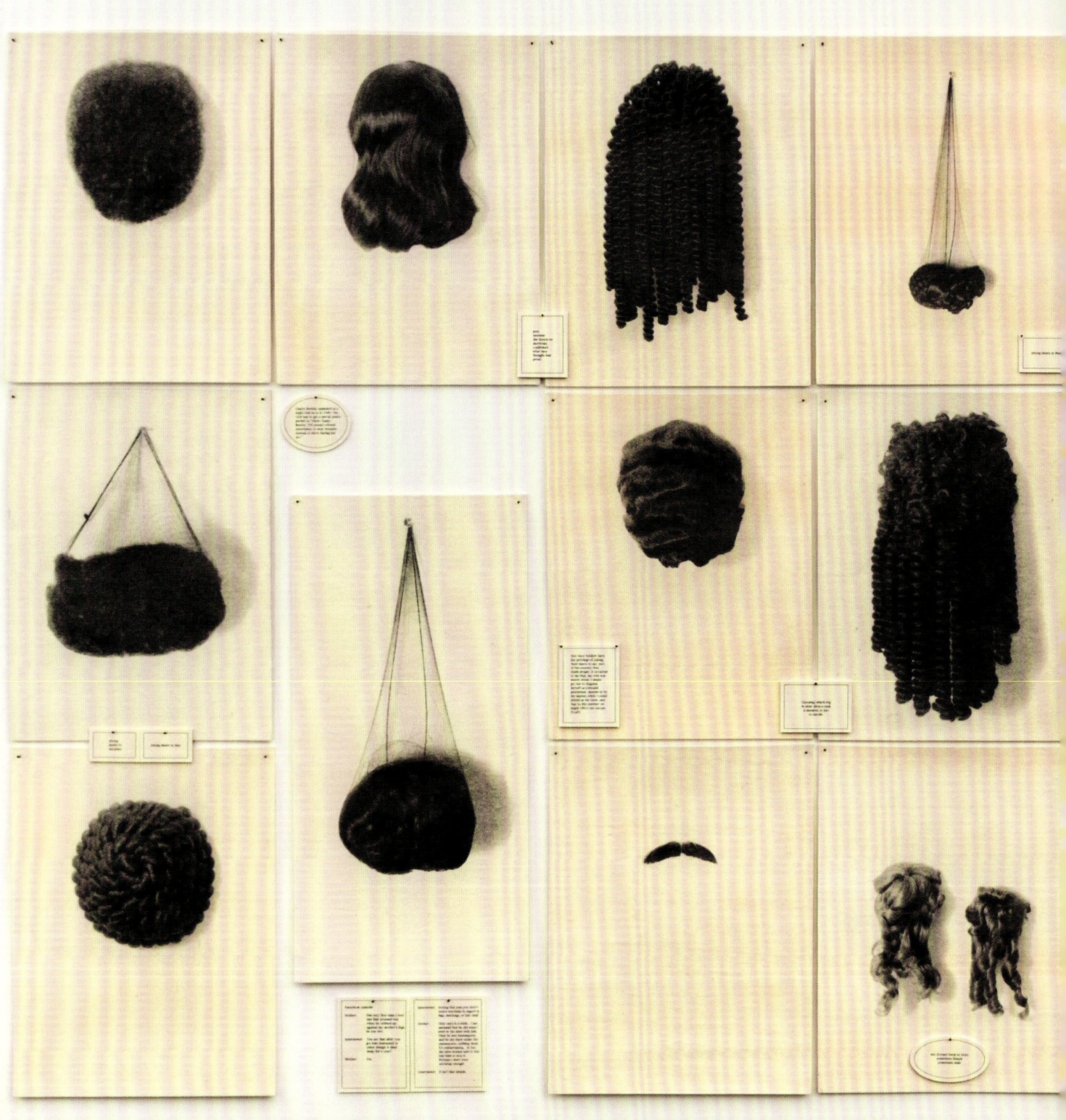

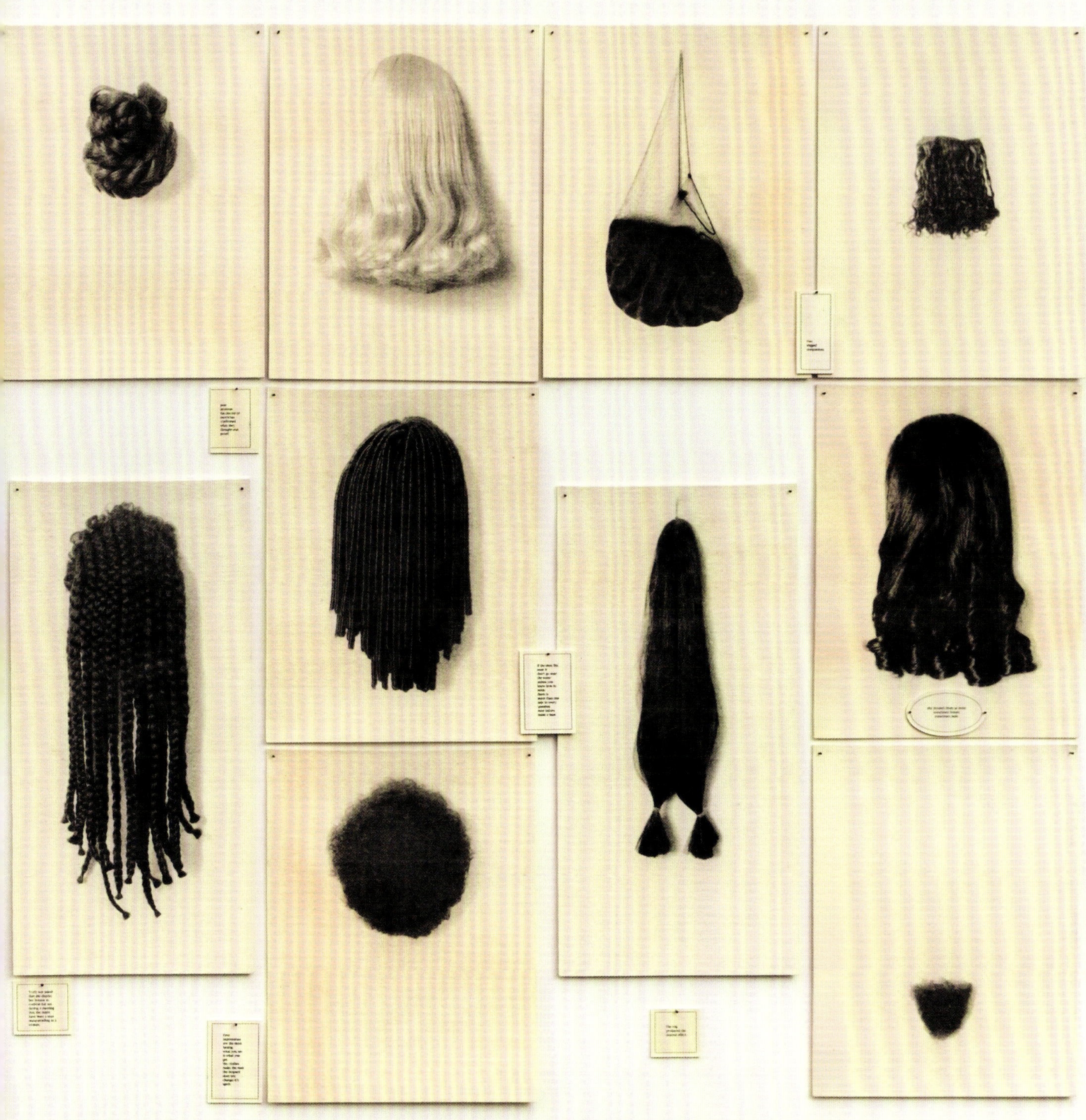

Swoon

The American artist Swoon (Caledonia Dance Curry, b. 1977) is widely associated with the street-art movement, often seeking to embed her works within urban and communal spaces; she is particularly known for the large prints she affixes to the exterior walls of public buildings. In 2014, she created an indoor, site-specific installation in the fifth-floor rotunda of the Brooklyn Museum, titled *Swoon: Submerged Motherlands*; later that year, she was commissioned to execute a public wheat-paste mural in New Haven. Both projects incorporated an image of a woman nursing her infant child, in fact a portrait of a friend of Swoon's and her child, which she again repurposed for her 2017 multimedia work *Dawn and Gemma*. Across all three contexts, this maternal image occupies a central point of the composition, representing the "wellspring of the community."[1] At the Brooklyn Museum, it crowned a gazebo-like structure also featuring depictions of Swoon's own mother, part of the artist's process of mourning her after her recent passing.[2]

Beyond such personal reference points, Swoon has discussed the way her work seeks to help our communities reckon, on both a spiritual and an intellectual level, with urgent crises such as climate change.[3] This purpose is encapsulated in the title of the Brooklyn Museum solo show; and the multimedia work *Thalassa* (2020), whose title refers to the primeval spirit of the sea in Greek mythology, takes up a related issue. As with *Dawn and Gemma*, the imagery here first appeared in earlier public installations, those Swoon completed in New Orleans in 2011 and at the Detroit Institute of Arts in 2017. The female figure rises from the sea, her calm face looking upward. This recurrent installation was first created in the immediate aftermath and the immediate vicinity of the Deepwater Horizon oil spill. Swoon offers us a set of images—traveling across various contexts, both public and private—through which we might collectively grapple with crises such as this. —JO

1 "Swoon in New Haven 2014," Site Projects New Haven, http://siteprojects.org/swoon-dawn-and-gemma-new-haven-2014.

2 Sarah Rose Sharp, "Glimpses of the Afterlife in Swoon's New Installation," *Hyperallergic,* November 3, 2016, https://hyperallergic.com/330700/glimpses-of-the-afterlife-in-swoons-new-installation/.

3 Swoon speaks about *Submerged Motherlands*, video, "Swoon: Submerged Motherlands," Brooklyn Museum website, https://www.brooklynmuseum.org/exhibitions/swoon/.

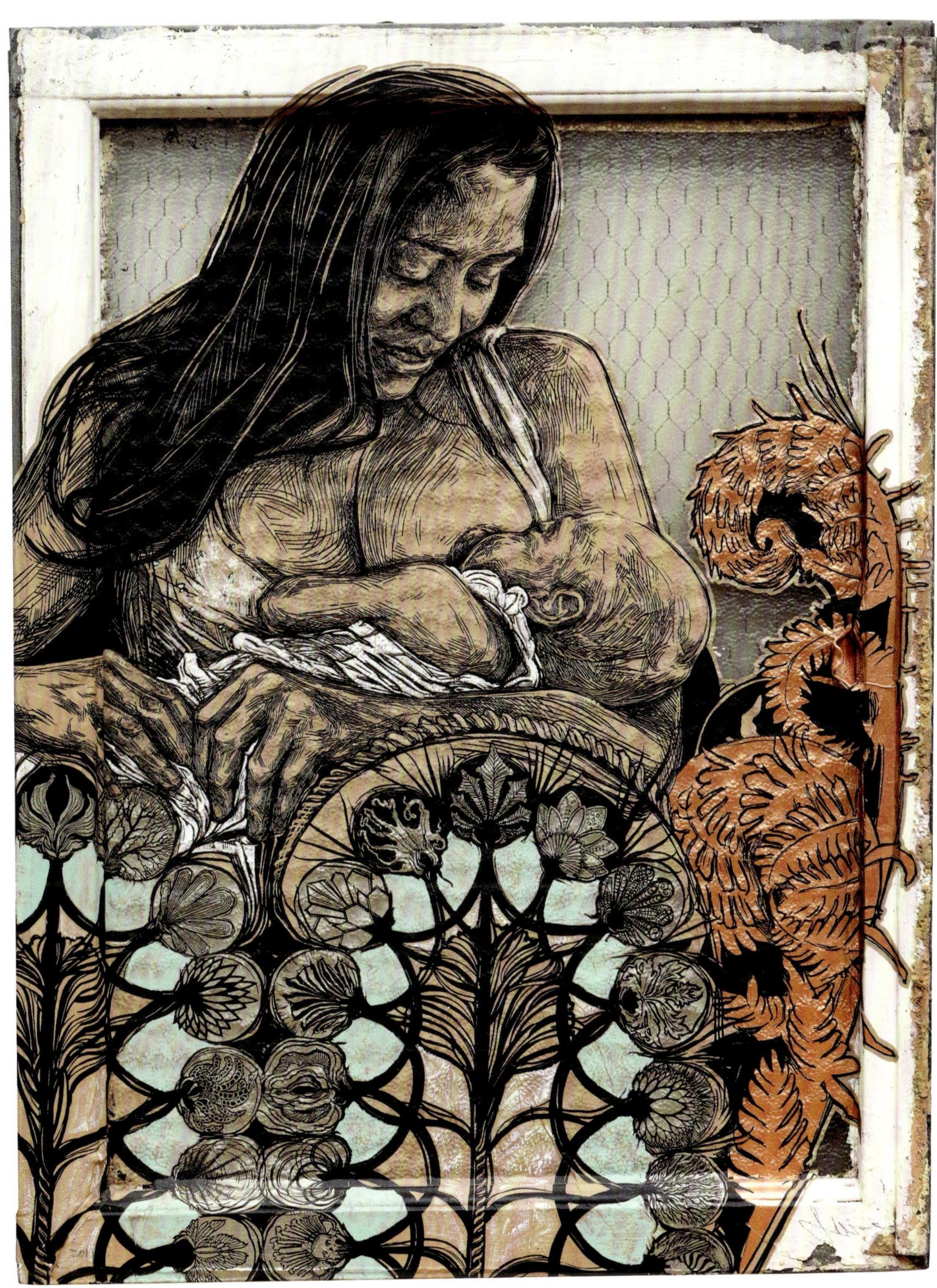

Swoon
(Caledonia Dance Curry)
(American, b. 1977)
Dawn and Gemma, edition AP, 2017
silkscreen and acrylic gouache on paper and found object (glass and wood)
24 × 32 × 2 in.
(61 × 81.3 × 5.1 cm)

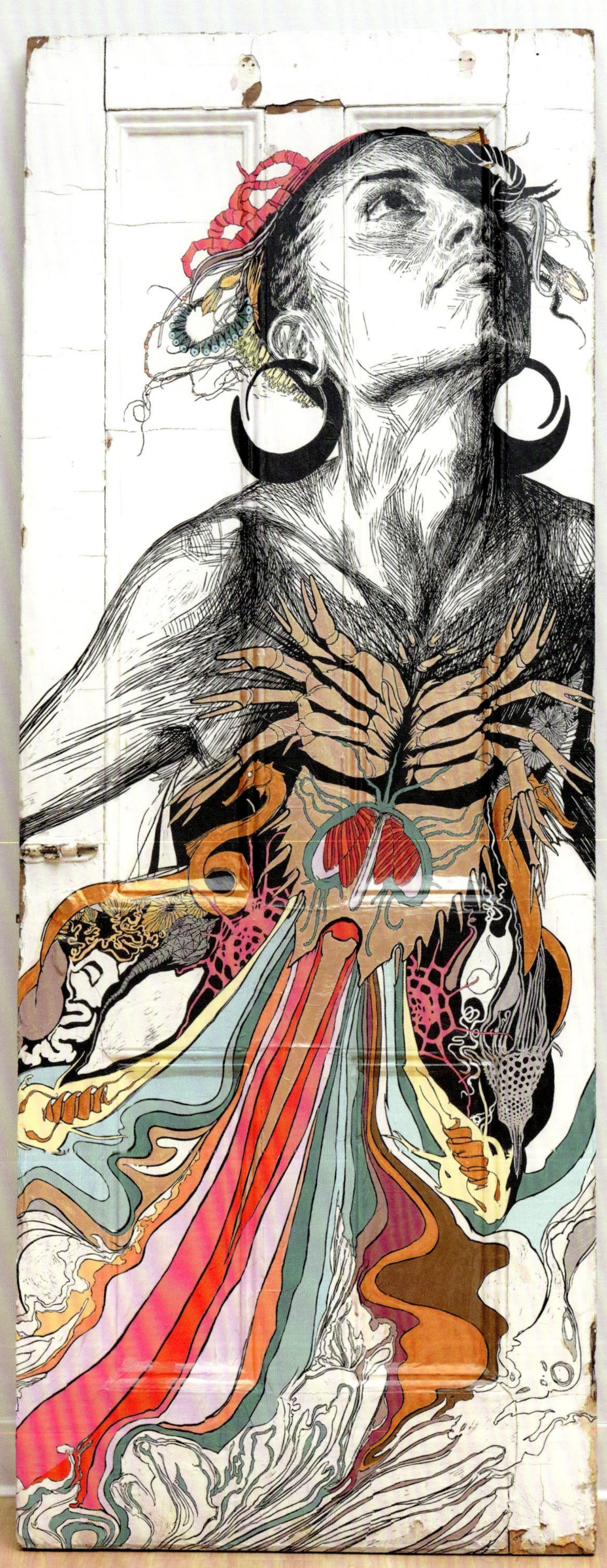

Swoon
(Caledonia Dance Curry)
(American, b. 1977)
Thalassa, 2020
silkscreen with hand-painted acrylic gouache colors on paper mounted to wooden door
77 × 30 × 1 in.
(195.6 × 76.2 × 2.5 cm)

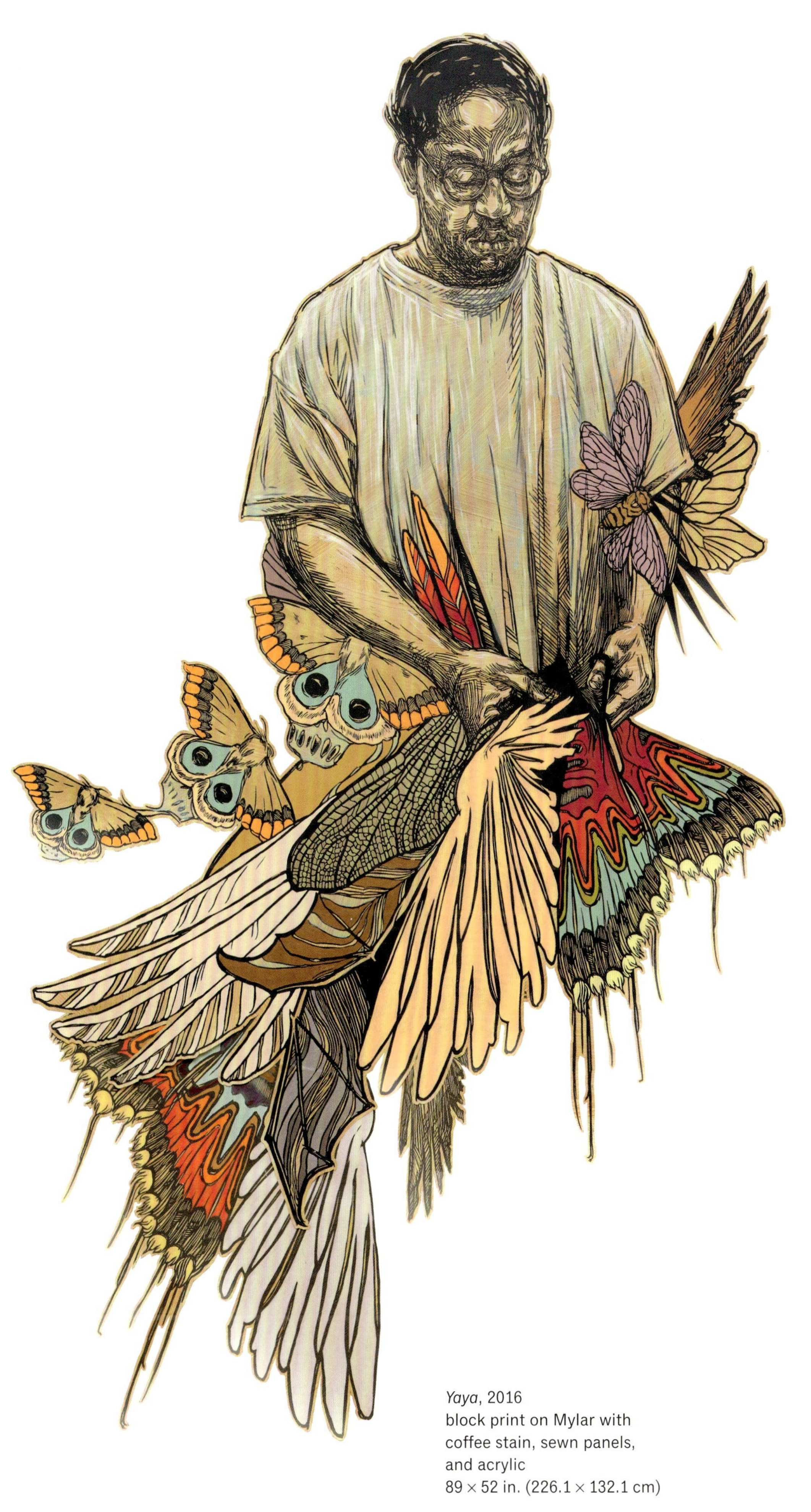

Yaya, 2016
block print on Mylar with
coffee stain, sewn panels,
and acrylic
89 × 52 in. (226.1 × 132.1 cm)

Barbara Takenaga

The American artist Barbara Takenaga (b. 1949) creates abstract compositions that resemble op art in their entrancing, highly constructed repetition of forms. Though primarily known as a painter, the artist is also active in the medium of print and holds an MFA in printmaking. A 2018 description of Takenaga, as "an abstractionist with a mystic's interest in how the ecstatic can emerge from the laborious,"[1] imparts a sense of the cosmic look of her works as well as of their meticulous detail.

Her lithograph *Small Springs (Backsplash)* confronts the viewer with an abstracted and emotive field—one that illuminates the comparison Takenaga has drawn between the grounds of her works (in painting) and those of abstract expressionism.[2] At the same time, the artist sets against this abstract ground patterned elements with a strong graphic quality, and the viewer also identifies raindrop and puddle motifs—representations of the natural world. *Small Springs (Backsplash)* thus revisits what John Yau has defined as a recurrent subject in Takenaga's oeuvre, namely a view of nature that is simultaneously real and imagined.[3] Moving from her earlier lithographs *Shaker Blue* (2004) and *Angel (Little Egypt) State I* (2007) to *Lines of Force (Fire Red)* and *Lines of Force (TBR)*—both from 2013—the viewer notes the introduction of the horizon line, evoking a recession into depth and thereby longer traditions of illusionistic art, particularly landscape. —JO

---

1 Andrea K. Scott, "Five Female Painters to See in New York Art Galleries," *New Yorker*, September 8, 2018, https://www.newyorker.com/culture/culture-desk/five-female-painters-to-see-in-new-york-art-galleries.

2 Conversation between Barbara Takenaga and Robert Kushner, in *Barbara Takenaga: New Paintings* (New York: DC Moore Gallery, 2013), 11. See also John Yau, "The Face of Infinity Is Not a Picture: New Paintings by Barbara Takenaga," *Hyperallergic,* September 22, 2013, https://hyperallergic.com/84834/the-face-of-infinity-is-not-a-picture-new-paintings-by-barbara-takenaga/.

3 John Yau, "Demotic Abstraction with a Twist," *Hyperallergic,* September 9, 2019, https://hyperallergic.com/459292/barbara-takenaga-outset-dc-moore-gallery/.

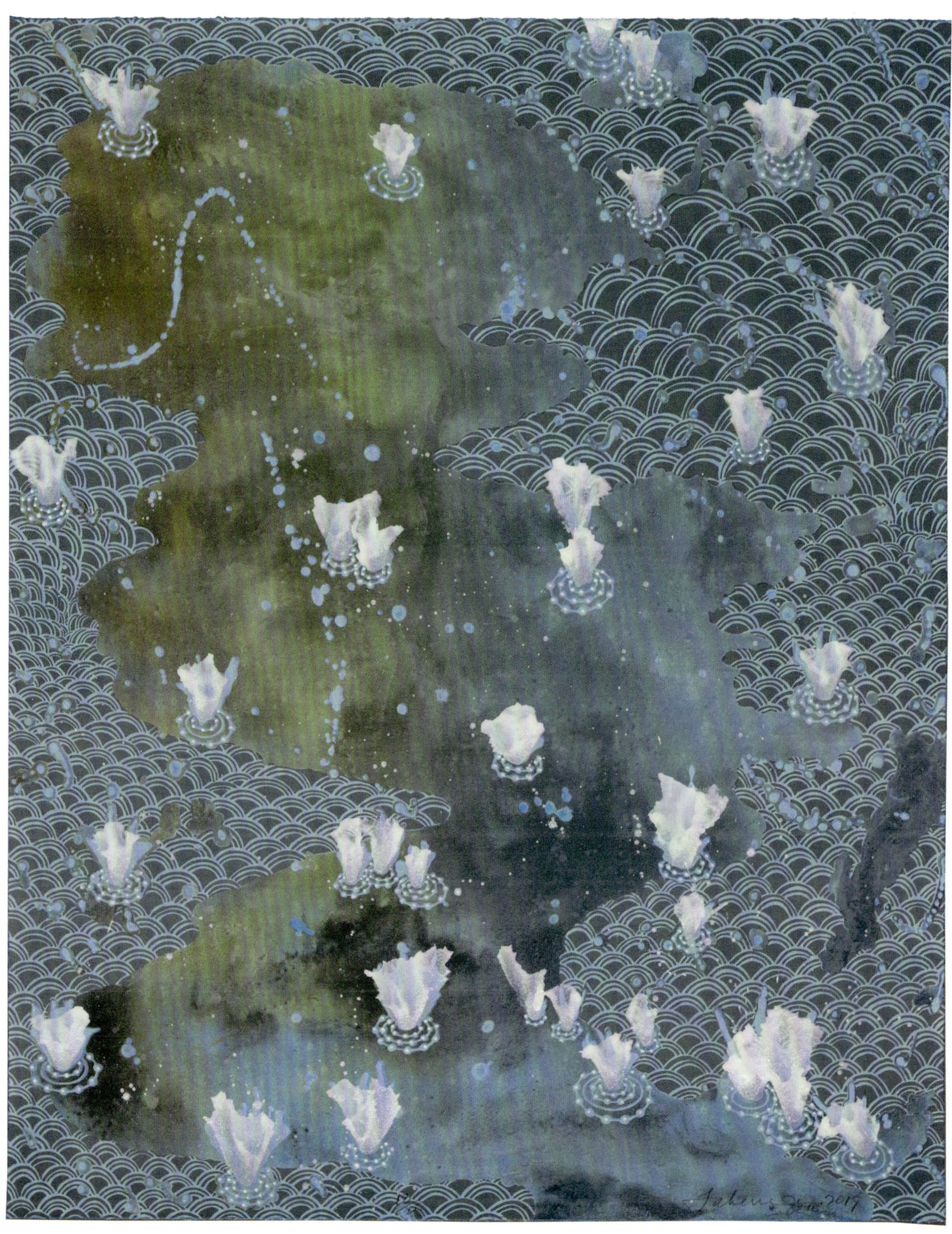

Barbara Takenaga
(American, b. 1949)
Small Springs (Backsplash),
edition 13/25, 2019
color lithograph with hand coloring and pearlescent powder
24 × 19½ in. (61 × 49.5 cm)

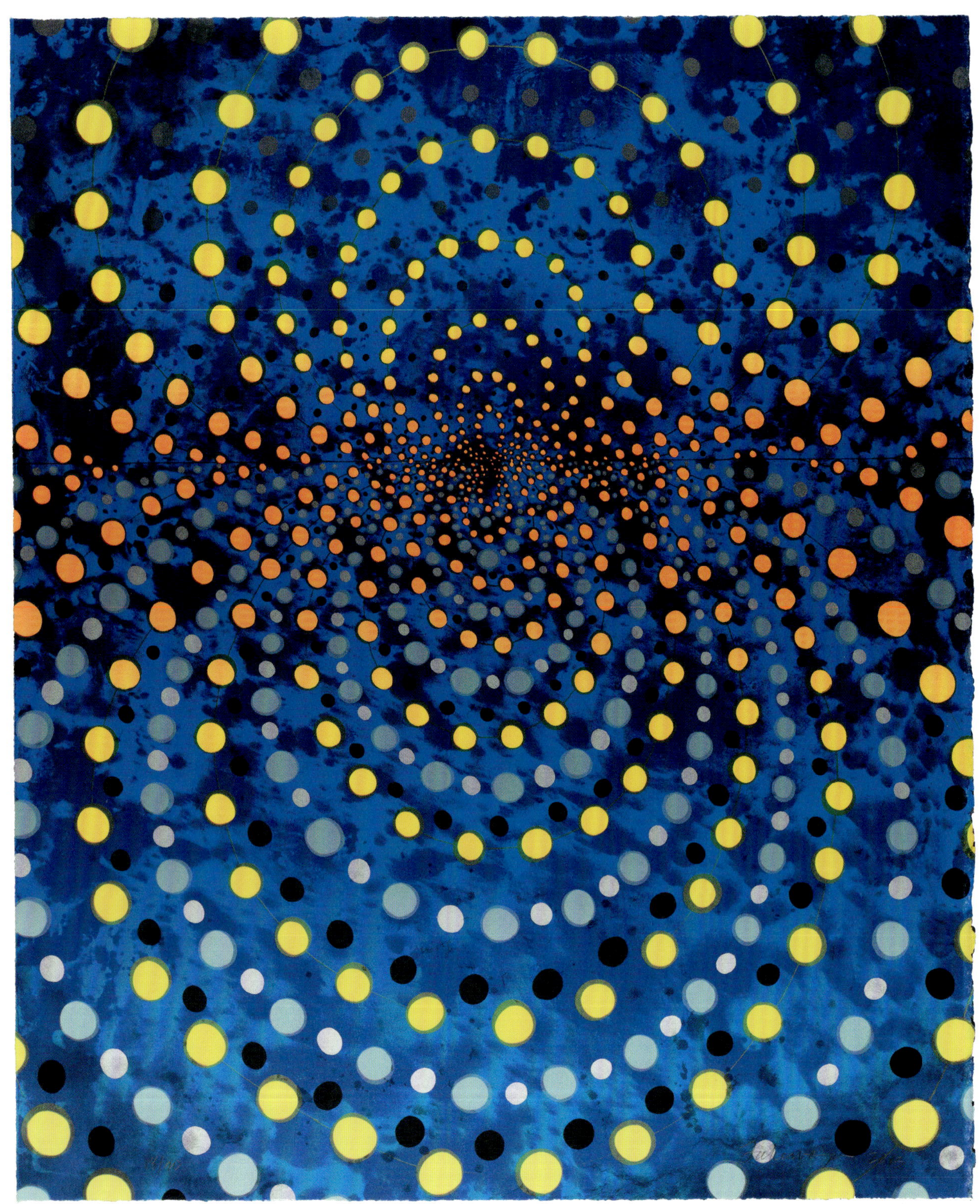

Barbara Takenaga
(American, b. 1949)
Lines of Force (TBR),
edition 18/20, 2013
color lithograph
24¼ × 20¼ in. (61.6 × 51.4 cm)

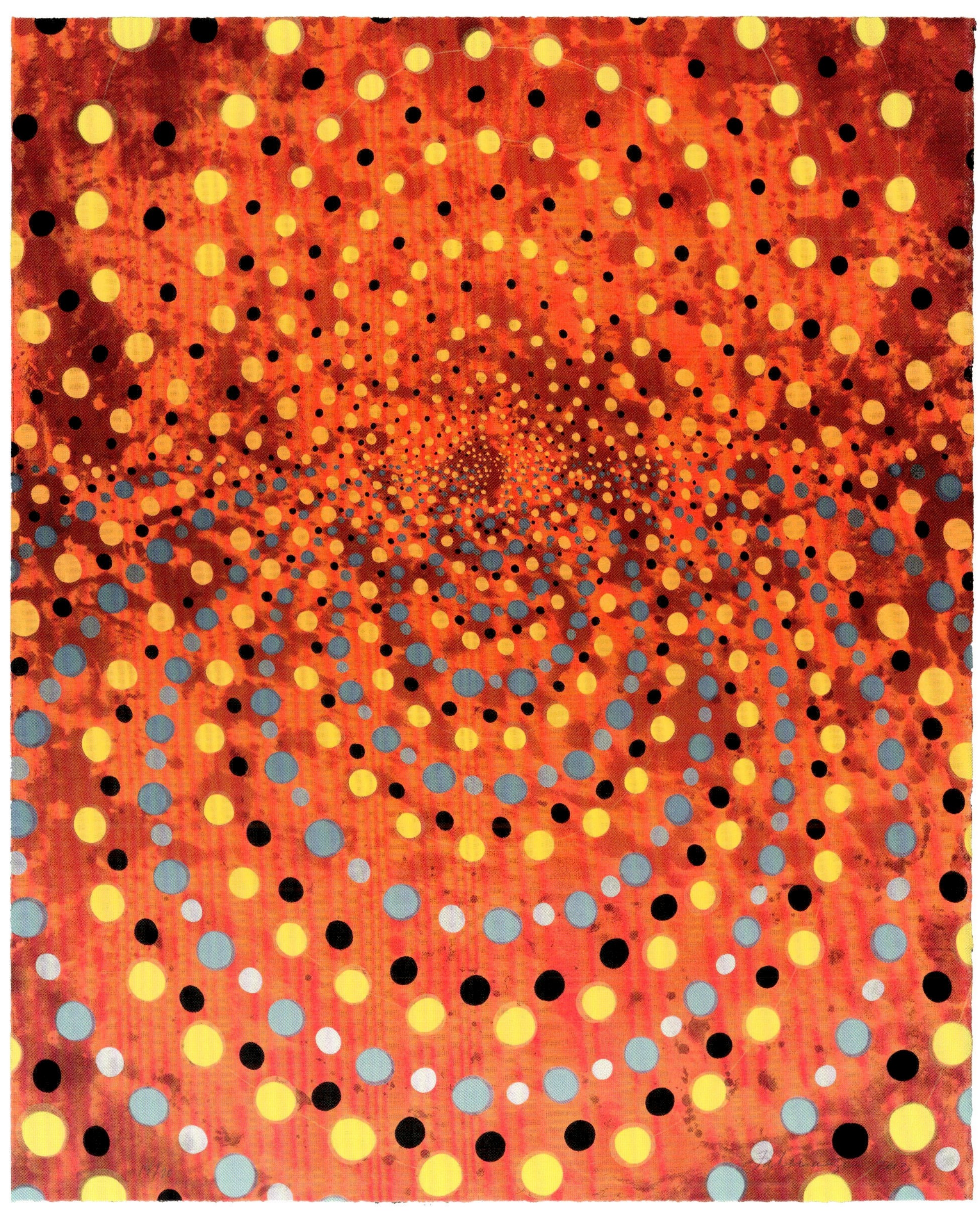

Lines of Force (Fire Red),
edition 18/20, 2013
color lithograph
24¼ × 20¼ in. (61.6 × 51.4 cm)

Mickalene Thomas

The American artist Mickalene Thomas (b. 1971) is best known for her large acrylic paintings of Black women within interior spaces, often finished with enamel and rhinestones. Central to Thomas's practice is revision of the legacy of representing the Black female figure, particularly that of modernist painting, as Denise Murrell has argued.[1] Exemplary of the artist's larger concern with reimagining "past masterworks as vivid evocations of the contemporary moment"[2] is her editioned collage *Sleep: Deux Femmes Noires* (2013), which makes explicit reference to Gustave Courbet's 1866 painting *Le Sommeil*. At the center of the monumentally scaled image, measuring 80½ inches in length, two Black women embrace on a surface of patterned textiles. The landscape that surrounds them is interspersed with wood paneling, a motif that Thomas recurrently calls upon to signal nostalgia, as the artist Kara Walker has observed.[3] Together, these elements position the figures on a dreamlike threshold between interior and exterior, past and present. The wood-grained surfaces, unsurprisingly, reappear in one of Thomas's more direct engagements with the long history of Western landscape painting, *Landscape Majestic* (2011), where they evoke trees.

Setting them in continuity with her landscapes, Thomas has described her *Interior* series of editioned collages as "interior landscapes."[4] The three examples featured here, *Interior: Zebra with Two Chairs and Funky Fur* (2014), *Interior: Fireplace with Blackbird* (2016), and *Interior: Blue Couch and Green Owl* (2016), are each based on earlier paintings of the same title, which were inspired by photographs Thomas encountered in *The Practical Encyclopedia of Good Decorating and Home Improvement*, from the early 1970s.[5] While no figures appear in these interiors, the works take up questions closely related to portraiture. As Thomas notes, the interior is often "created as a sort of mask, a way of not only hiding what is beneath the surface but also of projecting an image of beauty, power, or elegance."[6] Thomas aptly explores such concepts through her specific approach to collage, characterized not only by a layering of images but also by the application of further materials including enamel, gold leaf, and wood veneer. —JO

1 Denise Murrell, *Posing Modernity: The Black Model from Manet and Matisse to Today* (New Haven: Yale University Press, 2018), 161.
2 Murrell, *Posing*, 168.
3 Kara Walker, "Mickalene Thomas," *BOMB* 107 (2009), https://bombmagazine.org/articles/mickalene-thomas/.
4 "New Release: Mickalene Thomas. *Interiors*," Durham Press, August 16, 2017, https://www.durhampress.com/2017/08/new-release-mickalene-thomas-interiors/.
5 "New Release."
6 "New Release."

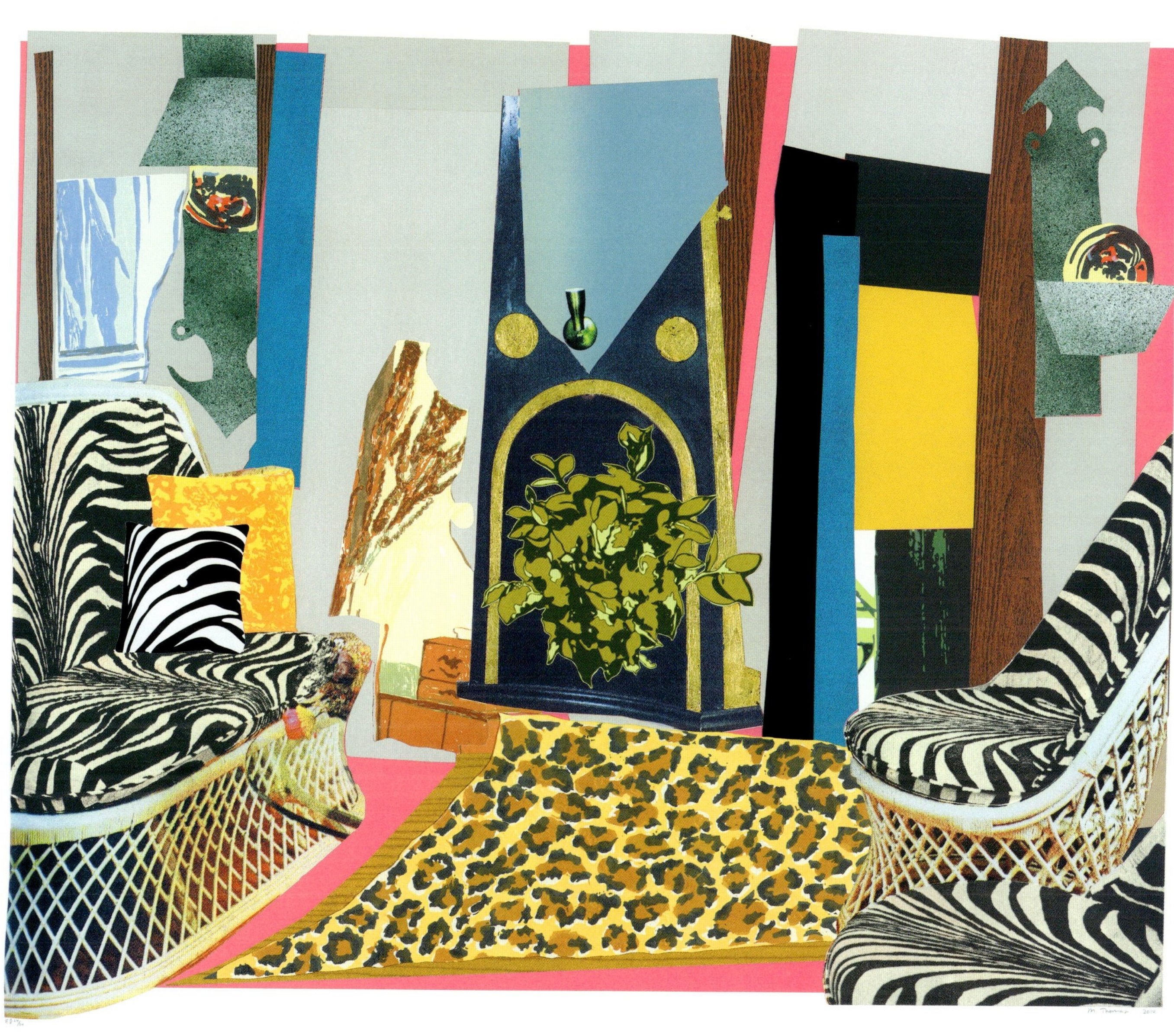

Mickalene Thomas
(American, b. 1971)
Interior: Zebra with Two Chairs and Funky Fur, edition 24/24, 2014
relief, intaglio, lithography, digital collage, enamel paint, gold leaf, colored pencil
44 × 53 in. (111.8 × 134.6 cm)

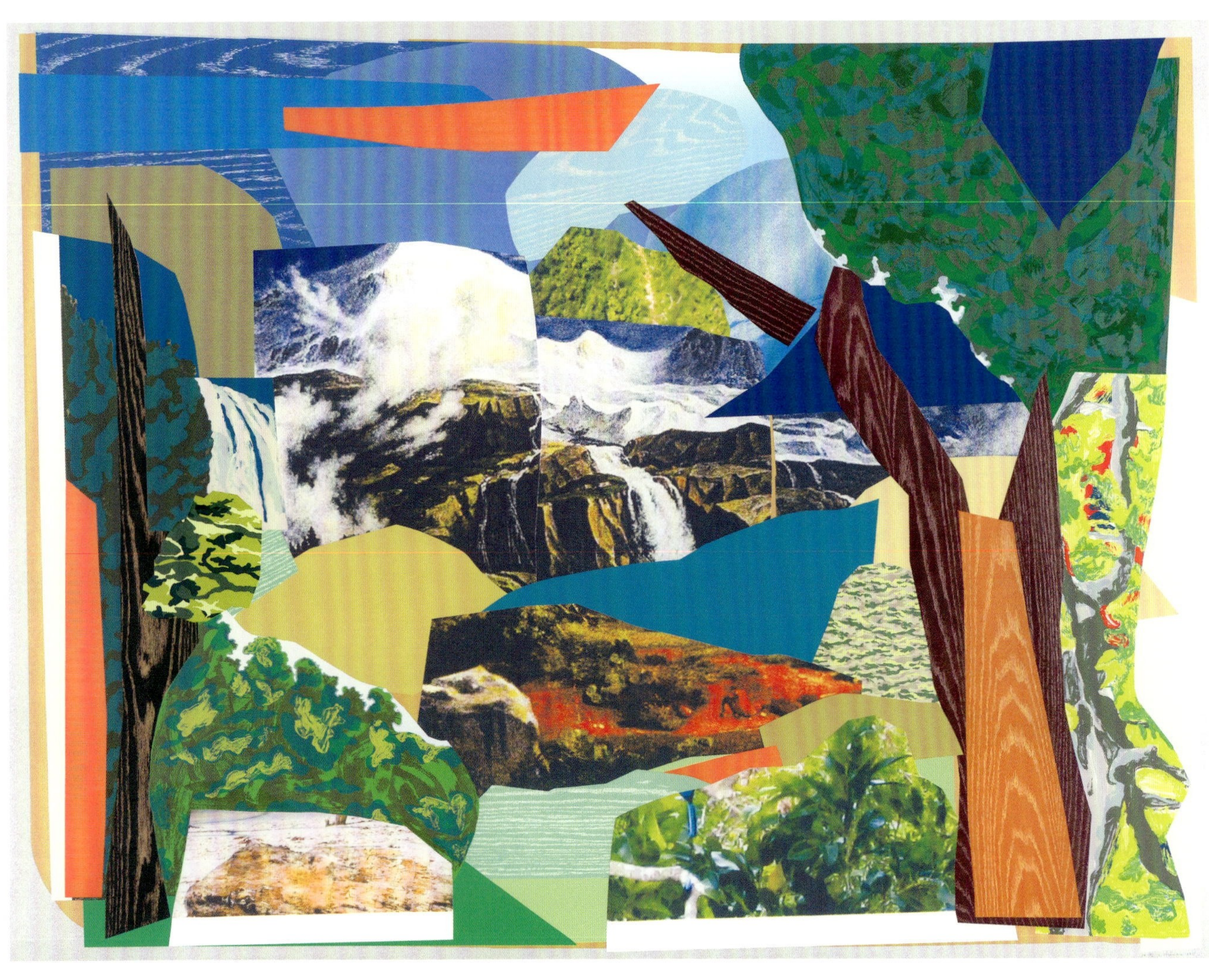

Mickalene Thomas
(American, b. 1971)
Landscape Majestic,
edition 25/30, 2011
woodblock, silkscreen, and
digital print collage
52 × 68⅝ in.
(132.1 × 174.3 cm)

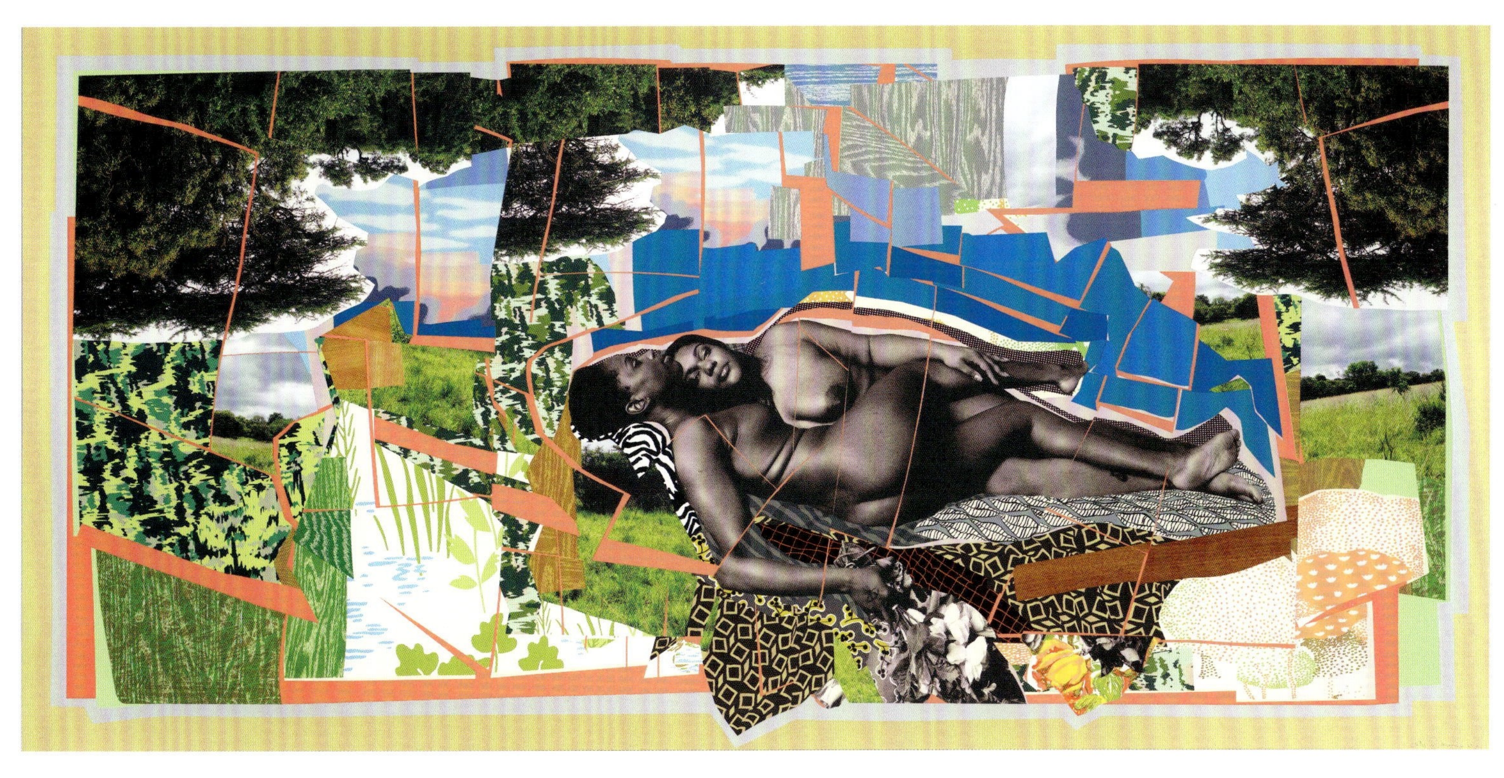

Sleep: Deux Femmes Noires,
edition 7/25, 2013
mixed-media collage,
woodblock, screenprint, and
digital print
38½ × 80½ in.
(97.8 × 204.5 cm)

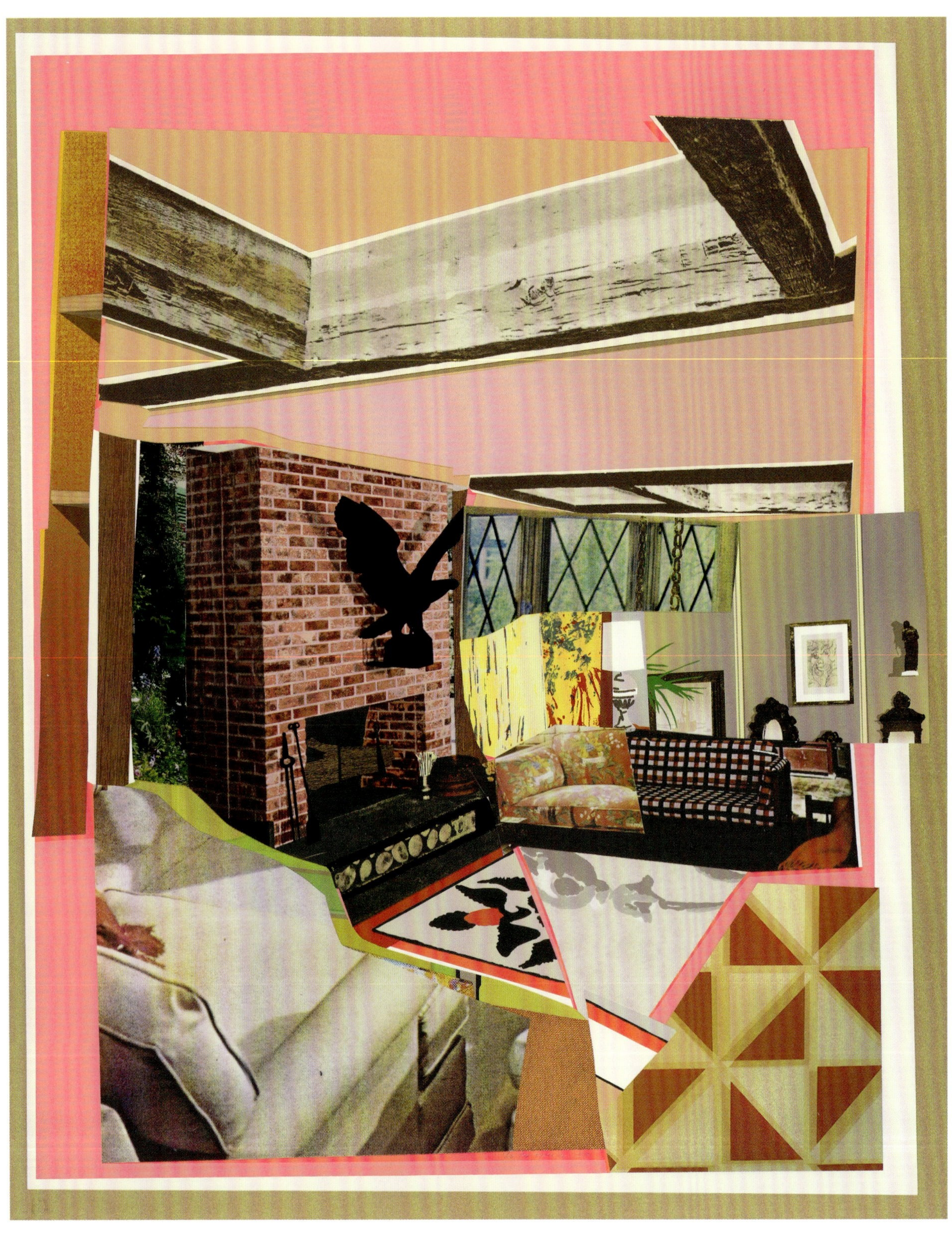

Mickalene Thomas
(American, b. 1971)
Interior: Fireplace with Blackbird, edition 5/26, 2016
mixed-media collage, screenprint, woodblock, digital print, etching, gold leaf, wood veneer, and flocking
42⅜ × 34¼ in. (107.6 × 87 cm)

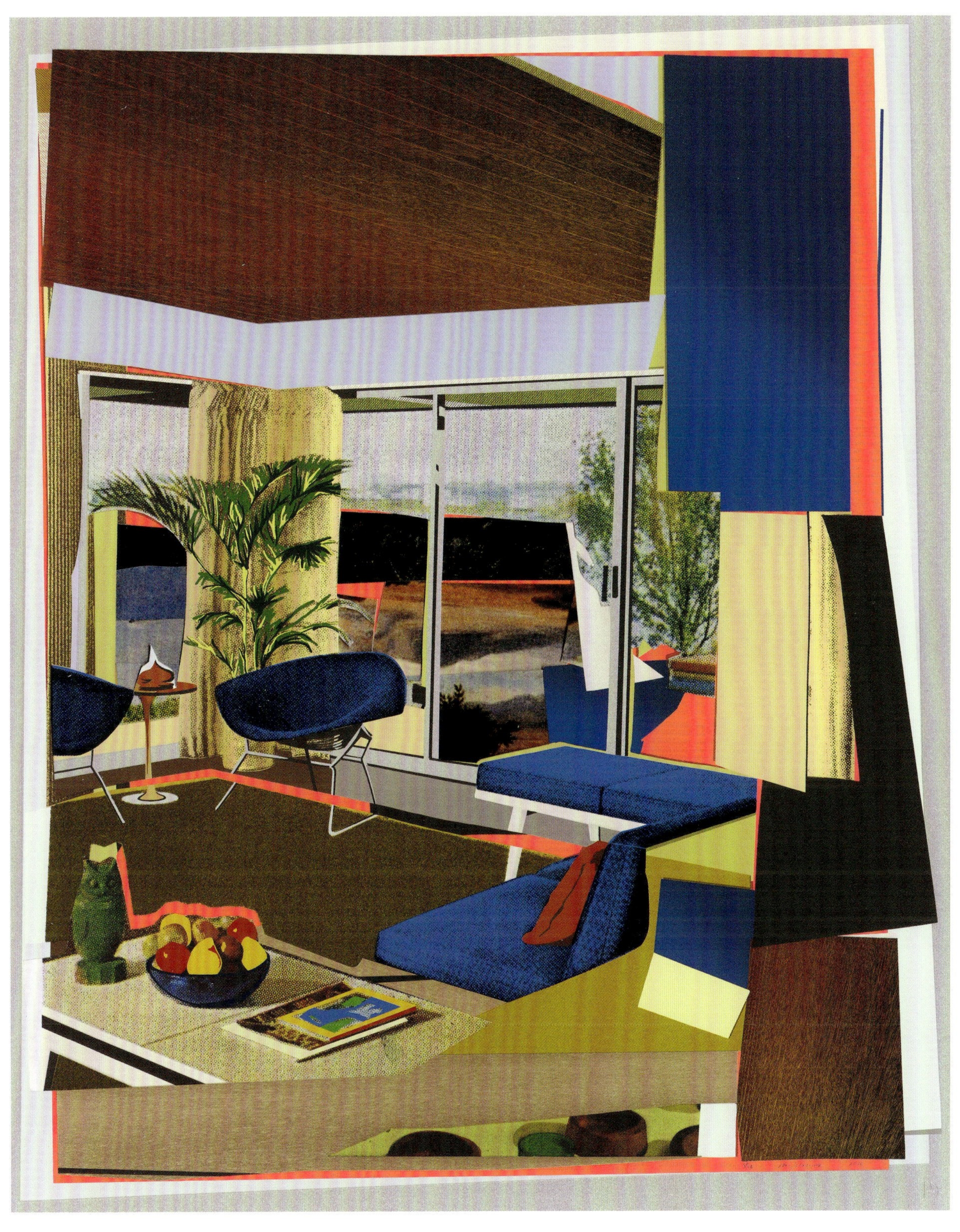

Interior: Blue Couch and Green Owl, edition 5/26, 2016
mixed-media collage,
screenprint, woodblock,
digital print, and flocking
42⅜ × 34¼ in. (107.6 × 87 cm)

Kara Walker

In her decades-long career spanning painting, installation, sculpture, puppetry, drawing, and printmaking, Kara Walker (b. 1969) probes the discontent of racial inequality and its origins in the United States. Interested in the foundational misrepresentations, violence, and economics of the eighteenth and nineteenth centuries that informed contemporary racism in America, Walker traffics in the visual culture of that time. She is best known for her use of the cut-paper silhouette, which once functioned as a precursor to photography as a way to capture a likeness. Walker, however, gives her silhouetted figures exaggerated characteristics that often play upon racial and gender stereotypes, and she often places her subjects in violent and nightmarish scenarios, requiring the viewers to acknowledge their own complicity in understanding the visual cues presented.

Harper's Pictorial History of the Civil War (Annotated) is a series of fifteen prints by Walker based on the two-volume anthology of the same name originally published in 1866. The artist selected and enlarged illustrations from the original text, which were reproduced for the portfolio using lithography at the LeRoy Neiman Center for Print Studies in New York. Silhouettes were then screenprinted onto the lithographs, punctuating the original scenes with what appear to be dismembered limbs and mutilated Black figures. Walker's insertions into the original illustrations point to discrepancies between historical narratives about the Civil War—of its victors and its victims—and calls into question the legacy of the Civil War as it pertains to today's racially divided society. —SD

Kara Walker
(American, b. 1969)
Harper's Pictorial History of the Civil War (Annotated): Buzzard's Roost Pass, edition 21/35, 2005
offset lithography and screenprint
53 × 39 in. (134.6 × 99.1 cm)

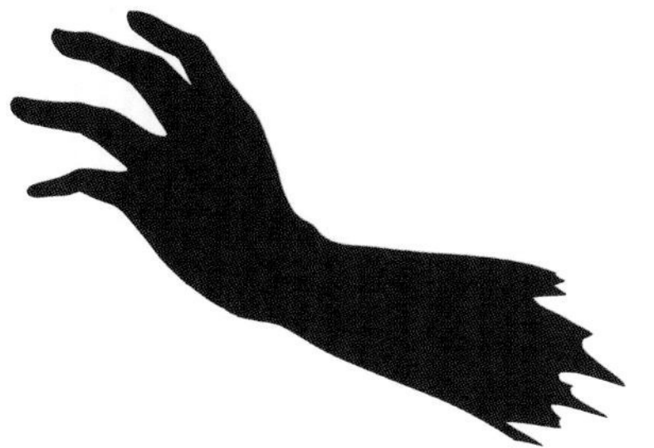

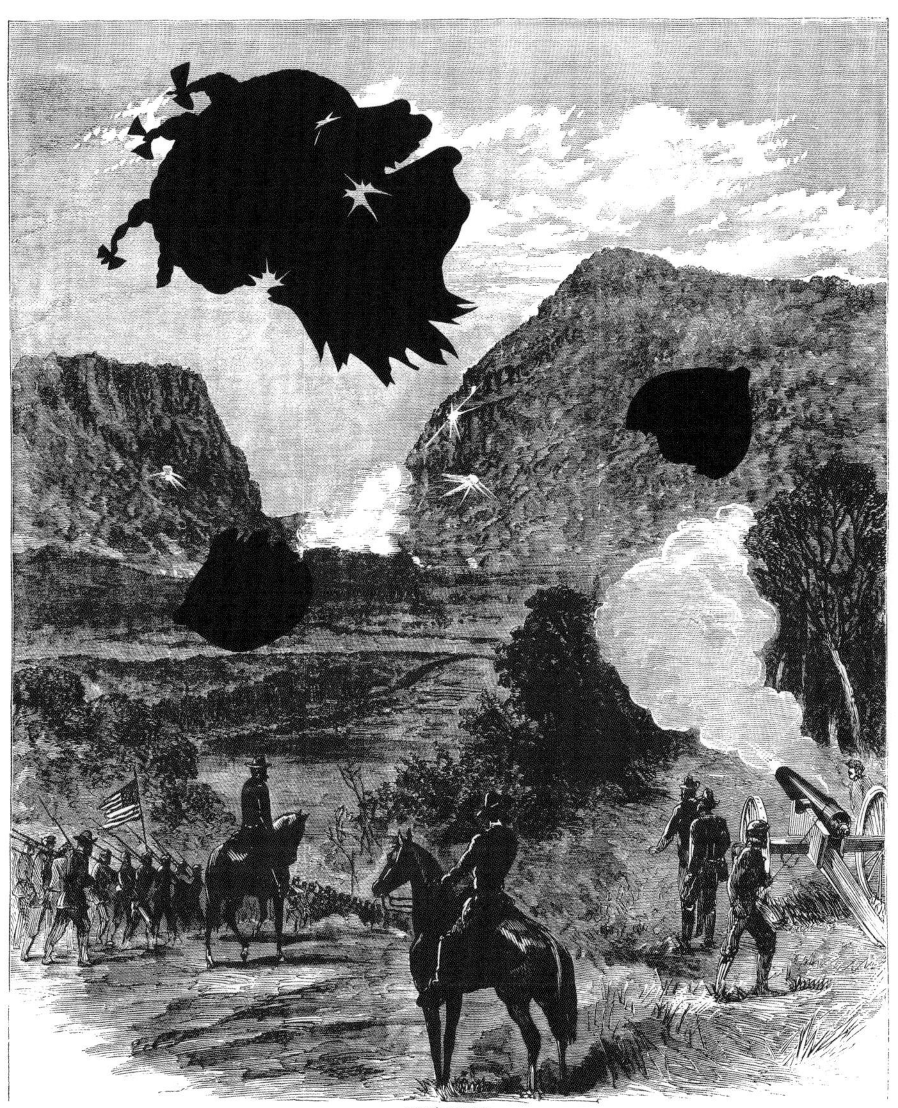

BUZZARD'S ROOST PASS.

Kara Walker
(American, b. 1969)
Harper's Pictorial History of the Civil War (Annotated): Scene of McPherson's Death, edition 21/35, 2005
offset lithography and screenprint
53 × 39 in. (134.6 × 99.1 cm)

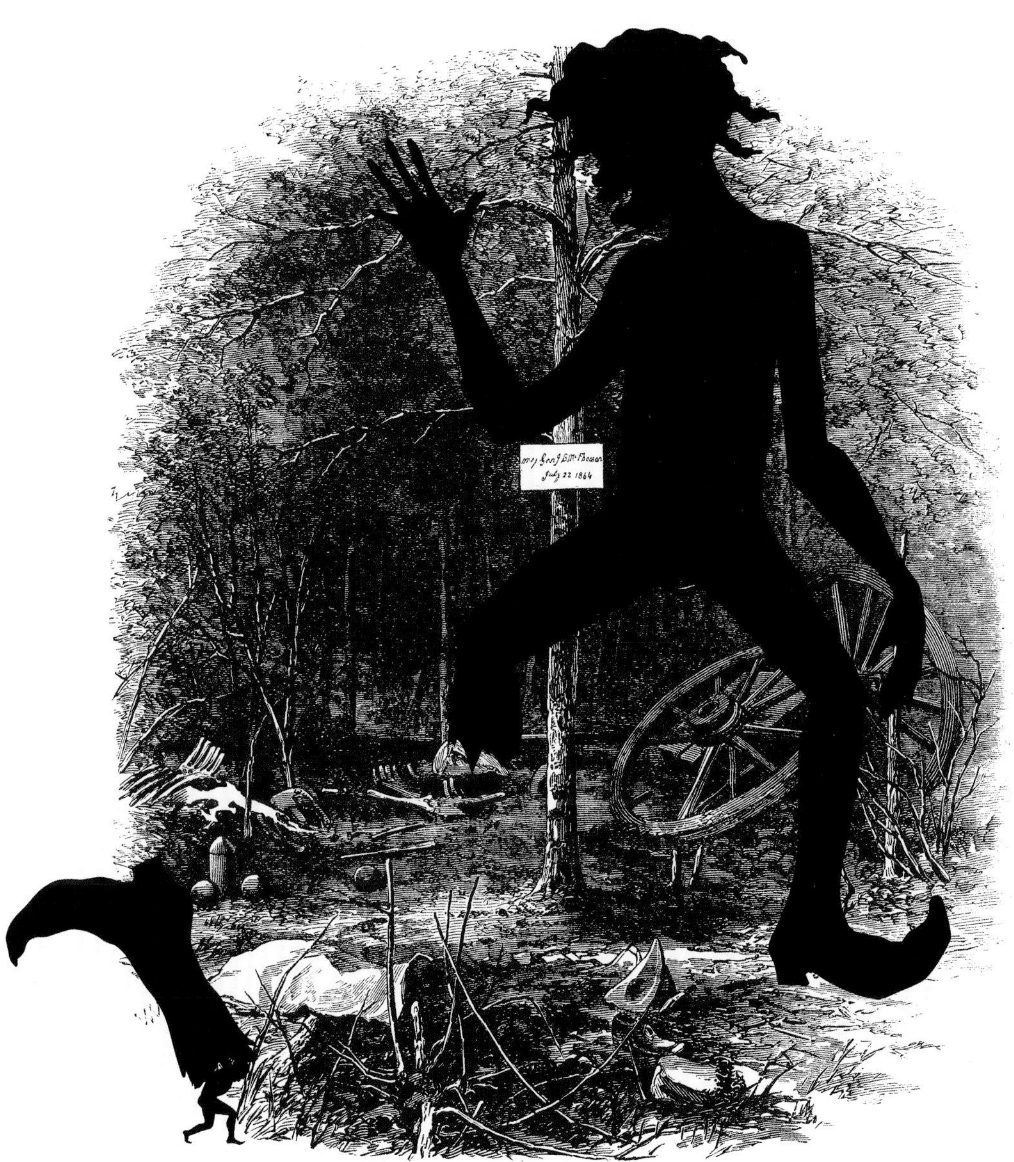

SCENE OF McPHERSON'S DEATH.

ALSO PUBLISHED BY THE JORDAN SCHNITZER FAMILY FOUNDATION

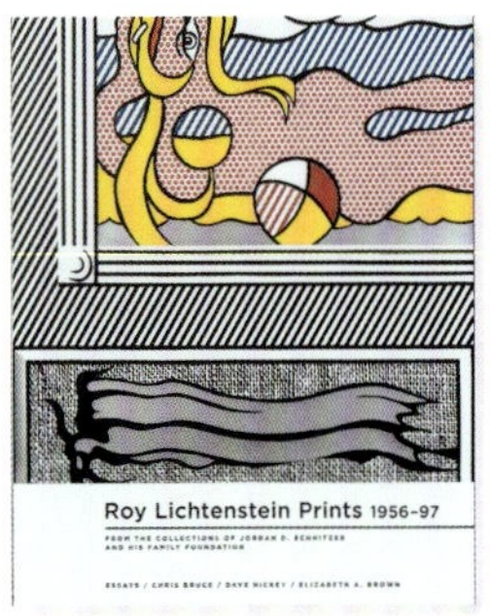

Roy Lichtenstein: Prints, 1956–1997 from the Collections of Jordan D. Schnitzer and His Family Foundation

Hardcover, 80 pages
ISBN: 978-0975566213

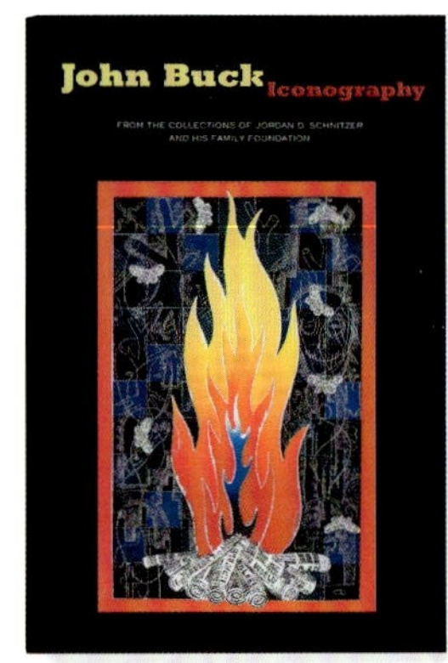

John Buck: Iconography

Hardcover, 144 pages
ISBN: 978-0910524377

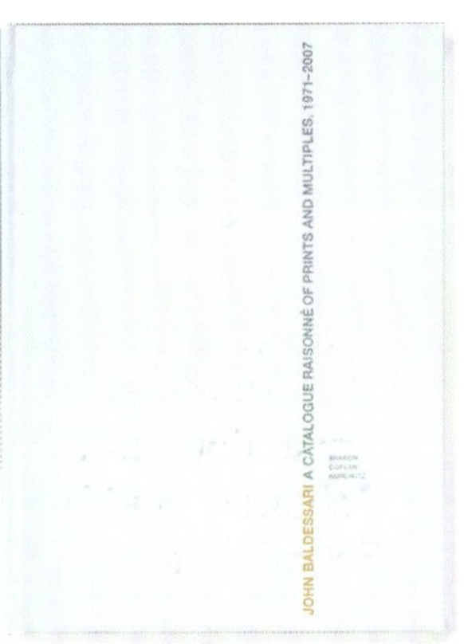

John Baldessari: A Catalogue Raisonné of Prints and Multiples, 1971–2007

Hardcover, 408 pages
ISBN: 978-1555952907

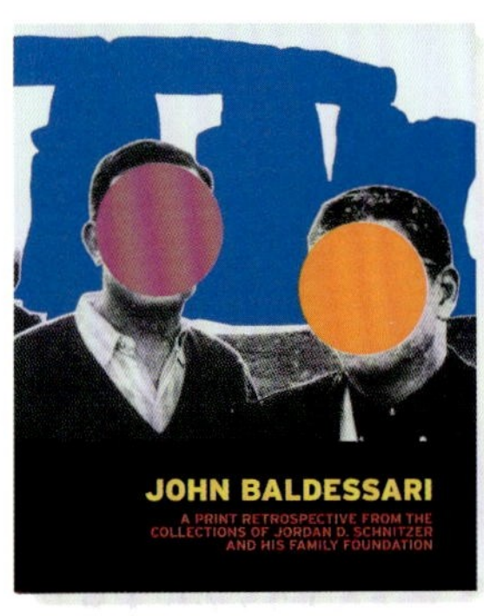

John Baldessari: A Print Retrospective from the Collections of Jordan D. Schnitzer and His Family Foundation

Hardcover, 160 pages
ISBN: 978-1935202103

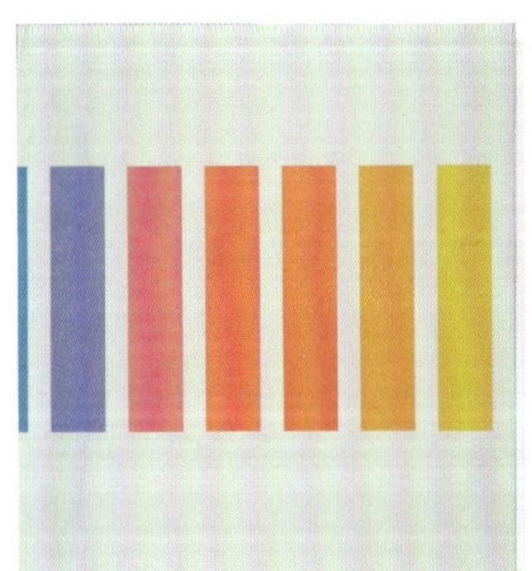

Letters to Ellsworth

Hardcover, 152 pages
ISBN-13: 978-0984986408

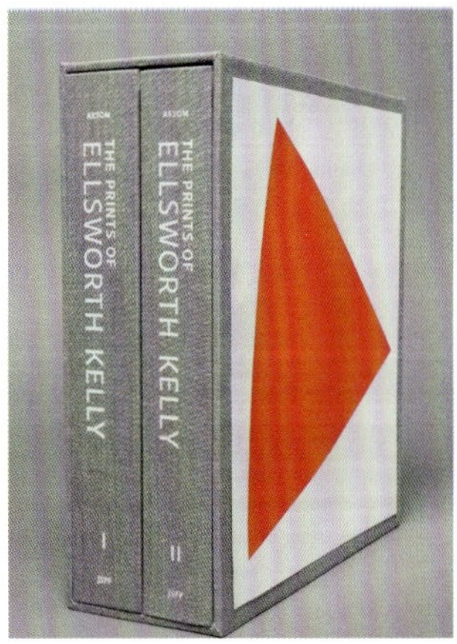

The Prints of Ellsworth Kelly: A Catalogue Raisonné

2 volumes
Hardcover with slipcase, 870 pages
ISBN: 978-0984986422

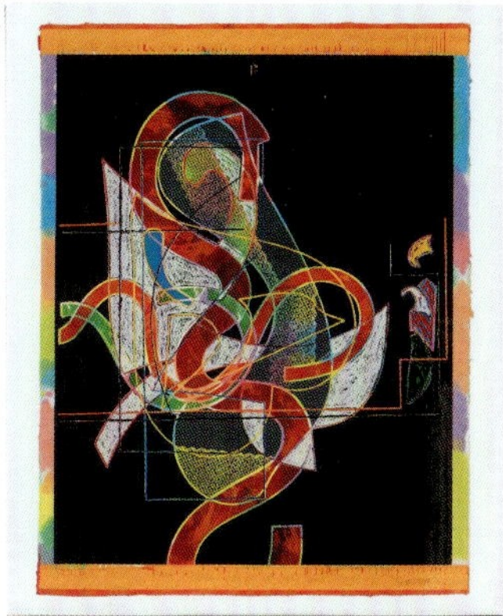

Frank Stella: Prints: A Catalogue Raisonné

Hardcover, 432 pages
ISBN: 978-0692587072

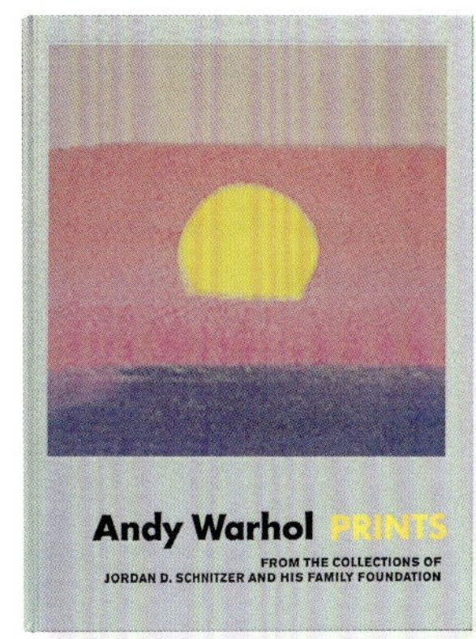

Andy Warhol Prints

Hardcover, 184 pages
ISBN: 978-0692764473

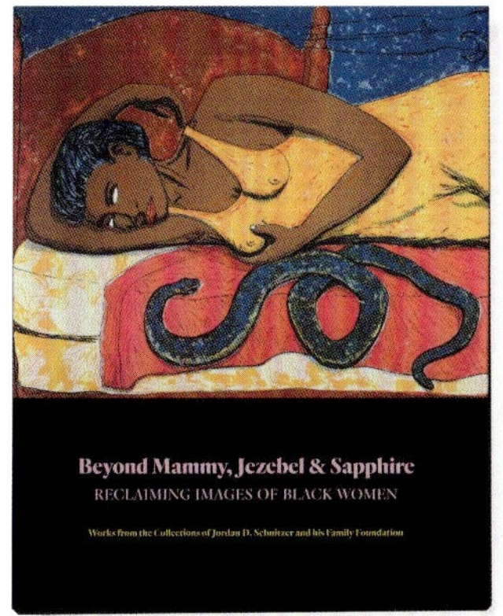

Beyond Mammy, Jezebel & Sapphire: Reclaiming Images of Black Women

Hardcover, 80 pages
ISBN: 978-0692803172

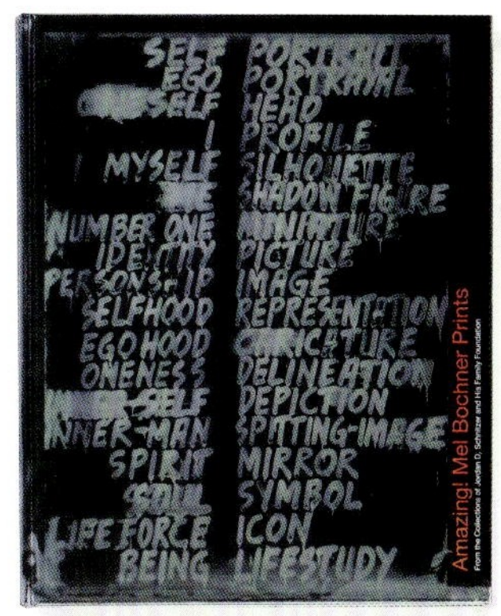

Amazing! Mel Bochner Prints from the Collections of Jordan D. Schnitzer and His Family Foundation

Hardcover, 256 pages
ISBN: 978-1732321205

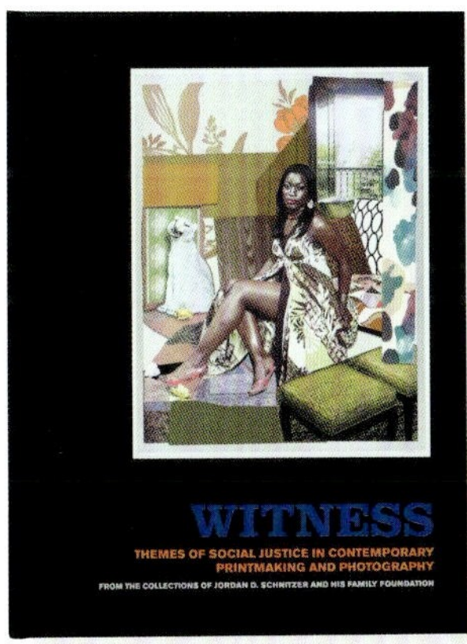

Witness: Themes of Social Justice in Contemporary Printmaking and Photography from the Collections of Jordan D. Schnitzer and His Family Foundation

Hardcover, 160 pages
ISBN 978-0-692-16298-9

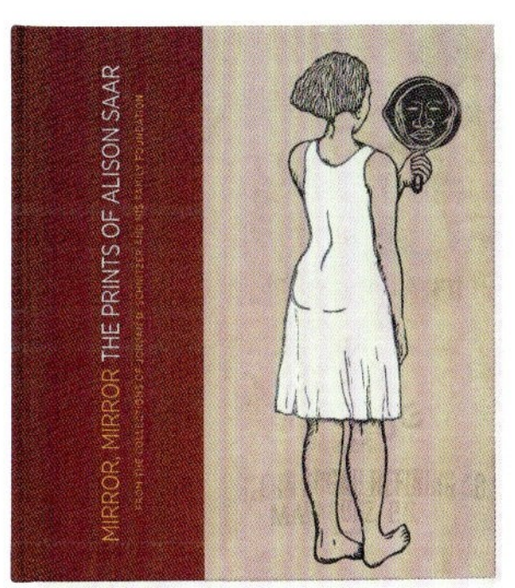

Mirror, Mirror: The Prints of Alison Saar from the Collections of Jordan D. Schnitzer and His Family Foundation

Hardcover, 128 pages
ISBN: 978-1-7323212-1-2

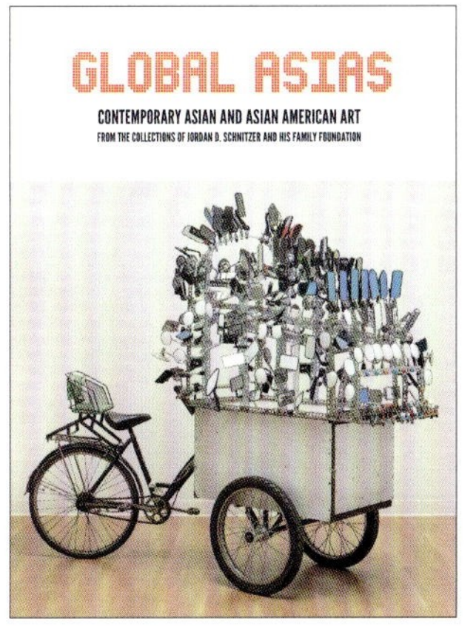

Global Asias: Contemporary Asian and Asian American Art from the Collections of Jordan D. Schnitzer and His Family Foundation

Hardcover, 104 pages
ISBN: 978-1-7323212-3-6

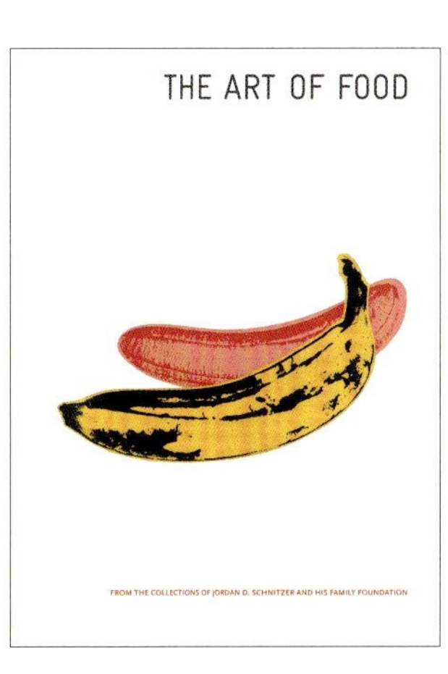

The Art of Food from the Collections of Jordan D. Schnitzer and His Family Foundation

Hardcover, 128 pages
ISBN: 978-1-7323212-4-3

Published by the Jordan Schnitzer Family Foundation

Designed by Phil Kovacevich

Edited by Carolyn Vaughan

Proofread by Nick Allison

All measurements are given in inches followed by centimeters. Height proceeds width.

Front cover: Sarah Morris, *Dulles (Capital): Panel 4* (detail), edition 32/45, 2001; screenprint, 29 × 29 in. (73.7 × 73.7 cm). © Sarah Morris.

Back cover: Julie Mehretu, *Six Bardos: Transmigration*, edition 23/25, 2018; aquatint, 98 × 74 in. (248.9 × 188 cm). © 2018 Julie Mehretu and Gemini G.E.L. LLC.

Frontispiece: Wangechi Mutu, *History of the Different Classes of Uterine Tumors: Fibroid Tumors of the Uterus,* edition 14/25, 2006; collage on found medical illustration paper, 23 × 17 in. (58.4 × 43.2 cm). Courtesy of the artist. © Wangechi Mutu.

Photography Credits

Alex Delfanne: pp. 26, 78, 79.

Courtesy of Gemini G.E.L: back cover, pp. 25 (right image), 37 (left image), 93, 95.

Courtesy of Nicola López: pp. 90, 91.

Strode Photographic, LLC: pp. 4, 6, 10, 17, 19, 22 (left image), 24 (right image), 33 (right image), 41, 53, 55–59, 75–77, 100, 101, 107–109, 125–29, 131, 133.

James Wang: pp. 114, 115.

Aaron Wessling Photography: front cover, pp. 14, 18, 20, 21, 22 (right image), 23, 24 (left image), 25 (left image), 27, 28, 30, 33 (left image), 35, 37 (right image), 43, 45, 47-49, 60, 61, 63–65, 67–71, 73, 81–83, 85–89, 97, 99, 103–5, 117–19, 121–23.

ISBN: 978-1-7323212-6-7

Library of Congress Control Number: 2021922882

Printed in Italy